Media, War and Postmodernity

Media, War and Postmodernity investigates how conflict and international intervention have changed since the end of the Cold War, asking why Western military operations are now conducted as high-tech media spectacles, apparently more important for their propaganda value than for any strategic aims.

Discussing the humanitarian interventions of the 1990s and the War on Terror, the book analyses the rise of a postmodern sensibility in domestic and international politics, and explores how the projection of power abroad is undermined by a lack of cohesion and purpose at home.

Drawing together debates from a variety of disciplinary and theoretical perspectives, Philip Hammond argues that contemporary warfare may be understood as 'postmodern' in that it is driven by the collapse of grand narratives in Western societies and constitutes an attempt to recapture a sense of purpose and meaning.

Philip Hammond is Reader in Media and Communications at London South Bank University. He is the author of *Framing Post-Cold War Conflicts* (2007) and co-editor, with Edward S. Herman, of *Degraded Capability: The Media and the Kosovo Crisis* (2000).

Media, War and Postmodernity

Philip Hammond

Routledge
Taylor & Francis Group

LONDON AND NEW YORK

First published 2007
by Routledge
2 Park Square, Milton Park, Abingdon, Oxon OX14 4RN

Simultaneously published in the USA and Canada
by Routledge
270 Madison Ave, New York, NY 10016

Transferred to Digital Printing 2008

Routledge is an imprint of the Taylor & Francis Group, an informa business

© 2007 Philip Hammond

Typeset in Bembo by
Keyword Group Ltd
Printed and bound in Great Britain by
TJI Digital, Padstow, Cornwall

British Library Cataloguing in Publication Data
A catalogue record for this book is available from the British Library

Library of Congress Cataloging in Publication Data
Hammond, Phil, 1962–
Media, war, and postmodernity / Philip Hammond.
    p. cm.
Includes bibliographical references and index.
    1. Mass media and war. 2. War in mass media. 3. War and society.
4. Postmodernism–Social aspects. 5. History, Modern–1945–1989.
6. History, Modern–1989– I. Title.
    P96.W35.H35 2007
    303.6'6–dc22   2007014296

ISBN10: 0-415-37493-6 (hbk)
ISBN10: 0-415-37494-4 (pbk)
ISBN10: 0-203-93417-2 (ebk)

ISBN13: 978-0-415-37493-4 (hbk)
ISBN13: 978-0-415-37494-1 (pbk)
ISBN13: 978-0-203-93417-3 (ebk)

For Saša, with hope for the future

Contents

Acknowledgements

This book started life as an essay for the online publication *spiked* (www.spiked-online.com). My thanks to all at *spiked*, particularly Josie Appleton, Mick Hume and Brendan O'Neill, both for their help and encouragement with the original essay, and, through their own writings on war and terrorism, for providing the inspiration to write it.

I am very grateful to all those friends and colleagues with whom I was fortunate to be able to discuss the ideas in the book, and who in many cases helped with advice on sections of the manuscript, especially Chris Bickerton, David Chandler, Barrie Collins, Phil Cunliffe, Terry Daniels, Bill Durodié, Tim Fenton, Joe Kaplinsky, Tara McCormack, Michael Savage and James Woudhuysen. My particular thanks to James Heartfield, for his help and advice throughout. Responsibility for any omissions or errors which remain is mine.

Finally, special thanks to my wife, Nena, without whom this book would not have been written.

Introduction

Postmodernism and 9/11

Among the many reactions to the 11 September 2001 attacks on New York and Washington, one of the most unexpected and striking was a public discussion of postmodernism. In his 22 September *The New York Times* column, for example, Edward Rothstein interpreted the World Trade Center attacks as a 'challenge' to postmodernists, arguing that: 'This destruction seems to cry out for a transcendent ethical perspective'.[1] On 24 September, *Time* magazine proclaimed, 'the end of the age of irony', with Roger Rosenblatt asking combatively: 'Are you looking for something to take seriously? Begin with evil'. Despite the devastation, Rosenblatt suggested, 'one good thing' would come out of 9/11: postmodernists would no longer be able to say that 'nothing was real'.[2] Similar views were expressed in academia. Conservative academic Andrew Busch argued that 'postmodernism has run smack dab into original sin, and original sin has won'; while Kenneth Westhues recalled telling his sociology undergraduates after 9/11: 'Hey, students, there is a real world. It's not all social construction .... It's not a matter of point of view. It's a fact'.[3] Finally, said these commentators, here was an event so undeniably real and shockingly immoral that it would make a disengaged, ironic attitude untenable, and would instead prompt people to reaffirm traditional notions of right and wrong.

Of course, the declaration of the end of the age of irony was premature. Before the month was out, *US News and World Report* editor John Leo was complaining that the reaction to 9/11 on university campuses was characterised by: 'radical cultural relativism, non-judgmentalism, and a post-modern conviction that there are no moral norms or truths worth defending – all knowledge and morality are constructions built by the powerful'.[4] A November 2001 report compiled by the American Council of Trustees and Alumni on responses to 9/11 in US universities claimed to have found evidence that: 'professors across the country sponsored teach-ins that typically ranged from moral equivocation to explicit condemnations of America' (Martin and Neal 2001: 1). By the first anniversary of the attacks, Charles Kesler conceded in the conservative *National Review*: 'September 11 was a deathblow to postmodernism, we are often told. I wish this were true'.[5]

Indeed, some observers argued that, far from signalling the end of postmodernity, 9/11 epitomised it. Christine Nicholls, for example, offered: 'a reading of September 11 2001 as the first world crisis expressing postmodernity'. Noting that the attacks were evocative of: 'the most spectacular of the Hollywood disaster movies', she suggested that:

> the main external referent for September 11 2001, at least as visual spectacle, seemed not to be 'the real' or 'reality' but the movies, specifically Hollywood movies. In a bizarre inversion of what is supposed to be the norm, *simulacra* of reality, at least in some respects, became the major referent for the real in this case.
>
> (Nicholls 2004)

Rather than marking a return to the real, the spectacular destruction, captured live on television and continually replayed, looked more like fiction. The point was inspired by Slavoj Žižek's argument that 9/11 seemed irreconcilable with our normal expectations of reality. Taking his cue from the 1999 film *The Matrix*, Žižek suggested that in the West:

> the virtualisation of our lives, the experience that we are living more and more in an artificially constructed universe, gives rise to an irresistible urge to 'return to the Real', to regain firm ground in some 'real reality'.

This urge appeared to animate both the terrorist act and the conservative reaction to it. Yet the intrusion of a catastrophic event did not have the effect of jolting us out of our virtual stasis. Instead, it seemed so incompatible that we could only comprehend it as unreal:

> precisely because it is real, that is, on account of its traumatic/excessive character, we are unable to integrate it into (what we experience as) our reality, and are therefore compelled to experience it as a nightmarish apparition.
>
> (Žižek 2002: 19)

Rather than shattering the image with a brutal 'return to the Real', argued Žižek, it would be more accurate to say that something which had formerly existed only as a screen image intruded into our 'reality' (2002: 16).

The implication of Žižek's argument was that the US had imagined its own destruction, even fantasised about it:

> poor people around the world dream about becoming Americans – so what do the well-to-do Americans, immobilized in their well-being, dream about? About a global catastrophe that would shatter their lives.
>
> (Žižek 2002: 17)

Hence the parallels with disaster movies: 'the September 11 attacks were the stuff of popular fantasies long before they actually took place' (2002: 17). So much so, indeed, that a number of popular cultural products were hastily withdrawn or postponed because of their close resemblance to the actual events, such as an album cover depicting hip-hop musicians The Coup blowing up the World Trade Center, and *Collateral Damage*, a film starring Arnold Schwarzenegger as a firefighter whose family is killed by a terrorist bomb.[6]

Somewhat similar points were made by the French philosopher Jean Baudrillard: although Žižek attributed the title of his collection of essays on 9/11 – 'Welcome to the Desert of the Real' – to *The Matrix* (Žižek 2002: 15), the line from the film was itself famously a quotation from Baudrillard's 1981 book *Simulacra and Simulations*. Writing about September 11, Baudrillard also noted the resemblance to, 'countless disaster movies'. He too suggested that 'we have dreamt of this event', arguing that 'they *did it*, but we *wished for* it' (Baudrillard 2002: 5–7). Contemplating the unexpectedly total collapse of the Twin Towers, Baudrillard took it as a symbol of the West's collusion in its own destruction:

> The symbolic collapse of a whole system came about by an unpredictable complicity, as though the towers, by collapsing on their own, by committing suicide, had joined in to round off the event. In a sense, the entire system, by its internal fragility, lent the initial action a helping hand.
>
> (Baudrillard 2002: 8)

Such arguments did not go down well among American conservatives concerned to restore a sense of moral certainty, and no doubt the suggestion that the towers had symbolically 'committed suicide' was calculated to *épater les bourgeoises*.[7] Yet Baudrillard's audacious metaphor highlighted the way that 9/11 brought to the surface the West's own internal conflict, vulnerability and self-doubt. The very fact that conservative commentators seized on the attack as an opportunity to vent their frustrations at postmodernist relativism was a sign of their own ideological insecurities.

'Who would have thought, in those first few minutes, hours, days, that what we now call 9/11 was to become an event in the Culture Wars?', asked literary critic Stanley Fish in *Harper's Magazine*, coming to postmodernism's defence after September 11.[8] Yet that is precisely what it did become: another issue through which conservatives attempted to cohere society around a common set of patriotic, moral values. In the Culture Wars – launched by the political Right against the perceived legacy of the 'anything goes' culture of the 1960s – conservatives have often seemed to be winning. The 1980s saw the promotion of an aggressively pro-capitalist ideology under the governments of Margaret Thatcher and Ronald Reagan and the decade culminated in the ending of the Cold War, appearing to signal an epochal victory: the 'end of history' as Francis Fukuyama (1989) famously put it. After the interlude of President Bill Clinton's two terms of office in the 1990s, the election of George W. Bush in 2000 was widely understood as a further resurgence of neo-conservatism. Yet, as the reaction to 9/11 suggested, conservatives were still on the defensive ideologically, seeing allegedly unpatriotic college professors and postmodern ironists as a threat to the American way of life. In arguing that 'The West ... has become suicidal, and declared war on itself', Baudrillard (2002: 7) pointed up the lack of unifying values in Western societies. In the absence of any confident vision of the future, 9/11 further intensified an already heightened sense of vulnerability and fear. In Baudrillard's terms, the attack could indeed be said to have revealed the 'internal fragility' of the system.

Baudrillard had made similar points ten years earlier, writing about the 1991 Persian Gulf War. Then too, the argument was provocatively overstated: Baudrillard notoriously predicted that the war 'would not take place'; asked, once it had started, if it was 'really' taking place; and maintained afterwards that it 'did not take place'. At the time, he was widely dismissed as irrelevant. Even some critics who were sympathetic to post-structuralist thought derided Baudrillard's Gulf War commentaries as rarefied nonsense (Norris 1992). Yet his essays did seem to capture the inauthenticity of the high-tech, television war; the feeling that it was somehow fake. A decade later, the notion of 'postmodern war' had become mainstream. In the wake of 9/11, commentators across the political spectrum discussed the War on Terrorism as a 'postmodern' phenomenon. Left-wing academic Douglas Kellner saw the October 2001 bombing of Afghanistan as 'a new step toward postmodern war'; while in the *National Review* Victor Davis Hanson complained that, with the 2003 invasion of Iraq, war had 'become fully postmodern'; and in the Pakistani newspaper *Dawn* Anis Shivani condemned 'America's hyperreal war on terrorism', describing it as 'an intended replay of the Cold War with a new postmodern gloss'.[9] What was formerly seen as an esoteric cultural theory had moved from the margins of academia to the mainstream of public debate.

Postmodernism and postmodernity

'Postmodern' is of course a notoriously slippery term, used by different writers to mean different things, and used sometimes to mean not very much. This book adopts Jean-François Lyotard's (1984: xxiv) definition of postmodernism as 'incredulity toward metanarratives'. That is to say, postmodernism is an attitude: one which rejects grand narratives purporting to explain historical reality. Such 'totalising' theories are rejected by postmodernists as mere language games: discursive constructions, or ways of looking at the world, with no objective validity. There is, in this perspective, no Truth about Reality, only contingent, local 'truths' about multiple, discursive 'realities'. Lyotard's definition implies exactly the ironic, sceptical attitude toward truth claims and toward political and moral values which so troubled conservatives in the reaction to 9/11.

Yet, as Perry Anderson (1998: 29) notes, 'Just one "master narrative" lay at the origin of the term: Marxism'. In other words, Lyotard's incredulity was aimed, in the first instance, at the promise of liberation and freedom offered by the 'grand narrative' of Marxism. He attempted a critique of capitalism of sorts, but one which was directed primarily at the alternative to it:

> Reason is already in power in kapital. We do not want to destroy kapital because it is not rational, but because it is. Reason and power are one .... socialism, it is now plain to all, is identical to kapitalism. All critique, far from surpassing, merely consolidates it.
>
> (Lyotard quoted in Anderson 1998: 27)

The modernity that we are supposed to be 'post' is that of the Enlightenment. It is the belief in progress through scientific knowledge and in humanity's history-making potential which is the object of scepticism. Where Marxism had claimed to be the Enlightenment's true heir, upholding values of reason, progress and emancipation as the bourgeois order could not, postmodernists rejected those values as inevitably compromised, as not worth defending, as complicit with power.

While, in its origins, postmodernism is the outlook of a minority of disillusioned French leftists, it also claims to describe an epoch ('postmodernity'), or a general state of the world ('the postmodern condition'), which provides the basis for this outlook. The apparent distinction here between subjective perceptions and objective changes out there in the world is deceptive, however. As Frank Webster (1995: 164) argues, both postmodernism, as an intellectual perspective, and postmodernity, as a general condition or era, are defined by 'a rejection of modernist ways of seeing'. Although various events and developments are identified as ushering in the postmodern age – Webster (1995: 167) suggests 'Fascism, Communism, the Holocaust, super-sophisticated military technologies, Chernobyl, AIDS, an epidemic of heart disease, [and] environmentally-induced cancers', as a representative list – it is less the events themselves than the perception of them which is important.[10] Different writers have different items on their shopping-lists of phenomena to be associated with postmodernity, but whichever developments are held to justify it, the result is the same: postmodern scepticism. What 'postmodernity' really means is that the outlook initially associated only with a few intellectuals has now become more generalised. This is not to say, of course, that everybody is familiar with the intricacies of academic theorising about postmodernism. But it is to suggest that today the ironic and sceptical postmodern attitude is widespread.

At the heart of the postmodernist perspective is a profound doubt about political agency, often summed up as the 'death of the subject'. The concept of the active and autonomous individual is seen by postmodernist thinkers as an illusion, a product of discourse. For Jacques Derrida, for example, the logical conclusion of structuralist linguistics, whereby meaning is understood to be produced by the system of signs rather than by the speaker, is that the subject is 'a "function" of language' (1982: 12). According to Michel Foucault's historical study of the French penal system, *Discipline and Punish*, 'it is not that ... the individual is amputated, repressed, altered by our social order, it is rather that the individual is carefully fabricated in it' (1991: 217). The implication is that the subject cannot challenge the rule of power and ideology since she is herself a product of it. Our very sense of ourselves as free and autonomous individuals is no more than an 'effect' of discourse. Language 'speaks us', rather than the other way round. The theoretical or historical terms in which this view is usually presented tend to mask its direct significance, but in reaching these conclusions postmodernists had a very specific subject in mind: the working class. For Marx, the working class was the collective 'universal subject', the potential active agent of historical change and progress. This was the subject who postmodernists pronounced dead.

Today the crisis of political agency is not just a theoretical proposition but a fact of everyday life. The world as described by the postmodernists, in which grand historical projects are viewed with extreme scepticism and there is no apparent agency for effecting political and social change, would seem to have arrived. We have entered the twenty-first century with little vision of the future and less debate about what would constitute the good society than at any time since the French Revolution. The working class has ceased to exist as a political force, and the political sphere has become impossibly narrow as old ideologies appear discredited but no new ideas have replaced them. Scientific advances are commonly viewed with suspicion, economic and industrial development is widely condemned as a threat to the natural environment, and in place of the history-making subject stands the vulnerable individual, permanently 'at risk' and in need of protection.

If this state of affairs may be characterised as the postmodern condition, however, it does not prove that the postmodernists were right all along. What they theorised as the impossibility of historical agency was the political weakness of the Left. The postmodernists (and others) sought to provide a philosophical justification for this subjective political weakness or to endow it with the appearance of historical inevitability. Yet the main development which brought reality into line with their bleak prognosis was the Left's own long-drawn-out demise. In fact, if one wanted to identify a single historical event as signalling the emergence of postmodernity it would be the end of the Cold War. When Lyotard announced postmodernism's 'incredulity toward metanarratives' in 1979, he expressed a disenchantment that others shared: around the same time, André Gorz was bidding 'Farewell to the Working Class', for example, and Eric Hobsbawm was declaring the 'Forward March of Labour Halted' (Gorz 1982; Hobsbawm 1981). Yet even at that low point the Left was not entirely defeated, though it was weak enough for the Right to go on the offensive successfully throughout the 1980s. It was when the Berlin Wall came down at the end of the decade that Margaret Thatcher's famous insistence that: 'There Is Nc Alternative' to capitalism seemed to have been borne out by events.

There is, though, a twist in the tale. For the Left, of course the end of the Cold War delivered the *coup de grâce*, but perhaps surprisingly the result was not much better for the Right. Although attempts were made to suggest that Western governments had defeated the USSR through escalating the arms race and dragging the Soviets into a proxy war in Afghanistan, the West's 'victory' was accidental and unexpected, brought about more by the internal collapse of the decrepit Soviet system than by anything else. Having won by default, the Western elite found themselves wondering what to do next. It was as if they had been kept going only by having something against which to fight: so long as state socialism staggered on, the Right could appear dynamic and purposeful. Even as they celebrated their triumph, the more perceptive elite thinkers quickly realised that with nothing to define themselves against, their own underlying weakness would be exposed. Irving Kristol, for example, arch neo-conservative and the publisher of the magazine in which Fukuyama's 'end of history' article appeared, observed that 'our American democracy, though seemingly triumphant, is at risk':

> it is at risk precisely because it is the kind of democracy it is, with all the problematics – as distinct from mere problems – that fester within such a democracy. Among such problematics are the longing for community, for spirituality, a growing distrust of technology, the confusion of liberty with license, and many others besides.

> We may have won the Cold War, which is nice – it's more than nice, it's wonderful. But this means that now the enemy is us, not them.[11]

Kristol found it hard to work up much enthusiasm for the 'nice' historic victory because he knew it exposed the elite to scrutiny and he feared that the emperor had no clothes. His 'problematics' are a series of absences – of a strong shared identity, of clear common values, of a vision of progress, of agreed traditions and mores – which could no longer be disguised. With the ideology of anti-communism suddenly unavailable, awkward questions began to be asked about what exactly the West did stand for.

This, to return to where we started, is the reason for conservatives' continuing discomfort with postmodernism. When they get agitated about 'un-American' intellectuals, what conservative commentators are really railing against is their own inability to project a clear and inspiring cause. In reality, the *recherché* pursuits of academic postmodernists present little challenge. Responding to conservatives' fulminations against unpatriotic cultural relativists in US universities, for example, Stanley Fish resented what he saw as a contemporary equivalent of the red-baiting scares of the McCarthy era, but was at pains to show that he was not unpatriotic. Indeed, postmodernism might even make

the War on Terrorism more effective, he suggested, by allowing greater understanding of the motives and goals of the enemy. We 'can and should invoke
the particular lived values that unite us and inform the institutions we cherish
and wish to defend', argued Fish, but we should do so 'without grasping for
the empty rhetoric of universal absolutes' such as 'abstract notions of justice
and truth'.[12] Fish's pragmatic acceptance of relativism, whereby 'there can be
no independent standard for determining which of many rival interpretations
of an event is the true one', and no 'hope of justifying our response to the
[9/11] attacks in universal terms', is fine for the seminar room, where it no
doubt makes for lively, if inconclusive, discussions about any number of texts.
It is of limited use to the political elite, however, since it presumes the presence of precisely that which is lacking: a society united around agreed values
and institutions. The problem is that, far from exhibiting a fervent belief in
common 'cherished' values, contemporary Western societies are characterised
by a conspicuous lack of shared meanings. This is not to imply, of course, that
the past was a golden age of social harmony and unity which has now ended.
Rather, it is to suggest that the framework of Left and Right provided a common vocabulary with which to discuss and dispute how society could be taken
forward. This is what is now absent.

This book is not written from a postmodernist perspective, and the terms
'postmodernism' and 'postmodernity' are used here in a way that some readers
may find annoying. Those sympathetic to postmodernism may well object to
the fact that the book takes a critical view of postmodernism while treating its
terminology and concepts in a rather cavalier fashion. They will be disappointed
to find little reference to jargon-laden academic debates, and may think it scan-
dalous that various writers, ideas and events are nevertheless bandied about
freely as examples of the postmodern in the pages that follow. Those unsym-
pathetic to postmodernism, if you have got even this far, may feel on the
contrary that postmodernist theory and the concept of postmodernity are given
far too much credence and treated with excessive respect. It is accepted here as
a premise that the contemporary period may usefully be characterised as 'postmodernity' along the lines suggested above, and it is suggested that thinkers,
such as Baudrillard, usually classified as postmodernists have something interesting to say about it. The aim is to take the postmodernist approach for what
it is: an often illuminating description of contemporary realities, but one which
allows only a limited critique. As an outlook of disillusionment, postmodernism accurately describes the uncertainty, relativism and lack of self-belief
which characterises society today, but is unable to transcend it.

Globalisation, risk and war

There are, of course, alternative ways of describing the present epoch, most
influentially with the ideas of 'risk society' and 'globalisation'. Despite their
obvious differences from the concept of 'postmodernity', in certain key

respects these ideas are also similar – perhaps not surprisingly, since they are concerned with explaining the same developments. Look again, for example, at Webster's (1995: 167) list of events often seen as marking the onset of postmodernity, quoted above. Most of them are concerned with risk and 'manufactured uncertainty': 'super-sophisticated military technologies, Chernobyl, AIDS, an epidemic of heart disease, environmentally-induced cancers'. Anthony Giddens, who together with Ulrich Beck is the most influential exponent of the 'risk society' concept, argues that globalisation is related to the 'emergence of means of instantaneous global communications and mass transportation' and is 'really about the transformation of space and time' (Giddens 1994: 4–5), an explanation which is strikingly similar to David Harvey's (1989) argument that 'time-space compression' is the defining characteristic of 'the condition of postmodernity'. These are different ways of getting at the same thing. What makes the idea of postmodernity a potentially more useful starting point for thinking about the present is that it foregrounds the problem of political agency: this, it is argued here, is the key change that needs to be investigated and explained. It has to be said that postmodernist thought does not offer an entirely straightforward route to addressing this issue, but both the origins of postmodernism and the important place it gives to the 'death of the subject' mean that one does not have to scratch very hard at its surface to see that what is at stake is a failure of political subjectivity.

In the concepts of globalisation and risk society, on the other hand, the problem of political agency is even more mystified. This is partly a problem of explanation, and partly a result of the prescriptive uses to which these concepts are put. In terms of explanation, both of these ideas suggest that unavoidable processes – of globalisation or of 'reflexive modernisation' – have made the old political frameworks of class and nation untenable. In a global economy, for example, governments are said to have only limited room for manoeuvre in terms of national economic and social policy, while global risks such as environmental damage seem to demand solutions which are not conceivable within the bounds of single nation-states. Moreover, the way that people are said to experience this new world also has a corrosive effect on former patterns of political and social identification. The process of 'reflexive modernisation', whereby society confronts its own unintended risks and side-effects, entails a breakdown of traditional forms of identification, such as in fixed class and gender roles, leading to greater individualisation; while globalisation, it is claimed, entails the growing self-awareness of new 'placeless', trans-national communities which develop in the increasingly dense networks of 'global civil society' (Beck 2000a: 12). Prescriptively, globalisation and the coming of 'risk society' are supposed to have forced a new politics on to the agenda. The radical uncertainty of risk society both undercuts traditional political responses and relocates the political to this new ground of 'reflexive' debate over risk; globalisation both empties national politics of meaning and necessitates a new 'cosmopolitan' outlook.

On the one hand, then, change is objectified as the inevitable product of implacable forces beyond anyone's control. At the same time, the powerlessness of political actors who remain within the traditional Left-Right, nation-state framework is taken as the warrant for a new cosmopolitan politics. In this sense, the ideas of globalisation and risk society are attempts to explain the crisis of political agency. Yet they are also invoked in attempts to overcome the ideological vacuum left by the end of the Cold War, including – and this is their main interest for this discussion – in attempts to do so through war and international intervention. Particularly since 9/11, a politics of fear has been used in just the way suggested by the theorists of 'risk society' – as a means of bringing people together through a new 'solidarity from anxiety' (Beck 1992: 29) – and war is now understood as a preventive measure to pre-empt possible risks and threats. Similarly, the cosmopolitan outlook of 'global civil society' has been invoked repeatedly by Western leaders as the rationale for new forms of 'humanitarian' and human rights-based intervention.

Sceptics of globalisation argue that in fact not much has changed and that this much-vaunted development is really just the capitalist world market discussed by Marx. Viewed from this perspective, the fear-mongering of neoconservatives, or the 'cosmopolitan' justifications for international armed intervention just look like the latest ideological excuses for the pursuit of business as usual. The barriers to capital are broken down abroad as the borders of nation-states are either rendered irrelevant by trans-national economic activity or are crossed by Western armies, sent to intervene on 'human rights' grounds, who make the more unruly parts of the world stable enough for investment or resource-plundering. Meanwhile, at home the populace is kept in fear of the next terrorist attack, the better to neutralise opposition. Some such scenario is the traditional left-wing response, but it is an inadequate critique.

While cosmopolitanism does work as an ideological justification for intervention in weaker states, the sorts of military actions pursued by Western governments since the end of the Cold War have little or no direct relationship to the promotion of capitalist interests. Where was the self-interested advantage of intervention in Somalia or Kosovo, for example? Furthermore, with little opposition either at home or abroad, it is not obvious why Western governments should have sought to cloak their post-Cold War foreign interventions with the rhetoric of cosmopolitanism. In many instances – notably Bosnia and Rwanda – the West was criticised, both by liberals and leftists at home and by local actors, for *not intervening enough* rather than for projecting its power too aggressively. The problem with the traditional anti-imperialist critique is that it hugely overestimates the extent to which the Western elite are in control: they are themselves prone to the fear they promote, rather than coolly manipulating it for some hidden purpose; they are seeking a self-defining mission in the project of 'ethical', cosmopolitan interventionism, not simply using it instrumentally to conceal some darker, self-interested goal. The ideas of precautionary war and cosmopolitan interventionism, in other words, are attempts to give purpose and direction to Western foreign policy: they are an expression of the elite's attempt to establish some new sense of mission for the post-Cold War era.

About this book

This is the core argument of this book: that war and intervention since the Cold War have been driven by attempts on the part of Western leaders to recapture a sense of purpose and meaning, both for themselves and for their societies. This in turn has led to a heightened emphasis on image, spectacle and media presentation. Yet it is not really the media themselves that are the problem, even though some reporters and commentators have actively colluded in the process. Rather, it is the changing character of war which is at issue, and behind that, a fundamental shift in the politics of Western societies, summed up as the 'end of Left and Right'. For that reason, although the staging of war, and of acts of terrorism, as media events make it important to examine media coverage, the analysis developed here attempts to reach beyond a critique of the media to examine the events themselves and the broader political changes that give rise to them.

Chapter 1 examines the idea that the Western military and the wars they fight can be described as 'postmodern'. Through a re-reading of Baudrillard's essays on the 1991 Gulf conflict, it is argued that the distinctive features of contemporary warfare as waged by the West – particularly its emphasis on image and spectacle – derive from the fact that it is a response to what Zaki Laïdi (1998) calls the 'crisis of meaning' precipitated by the end of the Cold War. Critically assessing claims that some Western states are now 'postmodern', it is argued that the hollowing out of the national political sphere has led to the use of international activism as a means of manufacturing a sense of shared 'values'. At the same time, this attempt is undercut by the fact that the absence of meaning makes the conduct of war risk-averse and its media presentation self-conscious.

These tensions are explored further in Chapters 2 and 3. Chapter 2 examines the attempt to use 'humanitarian intervention' as a new source of common values, arguing that this gave rise to media distortions as Western journalists joined their leaders in a narcissistic search for meaning in the Balkans and elsewhere. Ultimately, it is suggested, the attempt was unsuccessful: the ersatz morality constructed around 'ethical foreign policy' could only evade, not overcome, the death of politics. The War on Terror is also assessed, in Chapter 3, as an ideological failure. The preoccupation with image and presentation reached new heights in the 2003 Iraq war, yet the effectiveness of the propaganda was undermined by the way that the news media self-consciously drew attention to its deliberately manufactured quality. The elite's own image-conscious conduct of war was counter-productive, encouraging media cynicism.

Chapter 4 begins to uncover the roots of this crisis of grand narratives, locating the problem of meaning in Western societies. This chapter looks at the origins of postmodernism and at how it became influential among a Left which had grown disillusioned with universalism and humanism, became sceptical of any 'grand narrative', and effectively abandoned the goal of progress. Examining the post-Vietnam Culture Wars, however, it suggests that the elite had its own 'postmodern moment', and outlines the consequences of this stalemate for contemporary political life.

These consequences are explored in Chapters 5 and 6. Chapter 5 addresses the idea of 'risk society' in relation to war and domestic terror alerts. A heightened sense vulnerability and risk, it is argued, is more a symptom of the death of politics than a sign of some new politicisation. Discussing how theories of international relations have changed since the end of the Cold War, Chapter 6 examines what David Chandler (2006) calls the 'Other-directed ethics' of contemporary Western foreign policy. It is suggested that the elevation of individual conscience represents an inability or unwillingness to engage others in political debate, as evident in Western societies as it is in the phenomenon of 'postmodern terrorism'.

The Conclusion returns to the issue raised here of how far postmodernism represents a challenge to, rather than only a description of, contemporary society.

Chapter 1

Postmodern war in a world without meaning

What is 'postmodern war'? As Steven Best and Douglas Kellner observe, although the term is very common today, it is often used loosely, sometimes as little more than a fashionable buzzword (Best and Kellner 2001: 63, 85). Even in the academic literature there is scant agreement about what is distinctive, and what is distinctly 'postmodern', about contemporary war. Writing on the topic is diverse in terms of the disciplinary background of different authors (from Media and Cultural Studies to International Relations), the perspectives adopted (some taking a broadly postmodernist perspective, others rejecting it), and the issues which are emphasised. The critics who have addressed the question of postmodern war most directly have tended to focus on technological change. Writers such as Chris Hables Gray and James Der Derian have investigated the new technologies of the digital battlefield, and the new military doctrines and media strategies which have accompanied their development. Yet while these authors offer some important insights into the nature of contemporary warfare, it is partly the emphasis on these essentially technical issues that has sometimes led to a lack of clarity about war's relationship to postmodernity. There is a tendency toward technological-determinism in this discussion, as when Der Derian argues that 'a revolution in networked forms of digital media has transformed the way advanced societies conduct war and make peace'. For Der Derian, information technology is not 'a neutral tool of human agency'; rather, 'it determines our way of being' (Der Derian 2003: 447, 449). Though it is undoubtedly the case that warfare as waged by the Western military is more high-tech than ever before, this in itself provides no grounds for claiming that it has become 'postmodern'. It would be just as logical to understand the role of technology in terms of modernity, as Kevin Robins and Frank Webster (1999: 161) implicitly do in describing military 'technophilia' as expressing 'an entirely rationalistic and technocratic attitude towards the world'.

There is, however, a second, very different and apparently unrelated discussion of postmodernity, which has little to say about technology, and which has instead focused on shifts in politics and international relations. Here, writers such as Zaki Laïdi and Christopher Coker have argued that, for better or worse, the system of sovereign nation-states which arose in the modern era has undergone some fundamental changes since the end of the Cold War. Conflict and international politics are 'postmodern' in that the era of the modern nation-state has passed. Works by the one set of writers almost never acknowledge the existence of the other discussion, but this chapter contends that these two camps are not as unconnected as they may appear. It is just that those authors who concentrate on developments in military technology or the production of media spectacles tend to confuse cause and effect. The focus on these relatively superficial factors leads to a correspondingly weak sense of the underlying roots of the changes they identify. Instead, this chapter argues, the most important shifts to consider in seeking to understand postmodern war are political. Within each discussion, there are varying assessments of whether the new forms of postmodern war are positive or negative for Western societies and for their governing elites. It is argued here that they are negative: contemporary warfare is 'postmodern' in so far as it is driven by a collapse of 'grand narratives' in Western societies.

The end of the Cold War

In a brilliant analysis, Zaki Laïdi argues that the end of Cold War has left us in 'a world without meaning'. His key insight is that the end of the Cold War 'buried two centuries of Enlightenment' (1998: 1). That is to say, the fall of the Berlin Wall signalled the end, not only of communism, but of all forward-looking collective projects for the foreseeable future. In postmodernist terms, one might say that the end of the Cold War represented a collapse of grand narratives (1998: 8). This has most obviously had a debilitating effect on the Left and on national liberation movements in the Third World, for whom the ideas through which they had staked a claim on the future now stand discredited. Less obviously, but just as importantly, what Laïdi calls the 'crisis of meaning' has fundamentally affected Western societies and their governing elites. Put at its simplest, the West has lost its cohesion because it has lost its enemy. The ideological cement which anti-communism provided as a negative justification of Western capitalism has crumbled away, and the system of institutions through which international relations were organised throughout most of the post-Second World War era has lost its justification. These are significant problems, but the crisis of meaning entails yet more than that. Western elites have lost the political wherewithal to cohere their own societies around a meaningful project and to give them a sense of a future goal.

In the immediate aftermath of the fall of the Berlin Wall, assessments of the future were highly positive. Scenes of jubilant East Berliners marching toward political freedom and capitalist prosperity, soon replicated in other East European countries, provided a powerful vindication of Western societies. Indeed, Laïdi argues that the ending of the Cold War was itself initially understood by reference to familiar Enlightenment themes: the apparent validation of the market and of liberal democracy seemed to affirm the notion that history had been following a teleology of freedom and liberation. The moment of triumph, however, was also a moment of terminus: the project was at an end. Francis Fukuyama's 'end of history' thesis captures this double-edged character of the end of the Cold War: his argument is at once triumphalist and an acknowledgement that there is no longer any vision of the future:

> The end of history will be a very sad time ... the worldwide ideological struggle that called forth daring, courage, imagination, and idealism, will be replaced by economic calculation, the endless solving of technical problems, environmental concerns, and the satisfaction of sophisticated consumer demands.
>
> (Fukuyama 1989)

Fukuyama admitted feeling 'ambivalent' about the West's triumph, anticipating the 'prospect of centuries of boredom'. The end of history did not represent a transcendence of the previous state of affairs, but offered only the prospect of its gradual generalisation. Market democracy, Laïdi (1998: 35) remarks, 'aspires neither to reach a new objective nor to construct a new horizon of meaning. It seeks simply to confirm the viability of the existing reality'. Fukuyama's diagnosis was that other ideologies, notably Islam, did not pose the same kind of challenge as communism had in the past. In place of the clash of world systems of the Cold War, there was henceforth only the prospect of *ad hoc* responses to relatively minor, local threats. Leaving aside, for the time being, the question of whether this assessment has to be revised in light of the War on Terror, it should be noted that, in terms of conflict too, the moment of victory also implied purposelessness. In the post-Cold War era: 'Political actions no longer find their legitimacy in a vision of the future, but have been reduced to managing the ordinary present' (Laïdi 1998: 7).

This is not to say that there have been no attempts to recover a sense of purpose and meaning. On the contrary, Western intervention in the international arena has been driven by a desire to do just that. Furthermore, the end of the Cold War offered new opportunities for foreign intervention: there was no longer any ideological alternative to Western capitalism, and no Soviet deterrent to the exercise of US military power. Initial assessments of these new realities were upbeat. Indeed, in retrospect, they appear wildly optimistic – a revivified United Nations (UN) would henceforth be able to act on moral principles and not be hampered by the Soviet veto; there would be a 'peace dividend' as money formerly spent on the arms race was put to better use; there would, in President George H. W. Bush's phrase, be a 'New World Order'. Yet although there were fewer restraints than ever on the use of military force and the open pursuit of US interests and influence around the globe, the overarching rationale for action had also collapsed. In Laïdi's terms there is a dislocation between power and meaning (1998: 8). If international intervention since the end of the Cold War has been driven by a search for a new sense of purpose, it has also been undermined by the crisis of meaning. As Laïdi (1998: 11) comments:

> The end of utopia has brought the sanctification of emergency, elevating it into a central political category. Thus our societies claim that the urgency of problems forbids them from reflecting on a project, while in fact it is their total absence of perspective that makes them slaves of emergencies. Emergency does not constitute the first stage of a project of meaning: it represents its active negation.

From the 1991 Gulf War to the War on Terror, launched a decade later, intervention has been opportunistic and reactive, responding to perceived threats and crises rather than acting in accordance with some strategic project.

If the Gulf War provided a focus for the initial optimism about the end of the Cold War, it soon became apparent that future conflicts were unlikely to follow the same pattern. No sooner had Bush Snr. proclaimed a New World Order than critics were pointing to the actual disorder which seemed to reign. The break-up of Yugoslavia and the USSR, from 1991, suggested to many commentators that a resurgence of ethnicity and nationalism was fuelling conflict. Analysts such as Samuel Huntington (1993) and Robert Kaplan (1994) argued that there were new sorts of divisions and threats emerging. For Huntington, the political Cold War divide had given way to more deep-seated cultural antagonisms, particularly between Western Christendom and Islam; while Kaplan contended that the security of the West was menaced by the existence of failed states and zones of 'anarchy'. In either analysis, there was little that could be done. The deep-rooted cultural divisions which Huntington claimed to have identified did not seem susceptible to change, and Kaplan said that the West was 'not in control' of the anarchic world he described (quoted in Kaldor 1999: 147). As Laïdi notes, the new importance of identity stemmed from an 'exhaustion of universalism'. Post-Cold War 'ethnic' conflicts could also be seen as 'the expression of a harshly felt loss of meaning' (1998: 53, 54). Rather than representing a revival of the national idea, conflict was driven by the collapse of existing nation-states: it arose less from a resurgence of formerly suppressed ethnic identities, than from the crisis of state legitimacy precipitated by the end of the Cold War. The rise of Croatian nationalism, for example, was a far from spontaneous process: linguistic and cultural differences had to be exaggerated or even invented in order to give the break-up of the federal Yugoslav state the appearance of a more positive demand for recognition. What appeared as new claims for sovereign autonomy were only 'a "moment" in the process of decomposition and disintegration' (Laïdi 1998: 61).

Furthermore, as Laïdi's analysis also makes clear, this process of disintegration was not confined to former Eastern bloc or Third World states. The same dynamic could be seen in demands for regional autonomy in Western countries such as Italy, Belgium or Canada (1998: 41–2). These demands may not have resulted in war, as they did elsewhere, but the crisis of legitimacy which gave rise to them was real enough. Just as the end of the Cold War threw the international order into question, it also undermined the established framework of Left and Right in domestic politics. The end of grand narratives robbed the political process of meaning: in place of competing visions of the good society, politics was reduced to a technical managerialism. If international intervention appeared to offer a way to offset this crisis of meaning, it was also undermined by it. It was, says Laïdi (1998: 37):

> as if the West were giving the impression of wanting to spread its values without knowing in what name it was acting ... wanting to advocate a sort of abstract, almost dogmatic universalism in a foreign territory at the same time as a destructive relativism [had] set up on its home ground.

Without a coherent and confident vision of the future of their own societies, Western elites have found the projection of power abroad to be uncertain and dangerous. While one might have expected the end of the Cold War to bring greater security, removing the threat of nuclear confrontation between the superpowers, it has instead brought a heightened sense of vulnerability and risk. With no 'horizon of meaning', it becomes difficult to make sense of the present and the future is regarded with fear. As Laïdi (1998: 13–14) puts it: 'Western societies ... feed on the theme of the unknown, because there really is a drying-up of references that could be the basis for constructing a new social or global order'.

Postmodern wars

Two very different types of conflict have been seen as exemplifying postmodern war. For many commentators, taking their cue from Jean Baudrillard, the Persian Gulf War is the main reference point (Baudrillard 1995; Best and Kellner 2001; Der Derian 2001; Gray 1997). In this perspective, it is the advanced Western countries, particularly the US, which wage 'postmodern war', using high-tech 'smart' weaponry. Others, however, take the term to be more or less synonymous with the intrastate conflicts, such as those in the former Yugoslavia, which emerged after 1991 (Duffield 1998; Kaldor 1999; Møller 1996). For these writers, it is relatively low-tech wars in Eastern Europe or the Third World which are key.

Both views are considered below in light of Laïdi's analysis. First, in relation to Baudrillard's essays about the Gulf War, it is argued that the conflict can indeed be understood as an instance of 'postmodern war', not so much because of the way it was fought as a high-tech media spectacle, but rather because it was a response to the Western elite's post-Cold War crisis of meaning. With regard to the second type of war, characterised by the disintegration of weaker states, Mary Kaldor's (1999) 'new wars' thesis is perhaps the most influential analysis. These 'new wars', and the West's response to them, are considered at greater length in the next chapter, but Kaldor's argument is briefly discussed here in order to outline the relationship between these two conceptions of postmodern war.

The 1991 Gulf War

Baudrillard is usually interpreted as making two main observations about the 1991 Gulf War (see, for example, Hassan 2004: 70–3; Hegarty 2004: 98–9; Robins and Webster 1999: 155–6). Firstly, that the conduct of the war was new, using 'smart' computer-guided weapons to kill from a distance: America's technological superiority and use of overwhelming force made the conflict so one-sided that it could not properly be understood as war in the traditional sense. Secondly, that the deluge of information and images produced, not a representation of the reality of war, but a sanitised media spectacle in which it was impossible to distinguish the virtual from the actual. Baudrillard does make these points, and yet, as his English translator points out, similar arguments were also made by critics hostile to postmodernism (Patton 1995: 18). Noam Chomsky, for example, in an essay titled 'The Media and the War: What War?' wrote: 'As I understand the concept "war", it involves two sides in combat, say, shooting at each other. That did not happen in the Gulf' (Chomsky 1992: 51). Chomsky's essay appeared in a collection called *Triumph of the Image* which, like other studies of news coverage of the Gulf, examined how television images served to obscure, rather than to reveal, what was going on. As this suggests, there is nothing specifically postmodernist about Baudrillard's propositions regarding the way the war was fought or its media treatment. Furthermore, neither of these developments is new. As Susan Carruthers (2001: 676) notes, long-distance technological killing was as much a feature of First World War artillery as it is of today's computerised weapons systems: targets which appear as co-ordinates on a map are scarcely less impersonal than those which appear as pixels on a screen. As for propaganda, it is arguably as old as war itself (Taylor 2003), and as Binoy Kampmark (2004) points out, Baudrillard's critique seems to slip from a postmodernist notion of simulation toward a more traditional idea of dissimulation in which the existence of a knowable real is still assumed. If the Gulf War is to be interpreted as 'postmodern', it must be on other grounds than these.

Baudrillard's essays about the Gulf War are recognisably postmodernist in Lyotard's (1984: xxiv) sense of 'incredulity toward metanarratives'. Baudrillard could not see, in the Gulf War, any possibility of an alternative grand narrative to challenge the hegemony of the West: his essays are peppered with references to the decline of Arab nationalism, the containment of radical Islam, the collapse of communism in Eastern Europe, and the defeat of the 'revolutionary potential' (Baudrillard 1995: 85) of the Algerian uprising against colonial rule in the 1950s. From these past disappointments, postmodernists had drawn the conclusion that Enlightenment humanism was inherently flawed; this was the spirit in which Baudrillard wrote of: 'All these events, from Eastern Europe or from the Gulf, which under the colours of war and liberation led only to political and historical disillusionment' (1995: 77). His attempted critique of the 'consensual traditionalism' of the West was a rejection of 'the Enlightenment, the Rights of Man, the Left in power ... and sentimental humanism' (1995: 79).

It was from this perspective of disillusionment that the only option seemed to be the 'ironic' postmodern attitude, refusing to get excited by the propaganda, dismissing it all as only images. Hence Baudrillard's hyperbolic and seemingly nonsensical insistence that the war 'did not take place': it was meant as a refusal of the common ground of the debate about the war; the assumption that it was a significant historical event in that either supporting or opposing it could be tied to some grand narrative of liberation. 'To be for or against the war is idiotic if the question of the very probability of this war, its credibility or degree of reality has not been raised even for a moment' (1995: 67). In the absence, as he saw it, of any clear vantage point from which to oppose the war, Baudrillard's advice was to:

> Resist the probability of any image or information whatever. Be more virtual than events themselves, do not seek to re-establish the truth, we do not have the means, but do not be duped.
>
> (1995: 66)

Without any means to establish the truth, not being duped can only mean disbelieving everything. As Der Derian puts it: 'better strategically to play with apt critiques of the powerful new forces unleashed by cyberwar than to hold positions with antiquated tactics and nostalgic unities' (quoted in Chesterman 1998). This position of radical scepticism makes postmodernism a limited critique, since it is unable to pose any alternative.

However, the insight of Baudrillard's analysis is that the collapse of grand narratives is a problem, not only for would-be opponents of the war, but for the Western elite. As the first major conflict of the post-Cold War era, the Gulf crisis both exposed the fact that the old rules of international politics did not apply, and offered an opportunity to forge some new sense of purpose. As former US Defense Secretary James Schlesinger noted at the time: 'The nature of the international system in the post-Cold War world is now being shaped. Whether or not the US can effectively provide leadership remains to be demonstrated' (*Herald Tribune*, 7 August 1990). Bush Snr. seized on the Gulf War as a new source of meaning, a way to redefine what America stood for, declaring grandly: 'In the life of a nation, we're called upon to define who we are and what we believe' (quoted in Campbell 1992: 3). This was the president who famously had difficulties articulating what he clumsily called 'the vision thing', but the war seemed to offer moral clarity: 'It's black and white. ... The choice is unambiguous. Right vs. Wrong' (quoted in Chesterman 1998). This claim to have rediscovered a sense of political purpose and vision was the target of Baudrillard's attack.

The affected moral indignation rang false, given America's support for Saddam in the Iran–Iraq war of the 1980s. A few days before Iraq's invasion of Kuwait on 2 August 1990, the US ambassador to Iraq, April Glaspie, told Saddam that: 'we have no opinion on ... your dispute with Kuwait', a position which was repeated publicly by State Department officials (Keeble 1997: 84–5; Knightley 2000: 485–6). The sudden attempt to recast the invasion as a replay of the Second World War – with the US-led coalition commonly referred to as 'the allies' and Saddam cast in the role of a 'new Hitler' – was transparently an effort to invoke the moral certainties of a past era (Dorman and Livingston 1994). As Baudrillard noted, the exaggeration of the threat allegedly posed by Saddam was necessary in order to make the war seem meaningful. The Americans, he said, were 'hallucinating those opposite to be a threat of comparable size to themselves: otherwise they would not even have been able to believe in their own victory. ... They see Saddam as he should be, a modernist hero, worth defeating (the fourth biggest army in the world!)' (1995: 65). The assertion that Iraq had the 'fourth biggest army in the world' was a frequent theme of propaganda at the time, as was the entirely false story that Iraqi troops were 'massing' on the border of Saudi Arabia, poised for an invasion (Keeble 1997: 81–4; MacArthur 1993: 172–8). Saddam was, as Baudrillard pointed out, a 'fake enemy' (1995: 38).

When Baudrillard wrote sarcastically of the Gulf as a 'non-war', a war that 'never began', the outcome of which was 'decided in advance', he was pointing to what Laïdi (1998: 14) calls the 'divorce of meaning and power'. Despite having the most powerful military machine ever, there was no framework of meaning within which to use it; no metanarrative to allow the projection of power. Instead, the West had become 'paralysed by its own power, in which it does not believe' (Baudrillard 1995: 80). Baudrillard repeatedly emphasised this point in his Gulf War essays, writing of 'the profound self-deterrence of American power and of Western power in general, paralysed by its own strength and incapable of assuming it in the form of relations of force' (1995: 24). Without a grand narrative to make sense of the enterprise, war is unable to inspire belief or enthusiasm. Instead, it becomes meaningless and empty, a mere image, fought 'against a backdrop of spontaneous indifference' (1995: 50). The Gulf War was less a battle with Saddam than a struggle to make sense of the West's role in the post-Cold War world:

> It is not an important match which is being played out in the Gulf, between Western hegemony and the challenge from the rest of the world. It is the West in conflict with itself, by means of an interposed Saddam.
>
> (1995: 38)

It was this changed political context which, for Baudrillard, gave the Gulf War a sense of unreality:

> Unlike earlier wars, in which there were political aims either of conquest or domination, what is at stake in this one is war itself: its status, its meaning, its future. It is beholden not to have an objective but to prove its very existence. ... In effect, it has lost much of its credibility.
>
> (1995: 32)

Unlike in the past, war 'no longer proceeds from a political will to dominate or from a vital impulsion or an antagonistic violence'. Rather than being a means to realise definite political aims or interests, this 'non-war', he argued, was 'the absence of politics pursued by other means' (1995: 83).

It is the lack of political purpose and vision which gives rise to those phenomena that have been seen as typifying 'postmodern war': the use of hi-tech 'smart weapons' and the importance of media spectacle. When war is not 'born of an antagonistic, destructive but dual relation between two adversaries', Baudrillard contended, it becomes bloodless: 'an asexual surgical war, a matter of war-processing in which the enemy only appears as a computerised target' (1995: 62). In the propaganda, the emphasis is on the West's 'humane' approach to killing people, using 'smart weapons' to minimise 'collateral damage', but the more important aim is to eliminate the risk to Western troops themselves. As Baudrillard noted mockingly in 1991, American soldiers were actually safer in the war zone than at home: the casualties were lower than the rate of deaths from traffic accidents in the US (1995: 69). The fear of 'another Vietnam', which surfaces whenever the US military goes into action, is a fear that deaths cannot be justified when the political rationale for war is threadbare. As Colin Powell has argued, referring to the 1994 withdrawal from Somalia following the deaths of 18 US servicemen, the public are 'prepared to take casualties', but only 'as long as they believe it's for a solid purpose and for a cause that is understandable and for a cause that has something to do with an interest of ours' (quoted in Livingston 1997: 7). Conversely, the lack of any such 'solid purpose' means that the conduct of war becomes risk-averse. As Baudrillard put it, postmodern war is 'the bellicose equivalent of safe sex: make war like love with a condom!' (1995: 26).

For similar reasons, the media presentation of war assumed a disproportionate importance, as staging the spectacle of war became a substitute for an inspiring cause to rally public support. As Baudrillard wrote: 'The war ... watches itself in a mirror: am I pretty enough, am I operational enough, am I spectacular enough ... to make an entry onto the historical stage?' (1995: 31–2). In a sense, the attention to presentation was self-defeating. The emphasis on creating the right image heightened the sense that the war was somehow unreal; the feeling that it was, as many commentators remarked at the time, 'like a video game' (Knightley 2000). This was bound to be the case, since the prominence of presentation and propaganda was driven by the absence of meaning. As Baudrillard put it: 'The media mix has become the prerequisite to any orgasmic event. We need it precisely because the event escapes us, because conviction escapes us' (1995: 75).

In one respect, however, the propaganda had some lasting success. Although the proclamation of a New World Order was a short-lived ideological triumph, the aftermath of the Gulf War saw the beginnings of an idea which was to have a longer shelf-life: humanitarian intervention. In April 1991 'safe havens' for Kurdish refugees were established in northern Iraq, and 'no-fly zones' were imposed to protect the Kurds and other minorities. In what Martin Shaw (1996: 123) describes as 'the media's finest hour', television and press reporting played an important role in encouraging and endorsing this intervention. Shaw argues that the media's treatment of the Kurdish crisis can be understood as signalling the emergence of a 'global civil society', in which the media act as advocates for 'the globally vulnerable' (1996: 178). This idea is also at the centre of Mary Kaldor's analysis of 'new wars', to which we turn next.

'New wars'

Kaldor prefers the term 'new wars' to 'postmodern war', partly because the latter 'is also used to refer to virtual wars and wars in cyberspace'. Similarly, she distinguishes her argument from the discussion of the 'Revolution in Military Affairs', which essentially concerns technological changes, arguing that what is at stake is 'a revolution in the social relations of warfare, not in technology' (Kaldor 1999: 2–3). Despite this admirable emphasis on political factors, the weakness of Kaldor's explanation of them leads her back to claims about technologically-driven change at certain points in her argument. Examining this weakness, it turns out that what starts as a description of wars 'over there' has much more to do with politics 'over here'.

'New wars', Kaldor argues, taking Bosnia as her model, are: 'about identity politics in contrast to the geo-political or ideological goals of earlier wars'; war is no longer 'linked to a notion of state interest or to some forward-looking project – ideas about how society should be organized' (1999: 6). In this respect, her argument has something in common with Laïdi's (1998: 54) view of the violent decomposition of states as 'the expression of a harshly felt loss of meaning'. For Kaldor:

> The new identity politics arises out of the disintegration or erosion of modern state structures … it can be viewed as a reaction to the growing impotence and declining legitimacy of the established political classes.
>
> (1999: 78)

She focuses on former communist and Third World countries, for whom the loss of legitimacy consequent on the end of the Cold War is acutely felt, arguing that the growth of identity politics in such states entails a search, on the part of their ruling elites, for new forms of political mobilisation, and that it is supported by the development of new sorts of criminal or semi-criminal economic activity (1999: 78–9). The 'new wars' might be viewed as postmodern in that they result from a breakdown of the modern nation-state and entail a search for new sources of meaning.

For Kaldor, the cause of the 'erosion of the autonomy of the state and in some extreme cases the disintegration of the state' is globalisation (1999: 4). While she is no doubt correct to look for an international dimension to the 'new wars', her explanation of 'globalisation' leads her back to the very emphasis on technological factors which she initially set out to avoid. Globalisation, Kaldor argues: 'is a qualitatively new phenomenon which can, at least in part, be explained as a consequence of the revolution in information technologies and dramatic improvements in communication and data-processing' (1999: 3). 'What is new', she suggests, 'is the astonishing revolution in information and communications technology' (1999: 71). According to Kaldor, the new identity politics has a transnational dimension for two reasons: first, because of links between local particularists and diaspora communities abroad; second, because of an improved capacity for political mobilisation at home. The first development, she says, is made possible by new communications technologies such as email; the second because, in addition to improved education and literacy, 'more significantly, the widespread availability of television, videos and radio offers extremely rapid and effective ways of disseminating a particularist message' (1999: 86). On the first count, it seems highly unlikely that, to take one of her examples: 'pressure from Croatian groups in Germany' (1999: 85) caused the German government to lead the European Union (EU) in endorsing Croatian independence. As Diana Johnstone (2002: 184–8) shows, in the long-standing relationship between the German state and Croatian nationalist exiles, it was the former which was the active partner. Not only was there considerable continuity, in the 1991 recognition of Croatia, with Germany's previous Balkans policy, but it also presented new opportunities for the German elite:

> The crisis in Yugoslavia enabled German leaders to proclaim a new Germany, not only innocent of the *realpolitik* sins of the past, but moved by a special responsibility born of the Holocaust to play a prominent role in the crusade for universal human rights.
>
> (Johnstone 2002: 165–6)

On Kaldor's second point, it is by no means clear why communications, let alone education and literacy, should favour particularist ideas rather than others, and she is driven to exaggerate the power of the media, claiming that: 'The electronic media has [sic] an authority that newspapers cannot match; in parts of Africa, the radio is "magic"' (1999: 86). The resort to an image of primitive tribesmen worshipping the wireless belies the weakness of the argument. A more plausible explanation of the international dimension of what Kaldor calls the 'new wars', elaborated further in Chapter 2, is that the elites of powerful Western states have used intervention in other people's wars to offset their own crisis of meaning.

Any such explanation is unavailable from Kaldor's perspective, however, since her analysis is designed to advocate such intervention, presenting a set of tolerant, inclusive, democratic values – which she calls 'cosmopolitanism' – as the solution to conflict. Cosmopolitan values are linked with 'those who are part of global processes', while identity politics is associated with those who are excluded from such processes (1999: 6, 70). The equation is not entirely straightforward, since there are both globally-connected particularists and local groups who refuse exclusivist politics, but it is evidently Kaldor's intention to suggest that cosmopolitanism is the logical consequence of objective processes of globalisation, giving it the weight of historical inevitability. Yet it is also clear that she intends cosmopolitanism as a subjective political project:

> The key to any long-term solution is the restoration of legitimacy. ... An alternative forward-looking cosmopolitan political project which would ... reconstruct legitimacy around an inclusive, democratic set of values has to be counterposed against the politics of exclusivism.
>
> (1999: 10)

She means that in those East European and Third World countries where the state's legitimacy and monopoly on the use of violence has broken down, order must be restored through 'cosmopolitan law-enforcement' (1999: 124). The suspicion begins to dawn, however, that it is really the legitimacy of the intervening Western states which Kaldor's cosmopolitan project is designed to rescue. As Shaw (1996: 7) notes, 'The domestic political significance of a global crisis is a large part of its significance for Western states'.

Kaldor does acknowledge that similar processes to those she discusses in relation to the 'new wars' are also at work in the West:

> Even in Western Europe, the erosion of legitimacy associated with the declining autonomy of the nation-state and the corrosion of traditional, often industrially-based sources of social cohesion became much more transparent in the aftermath of 1989. It was no longer possible to defend democracy with reference to its absence elsewhere. A specifically Western identity defined in relation to the Soviet threat was undermined. And the distinctive character of national identity defined in relation to the Cold War lost its substance. ... Of equal significance is the political vacuum, the decline of the left and the narrowing space for substantive political difference.
>
> (1999: 82–3)

The West is also seen, however, as the source of the new cosmopolitan values. Kaldor identifies two key constituencies for cosmopolitanism: international organisations such as the EU, and non-governmental organisations (NGOs) such as Greenpeace. In both cases, the people involved are motivated by a disillusionment with politics. Kaldor says that 'committed idealistic officials' in international institutions 'have an interest in seeking alternative sources of legitimacy to their frustrating national masters'; while NGO activists are people who 'tend to be sceptical about politics' or who have a 'disaffection with conventional political forms' (1999: 88–9). In other words, though she does not make it explicit, it is clear that cosmopolitanism itself is also a response to the 'erosion of legitimacy' she identifies; an attempt to compensate for the loss of meaning in the narrow and insubstantial political sphere of the intervening states.

Kaldor's description of the relationship between the 'cosmopolitan project' and the particularists who 'spread fear and hatred' in the new wars inverts reality. In her telling, these are 'wars between exclusivism and cosmopolitanism' (1999: 9), in which it sounds as if the West is under threat. In Bosnia, she argues, both Serbs and Croats waged 'a war of exclusivist nationalists against a secular multi-cultural pluralistic society' (1999: 44). The society in question was not only mul-tiethnic Bosnia, but by extension, the West. The Bosnian war was: 'a conflict between a new form of ethnic nationalism and civilized values. The nationalists had a shared interest in eliminating an internationalist humanitarian outlook, both within the former Yugoslavia and globally' (1999: 58). It seems unlikely that nationalist Serbs and Croats were really aiming to 'eliminate' humanitari-anism worldwide. In reality, it is the intervention of the Western powers that threatens the integrity of weak states. In the April 1991 Kurdish crisis, by placing part of Iraq's territory and air space beyond its control, it was effectively estab-lished that humanitarianism and the protection of human rights could override the principle of non-intervention in the internal affairs of sovereign states. In 1991–1992 the leading Western powers dismembered multiethnic Yugoslavia by encouraging the secession of its constituent republics. Kaldor's rhetorical attack on 'territorially-tied' particularists is an ideological form of the actual assault on sovereign equality which humanitarian intervention entails.

Kaldor is dismissive of the type of war waged in the Gulf in 1991. Noting Baudrillard's 'famous remark that the Gulf War did not take place', she suggests that 'spectacular aerial bombing … reproduces the appearance of classical war for public consumption [but] has very little to do with reality on the ground' (1999: 3). Her preference is for global policing actions. Yet this is, in effect, a proposal that the Western powers fight postmodern wars. Her project seems to take Baudrillard's (1995: 84) dystopian description of the Americans at the time of the Gulf War as 'missionary people bearing electro-shocks which will shepherd everybody towards democracy' as a positive model:

This consensual violence … operates today on a global level which is conceived as an immense democracy governed by a homogeneous order which has as its emblem the UN and the Rights of Man. The Gulf War is the first consensual war, the first war conducted legally and globally with a view to putting an end to war and liquidating any confrontation likely to threaten the henceforward unified system of control.

(Baudrillard 1995: 83–4)

Kaldor envisages just such a system of control, recommending that Western states send their militaries into action on the basis, not of state interests, but of ethical principles or cosmopolitan values which are supposed to supply a new, forward-looking project.

Postmodern states

The idea that Western states, acting on the basis of values rather than national interests, are in some sense 'postmodern' is taken up by Robert Cooper, the EU's head of politico-military affairs and formerly a senior foreign policy advisor to Tony Blair. Cooper (2004) divides the world into postmodern states, exemplified by the members of the EU; modern states, such as Iraq under Saddam; and pre-modern 'states', such as Somalia, which effectively lack statehood. As this classification implies, Europe's postmodernity is taken as a positive development: European states are more advanced, having left behind the old world of competing national interests. Instead, they operate according to international rules and agreements, seeking consensus rather than conflict, and allowing mutual interference in each other's affairs.

The most notable response to Cooper has been Robert Kagan's book, *Paradise and Power*. Kagan (2004: 37) rightly points out that it is from a position of relative weakness *vis-à-vis* the United States that Europeans find international consensus a more attractive notion than the assertion of national sovereignty. He makes a strong case that Europeans use what the EU's foreign policy chief, Javier Solana, calls 'the legitimacy that comes through the collective action of a union of 25 sovereign states' as a bargaining chip to be 'bartered for influence' (2004: 120). Kagan also hits the mark in drawing attention to the hypocrisy of the Europeans' insistence on UN authorisation for the invasion of Iraq in 2003, despite having gone to war in Kosovo in 1999 without a UN mandate and in defiance of international law (2004: 128–9). Kagan's critique assumes that all the talk of European consensus and postmodernity is just a cover for the pursuit of interest and power by other means. Yet Cooper's claims demand to be taken more seriously, particularly since his argument about the limits of sovereignty is widely shared today. Cooper may be right to consider the EU 'postmodern', though not in quite the positive way he suggests.

There are two aspects of Cooper's argument which are of interest here. First, in so far as it is an argument specifically about the EU, it is worth asking whether Europe can work as a source of meaning. As Stefan Elbe (2003: 66) notes, during the 1990s there was a 'proliferation of pessimistic accounts of contemporary European culture which lament[ed] the inability to produce a meaningful idea of Europe'. The shared values which Cooper claims are the basis for European action can only be actualised through intervention and war. It is less that ethical principles are a guide to action; more that international activism is a means to work up a set of values. Second, as an argument about individual states, we should ask why national sovereignty seems an inadequate source of meaning. Looking a little more broadly at the intellectual background to Cooper's argument, it invokes the idea that today's 'postmodern' states are more humane than their modernist predecessors, and sees the nation–state as a constructed, or imagined community.

Postmodern Europe

Cooper presents a self-flattering picture of Europe, and one which appears to make a virtue of necessity. This is not to say that there is no substance to his claim that European integration has entailed an attenuation of national sovereignty. Rather, it is to suggest that the importance and authority of Europe have increased as those of national institutions have declined (Heartfield 2007). As Laïdi (1998: 84) comments: 'Europe is not managing to construct new post-national expectations by calling national experiences into question. It is at best managing to stem, through common rules of conduct, the perils of a solitary approach'. As an economic arrangement, European integration is more about 'technical standardization than an invitation to join a project' (1998: 84). Cooper's focus, however, is on security and defence. Indeed, he suggests that: 'The postmodern state defines itself by its security policy' (2004: 50). This, he argues, is because of Europe's past experience of nationalism and war. Having seen the dangers of the unbridled pursuit of national interest, European states have decided to subordinate their national sovereignty to the higher need for collective cooperation. His claims for the European approach to security – that postmodern states undertake 'intervention for values' and fight 'wars of principle' such as Kosovo – present Europe as the bearer of something resembling Kaldor's cosmopolitanism (2004: 61). As with Kaldor, however, the relationship between 'values' and intervention is the opposite of that proposed. Rather than values and principles guiding the European approach to security, it is through war and intervention that European leaders attempt to forge a sense of shared values and a collective project. Laïdi's (1998: 95) observation that, for some states: 'War becomes not the ultimate means to achieve an objective, but the most "efficient" way of finding one', might also be extended to Europe.

As Laïdi argues, Europe 'has trouble metaphorizing its own destiny, dramatizing it' (1998: 76). Kaldor presents her cosmopolitan project as the solution to this problem, claiming that international intervention in Bosnia could 'become ... a symbol of a new Europeanism or internationalism' (1999: 68). Bosnia did function in just this way in France during the 1994 European elections. Noting that the 'European Union is in need of a common identity more spiritual than a common currency', Johnstone describes how Bosnia became a *cause célèbre* for a number of prominent French intellectuals. Standing in the elections under the slogan 'Europe lives or dies at Sarajevo', they 'caught the need to associate "Europe" with a dramatic cause' (Johnstone 2000: 151). Cooper's conception of postmodern Europe is similar. As an administrative and economic arrangement it fails to engage public enthusiasm and offers no source of meaning. It is only when Europe proposes to 're-order the world', as Blair put it in a speech on 3 October 2001, that its claim to superior 'values' assumes any significance. In other words, the 'meaning' of Europe, in Cooper's argument, consists only in the warrant, allegedly given by its past experience of nationalism and war, to intervene against less advanced, modern and pre-modern states. It is no good Europeans sitting at home enjoying their postmodern peace. Instead, they need to go out into what Cooper calls 'the jungle', dealing with possible threats by reverting to 'the rougher methods of an earlier era – force, pre-emptive attack, deception, whatever is necessary for those who still live in the nineteenth-century world of every state for itself' (2004: 62). Indeed, Cooper's presentation of the argument is even more negative than Kaldor's, in that there is even less claim to a forward-looking project. Instead, the motivating factor is fear. This is, he suggests, 'a world in which Western governments are losing control': 'Civilization and order rests on the control of violence: if it becomes uncontrollable there will be no order and no civilization' (2004: viii–ix).

Deconstructing national identity

Notwithstanding his suggestion that it is external factors, such as the threat of weapons proliferation or the 'transformation of the state through globalization' (2004: x), which are leading to the emergence of postmodern states, the accent in Cooper's account is on states actively choosing to transform themselves from within. In response to Cooper, Kagan's defence of US foreign policy draws on what now seem old-fashioned ideas about the 'national character' (Kagan 2004: 86–7, 137). From this Kagan draws the warrant for what he claims to be America's continuing Enlightenment mission to spread democracy (2004: 95). In contrast, by seeing national identity as something which is 'a matter of choice' (Cooper 2004: 188, n1), Cooper's view of these matters is much more in tune with contemporary understandings of the nation-state, including postmodernist accounts, which see it as 'constructed' (see further Chapter 6).

For postmodernist critics of the nation-state, such as David Campbell, 'No state possesses a prediscursive, stable identity'. Instead, states are '"imagined communities" devoid of ontological being apart from the many and varied practices which constitute their reality' (Campbell 1992: 105). In this view, foreign policy is not the expression of some inner essence, such as national identity or the popular will; rather, it is one of the 'discursive practices' through which such concepts are created. One of the problems of this line of thought is that while it appears to historicise supposedly timeless notions of 'national identity' and expose their connection with the exercise of power, the outcome of the enquiry is curiously ahistorical. Hence in Campbell's analysis of the construction of American identity in foreign policy discourse, he ends up with an equally timeless notion of 'discursive economy' through which the American Self is defined in opposition to various marginalised domestic and foreign Others. Ranging across such diverse and distinct historical events as 'the "discovery" of the New World, the colonisation of Ireland, the Puritan settlement in America, and the subsequent moments of identity and conflict from colonial times through to the red scares of the nineteenth and twentieth centuries', Campbell's approach is to downplay 'all that was specific to the time and place', in favour of highlighting discursive 'techniques of exclusion' which he finds at play in all these contexts (1992: 249).

Such an ahistorical approach begs the question, why now? Why should national identity be seen as a questionable myth in the 1990s? The answer implied in Cooper's account is that European states have learned the lessons of the past and rejected the grand narratives of history. Cooper's development of the idea of 'postmodern states' appears to have been inspired by Stephen Toulmin's 1990 book, *Cosmopolis*.[1] It is worth briefly examining Toulmin's work, since the fact that Cooper is influenced by it reveals much about the elite's attitude to its own past.

Toulmin rewrites the history of modernity as an era, not of liberation, but of repression. Cartesian rationalism, he argues, did not come from nowhere: it was a response to the horrors of the Thirty Years' War (1618–1648). The scientific Quest for Certainty sought a neutral ground which could transcend religious divisions. It was, however, a limited and flawed response. Born in a period of crisis, modernity had a 'hidden agenda': to restore 'cosmopolitical' balance and stability between the natural and social worlds. Hence, for example, 'Newtonianism [was] a "cosmopolitical" justification for the "modern social order"' (1990: 133). Even though it was a response to religious hatred, rationalism 'perpetuated the dogmatism of the Religious Wars' (Toulmin 1990: 80). The social order of modernity, in Toulmin's view, was a highly repressive one: modernity's 'idolisation of social stability' gave rise to sexism, racism, sexual repression, class division and moral dogmatism (1990: 133–6). Against this, Toulmin sets out to recover the earlier tradition of Renaissance humanism. Instead of a Quest for Certainty, he argues, in the Renaissance tradition it was thought better to 'suspend judgement about matters of general theory, and to concentrate on accumulating a rich perspective, both on the natural world and on human affairs, as we encounter them in our actual experience' (1990: 27). Rather than a wish to impose order, there was a 'respect for complexity and diversity': in physics, 'everyone was free to believe what he liked'; in natural philosophy, many 'were driven to adopt attitudes of outright skepticism' (1990: 28–9). If this sounds similar to postmodernism, that is because Toulmin intends to suggest that we are beginning to recover this tradition – though he characterises this as 'humanizing modernity' rather than as 'postmodernity' (1990: 180).[2]

Toulmin's argument about modernity also entails a re-evaluation of the nation-state. The turning point ought to have come, he suggests, with the First World War, which led to 'a reappraisal of the "absolutely sovereign" nation-state': after 1914, 'the absolute sovereignty of the individual nation was seen to be dysfunctional and anachronistic' (1990: 152, 139). The recovery of humanism was delayed, however, and it was not until after the Second World War that there began to be 'a decent modesty about claims to sovereignty by the nation-state' (1990: 152). In the present, he points to the EU and to the activities of NGOs such as Amnesty International as positive signs of constraint on nation-states, although, as with Kaldor and Cooper, there is a hint that it is other people's sovereignty he finds most objectionable, as when he writes that: 'those peoples who develop a consciousness of "nationhood" late in the day are open to a pathological nationalism, which insists on anachronistic forms of unqualified sovereignty' (1990: 195).

Toulmin stops short of explicitly endorsing postmodernism, but his injunction to 'humanise' modernity implies a similar outlook. It is not coincidental that his critique of modernity takes Descartes as its starting point: his argument is an assault on the Cartesian Subject. Toulmin's 'humanism' aims to cut the Subject down to size, emphasising human fallibility. The Renaissance humanism he celebrates 'meant developing modesty about one's capacities and self-awareness about one's self-presentation' (1990: 199). Similarly, he suggests that: 'We need not be ashamed to limit our ambitions to the reach of humanity: such modesty does us credit'; and argues that: 'Tolerating ... plurality, ambiguity, or the lack of certainty is no error ... it is part of the price that we inevitably pay for being human beings, and not gods' (1990: 30). In this version of 'humanism', humanity must not be over-ambitious but should be aware of its limitations.

Again we might ask, why now? Why does the project of modernity seem to have lost its credibility at the start of the 1990s? It is at the point when history seems to have ground to a halt; when, in Laïdi's terms, there is no 'horizon of meaning', that the project of modernity appears open to question. Presenting this as a positive transcendence of the past cannot disguise the fact that it involves a drastic lowering of expectations, from the ambition to make history to a 'proper modesty' about human capabilities. For Cooper, it is at the point when it no longer seems credible as a source of meaning that the nation-state is called into question. He argues that the 'development of state structures is matched by a society that is more sceptical of state power, less nationalistic, in which multiple identities thrive and personal development and personal consumption have become the central goals of most people's lives' (2004: 51). It is the failure to engage people's belief in the state or the nation which makes these appear as artificial constructs. Indeed, if institutions lose the appearance of representing the will of the people, there would seem to be no reason why those institutions should not 'decide' to change their identities in an effort to re-legitimise themselves. If, as Cooper argues, 'for the postmodern state as for the individual identity is a matter of choice' (2004: 188, n1), this is not so much a transcendence of sovereignty as a consequence of the emptying out of the content of sovereignty as the expression of popular will. The nation-state was always an imperfect form of democratic representation, but it did at least offer some framework of political contestation and engagement. Cooper's argument for 'postmodern' states, on the contrary, is that they reflect an absence of political involvement. The EU provides an ideal focus for articulating this refashioning of identity precisely because it has even less connection with a demos (Heartfield 2007).

Though Toulmin is sanguine about the prospects for 'humanizing modernity', the crisis of meaning is apt to make the future appear threatening. Writing in the same year as Toulmin, Jean Delumeau draws a similar historical comparison, arguing that there is 'a climate of anxiety in our civilization which, in certain respects, is comparable to that of our ancestors between the time of the plague and the end of the Wars of Religion'. As in Toulmin's analysis, the events and developments which he sees as prompting a reappraisal of the past are many and varied. They include the 'various holocausts' of the twentieth century, the nuclear threat, the 'rapid and often more and more troubling progress of technology', environmental degradation, genetic engineering, and 'the uncontrolled explosion of information' (quoted in Campbell 1992: 55). As noted above, for Cooper, too, the motivating factor is fear:

> most worrying is the encroachment of chaos on the civilized world – from around it and within it. Europe may be able to stop the approach of chaos through the Balkans or even from across the Mediterranean, but it may prove more difficult to deal with chaos in its own suburbs and declining industrial towns.
>
> (Cooper 2004: x)

It is telling that he sees the greatest threat as coming from within. When state institutions fail to engage popular enthusiasm, they begin to regard their citizens with trepidation. Despite the talk of states and individuals freely choosing their identities, Cooper's overarching concern is to regulate and control; to stem the tide of chaos. Just as domestic government policy increasingly seeks to police individuals' choices in order to ensure that they are 'responsible', so too in contemplating the international sphere Cooper's impulse is to regulate and constrain the exercise of sovereignty.

The postmodern military

In discussing the 1991 Gulf War above it was argued that the emphasis on waging high-tech, low-risk wars stemmed from a lack of clear political purpose and vision. This can now be further clarified in light of the foregoing discussion of the 'postmodern state'. As Charles Moskos *et al.* (2000: 4–5) perceptively point out, 'the nation-state is the *sine qua non* of the Modern military', but in the postmodern era, 'the sense of identity with and loyalty to the nation-state is "decomposed"'. Western societies, they observe, have seen a 'cultural shift in public attitudes and opinions':

> Old verities are questioned rather than accepted. There are fewer over-arching authorities to whom people are willing to defer. There is a shrinking consensus about what values constitute the public good, and little confidence that we know how, by the use of reason, to determine what the public good might be.
>
> (Moskos *et al.* 2000: 4)

The inability of Western elites to cohere their societies around a positive vision of the future has had a negative effect on the Western military. As Cooper acknowledges ruefully, societies which can offer their citizens no higher goal than 'personal development and personal consumption' find it hard to inspire people to risk their lives:

> Army recruitment becomes difficult – consumerism is the one cause for which it makes no sense to die – though fortunately technology means that fewer recruits are required. Where once recruitment posters proclaimed YOUR COUNTRY NEEDS YOU!, they now carry slogans such as JOIN THE ARMY: BE ALL THAT YOU CAN; self-realization has replaced patriotism as a motive for serving in the armed forces.
>
> (Cooper 2004: 51)

'Self-realization', however, is a poor substitute for an inspiring cause greater than oneself. In so far as it makes any sense as a reason to sacrifice one's life, self-realisation only has meaning for the individual. It is not just that technology means that the military can manage with fewer personnel, it also helps to offset the elite's inability to inspire their soldiers with a 'cause for which it makes sense to die' by reducing the risks of war. As Alvin and Heidi Toffler argued in a book reportedly 'revered' by the American military, 'One of the foremost objectives in the development of new weaponry should be the reduction or total elimination of risk' (quoted in Coker 2001: 15).

The risk-averse conduct of contemporary war is a source of anguish for some commentators. William Shawcross (2000: 374), for example, points to 'an uncomfortable paradox':

> We want more to be put right, but we are prepared to sacrifice less. … Western television audiences want to stop seeing children dying on their screens, but many political leaders believe we do not want our own soldiers (our own children) to be put at risk to rescue them. That could change

if political leaders ... were prepared to argue that intervention cannot be cost free.

Similarly, Michael Ignatieff (2000: 163) sees the 1999 Kosovo conflict as the 'paradigm of [a] paradoxical form of warfare', whereby 'precision violence is now at the disposal of a risk-averse culture, unconvinced by the language of military sacrifice'. To resolve the paradox, he advises that: 'we need to stay away from ... fables of self-righteous invulnerability. Only then can we get our hands dirty. Only then can we do what is right'. The apparent bloodthirstiness of liberal writers such as Ignatieff may seem odd. What troubles them is that their own alternative frameworks for justifying military sacrifice do not seem to work. As Moskos *et al.* (2000: 2) note, one of the features of the postmodern military is that it is deployed in unconventional missions such as aid relief – 'Operations Other Than War', in the military jargon – which are 'authorized (or at least legitimated) by entities beyond the nation-state', such as the UN. With the declining authority and legitimacy of the nation-state, Cooper's 'postmodern Europe', or Kaldor's 'cosmopolitan values' are attempts to find alternate sources of legitimacy 'beyond the nation-state'. As far as Kaldor or Ignatieff are concerned, the new types of military intervention, for principles and values rather than state interest, are being hamstrung by the petty concerns of Western political leaders who are afraid of the adverse publicity if military personnel are killed. The problem, however, is not simply that politicians are reluctant to make the argument for sacrifice because, unlike the armchair interventionists, they are electorally accountable, it is that they lack the basis on which to do so.

Richard Devetak argues that the 'cosmopolitan vision might be thematised in terms of what [William] Connolly calls an "ironic" attitude toward community'. If the traditional foundations of community – such as race, nation or class – seem discredited in the postmodern era, definitions of community must do without 'sovereignty's usual understandings of identity and difference'. In place of the oppressive discourses of modernity, such as those identified in Campbell's deconstruction of American identity, a postmodern conception of community has to be 'conscious of its contingency and its incompleteness', without any 'fixed or permanent boundary to distinguish the inside from the outside' (Devetak 1995: 45). The problem with such a community, of course, is that it is hard to believe in. An 'ironic' attitude to community may avoid the pitfalls of modernity's 'discursive economy' but it cannot inspire conviction. Toulmin (1990: 160) suggests that the Second World War was 'the last time when the people of Europe could endorse, and act out, the ideals and ambitions of Modernity in a quite *unselfconscious* manner'. Coker adds that 'The same can be said of the United States in Vietnam':

Today even Americans find war ironic because they are deeply self-conscious. Our age is marked by a pervasive inability to take our own presuppositions seriously, and thus to be always at some ironic distance from ourselves. Nothing is more characteristic of the present mood than the ironic, detached self-consciousness that not only the public but many soldiers too now have of contemporary warfare and their own profession.

(Coker 2001: 42)

It is difficult to feel fully part of an 'imagined community' if we view it as such. If we are 'aware that the world is a constructed reality, a projection of our own cultural norms' (Coker 2001: 42), it is even more difficult to believe we should risk our lives for such a community.

Postmodern irony has had a disorientating effect on the military. As John Allen Williams (2000: 274) observes: 'Military culture is challenged by a relativistic civilian ethos from without and by the increasing civilianisation of military functions and personnel orientation from within'. The 'civilianisation of personnel orientation' is often discussed in terms of the 'feminisation' of the military (for example, van Creveld 2000), though the problem is not the recruitment of women *per se*. Stephanie Gutmann is closer to the mark when she identifies the issue as 'political correctness', one important aspect of which is the military 'working desperately to be "female friendly"' (Gutmann 2001: 15). A society unsure of its values – or at an ironic distance from any 'values' – is uncomfortable with the gung-ho aggression of traditional military culture. Madeline Morris, an American law professor who in 1997 worked as a consultant to the Secretary of the Army, argued for a change in 'military culture from a masculinist vision of unalloyed aggressivity to an ungendered vision' (quoted in Gutmann 2000: 151). The pursuit of the 'ungendered' ideal can often seem at odds with military objectives. A team redesigning a new amphibious landing craft, for example, declared that they were 'supporting standards developed to protect pregnant sailors' – hardly what one would expect to be a key concern in designing a ship to put troops ashore (Gutmann 2000: 96).

The US Navy personnel who Gutmann interviewed complained of feeling they were aboard a 'Mommy ship', which patronised them with endless 'Sailor of the Day' awards to bolster their self-esteem ('no matter what you do you get an award for it', remarked one bemused interviewee), fretted for their safety and hospitalised them for 'alcohol abuse' if they returned from leave drunk. As in wider society, the behaviour of the military is regulated to make sure it is not 'risky' or offensive. In a 'gender-integrated' military, this includes 'raising awareness' about sexual harassment, but it also extends to other areas, such as religion. During the 1998 'Desert Fox' bombing of Iraq, for example, not only were operations suspended during the first night of Ramadan, but when one sailor wrote 'Hey Saddam! Here's a Ramadan present from Chad Rickenberg' on a Navy bomb, the Pentagon issued an apology, saying it was 'distressed to learn of thoughtless graffiti mentioning the holy month of Ramadan written on a piece of ordnance' (quoted in Gutmann 2000: 176). As Moskos (2001) comments: 'The concept of "postmodernism", with its core meaning of the absence of absolute values, [is] increasingly applicable to the contemporary military'.

Coker takes up Toulmin's notion of 'humanising modernity', arguing that a similar logic extends to war. After the collapse of grand narratives, with no metaphysical principle to justify it, war is fought for humanity. Postmodern war, he argues, is 'humane', both in terms of its goals (humanitarianism and human rights) and its conduct (minimising casualties) (Coker 2001: 17–18). Coker is, however, sensitive to many of the contradictions of 'humanitarian war'. Among the problems it raises is how to 'create a sense of solidarity with mankind' (2001: 139). Absent the narratives of the past, which bound people together in a collective project, what is the basis of human solidarity? The cosmopolitan approach claims to be 'expanding our sense of "us" as far as we can' (2001: 139) – or at least, in Cooper's version, to the boundaries of the EU – but on what is such a community founded? The best answer Coker can suggest is that it is common awareness of human suffering, and an 'ability to sympathise with [other people's] pain', but as he acknowledges, the danger is that 'We no longer value others so much as *pity* them' (2001: 139, 127). Sympathy for others' pain and suffering is a lowest-common-denominator approach to humanity which emphasises individual human frailty and vulnerability. It is about as far away from a future-oriented collective project as one can get.

As Coker points out, without 'any transcendent ideal that extends beyond the immediate crisis', humanitarian war 'fails to offer a compelling reason to endure the cruelties that war usually brings' (2001: 142). Instead of a forward-looking project, society promises only 'the mundane satisfaction of mundane needs', and is in danger of becoming increasingly narcissistic (2001: 126–7, 138). With nothing to aspire to and nothing to fight for beyond the everyday, people increasingly turn inward. What starts out as sympathy for others can easily turn into self-pity. Although Coker, following Richard Rorty, couches his argument in terms of the death of metaphysics, this somewhat misstates the problem. Laïdi's way of putting it – that society lacks a collective project – is closer to the mark, since the problem is less the death of metaphysics than the death of politics. It is the hollowing out of the political sphere which puts social cohesion in question. As Moskos *et al.* (2000: 4) suggest, behind the erosion of the nation-state as the basis for the modern military lies the erosion of citizenship:

> Citizenship is a distinctively Modern institution, depending as it does on the conception of an autonomous individual, capable of free choice and self-regulation, participating in public affairs with expectations of affecting the outcome of political decisions.
>
> (2000: 4)

The inability of the elite to engage their citizens is posed sharply in the case of the military. Instead of viewing people as self-regulating, autonomous individuals, soldiers too are viewed as part-victims, part-victimisers.

Gutmann's account shows the politically correct US Navy treating its sailors as both incapable victims in need of protection, and as potential abusers who may run amok at any moment. Gutmann also offers some anecdotal evidence that soldiers sometimes internalise this victim status. One female reservist who was called up in the mobilisation for the Gulf War, for example, filed for conscientious objector status, complaining that: 'My recruiter told me I would never have to go to war, that I would travel and gain skills and an education ... I cannot kill another human being. I cannot even facilitate war' (Gutmann 2001: 135). Perhaps the recruiting sergeant was promising the kind of 'self-realisation' which the British Army now apparently offers. As Cooper (2004: 51) notes, possibly thinking of complaints of 'Gulf War Syndrome' after the 1991 war: 'while soldiers still die bravely for their countries, today they may also sue them for injuries sustained in war'. In the second Gulf War, the US military was reportedly 'fighting desertion, recruitment shortfalls and legal challenges from its own troops' (*The Times*, 10 December 2004).

Conclusion

Following Laïdi's argument that after the end of the Cold War modernity's grand narratives no longer seem to offer society a vision of the future, there are grounds for understanding both the 1991 Gulf War and intra-state 'ethnic' conflicts such as Bosnia as 'postmodern' wars. In both cases, there is a questioning of the nation-state as the focus for social cohesion and the basis for international action. Given that the declining legitimacy of the nation-state has had far more dramatic consequences in weaker, East European or Third World states, it may seem odd to focus, as this chapter has done, on the West. The problem with analyses that take wars 'over there' as their starting point, however, is that they tend to obscure the fact that, as Laïdi argues, the 'crisis of meaning' also affects Western societies. From this perspective, developments in Western states – whether understood in terms of 'cosmopolitanism', 'humanising modernity' or 'postmodernity' – tend to be seen as positive, and as offering a solution to conflict and disorder elsewhere.

Instead, this chapter has suggested, Western states have sought to offset their own crisis of meaning through international intervention, including humanitarian action. It is misleading to declare as, for example, Coker (2001: 133) does that: 'The postmodern age fights humanitarian wars because we have renounced metaphysics'. Rather, it is the hollowing out of the political sphere which leads to a repudiation of modernity and the modern nation-state, and which gives rise to a search for new sources of meaning or legitimacy in postmodern war. It is to the spectacle of armed humanitarianism that we turn next.

Chapter 2

The humanitarian spectacle

On Friday 4 December 1992, former US president Ronald Reagan gave a speech to the Oxford University Union in which he suggested that humanitarian military intervention could replace the Cold War as a new rationale for the projection of Western power. The 'end of communist tyranny', said Reagan, had 'robbed much of the West of its uplifting, common purpose'. Yet, he argued, 'Evil still stalks the planet', and combating it might provide a new 'cause' for people to rally round. Pointing to crises in Somalia, Sudan and Bosnia, Reagan asked:

> [M]ight we not now unite to impose civilised standards of behaviour on those who flout every measure of human decency? Are we not nearing a point in world history where civilised nations can in unison stand up to the most immoral and deadly excesses against humanity ...?

> [T]he world's democracies must enforce stricter humanitarian standards of international conduct. What I propose is a humanitarian velvet glove backed by a steel fist of military force.[1]

On the same day, Reagan's former vice president and successor in the White House, George Bush Snr., also gave a speech. In a national television address, President Bush explained his decision to send the US Marines to Somalia, where they would be authorised 'to take whatever military action is necessary':

> Let me be very clear: Our mission is humanitarian, but we will not tolerate armed gangs ripping off their own people, condemning them to death by starvation. ... The outlaw elements in Somalia must understand this is serious business.

The US troops in 'Operation Restore Hope', said Bush, would be 'doing God's work'. More importantly, they would also be demonstrating American leadership:

> I understand the United States alone cannot right the world's wrongs. But we also know that some crises in the world cannot be resolved without American involvement, that American action is often necessary as a catalyst for broader involvement of the community of nations. Only the United States has the global reach to place a large security force on the ground in such a distant place quickly and efficiently and thus save thousands of innocents from death.[2]

American military muscle was thus to be given new meaning in the post-Cold War era, no longer as a guarantor of the West's freedoms against the menace of communism but as the steel fist inside a humanitarian velvet glove.

This chapter explores the Western elite's attempt to discover a new source of meaning in humanitarian and human-rights intervention in the 1990s. It argues, firstly, that public discussion of the crises and conflicts targeted by such interventions was distorted and misleading. The justifications for action often misrepresented the actual situation and there was a sometimes extravagant concern on the part of the intervening states with generating good publicity. However, the gap between representation and reality is not equivalent to the traditional problem of wartime propaganda – in most cases the Western military was not at war and media misrepresentation was rarely the result of official control and censorship of information. Rather, journalists and other commentators were also engaged in a search for meaning, and it was primarily this which gave rise to distortion. Secondly, it is not only the media presentation but the interventions themselves which have to be understood in terms of the crisis of meaning. Instead of following a coherent strategy, policy was opportunistic and haphazard. Again the problem here is different from the past. Just as the distorted representation of crises and the international response to them is not reducible to the familiar issue of propaganda, so too the proclaimed goals of upholding humanitarian or human rights ideals were not merely a cover for hidden interests. That is to say, the rhetorical justifications for military action have often appeared arbitrary and inconsistent, not because the 'real' motivations were hidden, but because the key motivation for action was to demonstrate or exemplify proclaimed values; to construct some sense of an 'uplifting, common purpose' for Western societies. Finally, it is argued that the attempt to discover a new sense of purpose in humanitarian action has failed – inevitably so, since the orientation towards 'values' and 'ethics' in foreign policy was an attempt to evade the consequences of the death of politics through a search for moral absolutes.

Creating the spectacle

When the Marines dispatched by President Bush arrived in Somalia their first hostile engagement was with the massed ranks of the international media. Swarming up Mogadishu beach in camouflage gear, they were illuminated by television lights and camera flashbulbs which interfered with their night-vision equipment. Contemporary reports describe how the troops tried to hide as they were chased around the beach by journalists: 'the men pleaded with them to go away – like children discovered playing hide-and-seek by an adult' (*The Independent*, 10 December 1992). The military on the ground were confused and annoyed by the presence of the media, but the reporters had been invited to be there by the Pentagon, which had: 'made little effort to disguise the fact that the dawn landing had been set up in much the same way as a sporting event' (*The Times*, 10 December). 'We made an impressive show of force this morning', claimed a US Marines spokesman, 'we did it to make a play but we are not joking' (*The Independent*, 10 December). If this 'show' or 'play' was intended to impress the Somalis, it was equally aimed at television audiences back home. Some of the more cynical journalists suggested that the timing of the landing had been planned around the evening television schedules in the US. Yet as a publicity stunt it was largely unsuccessful because it was too obvious and heavy-handed: the absurd mismatch between the heavily-armed troops, behaving as if they were storming a military target, and the reporters clad in chinos and t-shirts, offering friendly greetings and attempting interviews, meant that the operation appeared farcical.

On other occasions too, the use of humanitarian crises to provide manufactured opportunities for good public relations (PR) has been patently self-serving. During the Bosnian war, for example, Prime Minister John Major personally intervened to arrange the evacuation by the Royal Air Force of an injured five-year-old girl, Irma Hadzimuratović, from Sarajevo to a London hospital. The main objective was the public display of caring, not saving the little girl: to ensure that the credit should not go to someone else, the government warned off two tabloid newspapers, *The Sun* and *The Mail*, both of which were attempting to mount their own rescue missions. Dismissing the government's mercy flight as a 'cheap publicity stunt' *The Guardian*'s Maggie O'Kane observed that there was 'a chilling cynicism in their actions' (10 August 1993). In such moments of contrived drama and pathos, the seams sometimes showed.[3] What was meant to appear edifying and noble just looked shoddy. This is not to say, however, that the overall illusion was entirely shattered, since critics tended to take it for granted that Western intervention was generally a good thing. O'Kane's main complaint, for example, was that 'the story of Irma diverted us down a tragic side road ... distracting attention from the central issue of military intervention'.

In Somalia, although few among the foreign media could stifle their sniggers at the Americans' clumsy attempt to look impressive, there were fewer still who were not complicit in creating the spectacle. Journalists sought out the most sensational stories of suffering, asking aid workers where they might find some 'stick action' – emaciated infants who could be filmed at the point of death (Carruthers 2000: 240; Lyman 1995: 122–3) – and in one incident they reportedly 'trampled starving children ... in their desperation to obtain the best photographs' (*The Guardian*, 16 December 1992). The picture they produced was of a wretched and chaotic country with no government, where warlords and gunmen preyed on the weak, looting shipments of aid intended for the starving. As Africa correspondent Richard Dowden (1995: 94) wrote afterwards: 'it seemed a self-evident truth that Somalia had to be rescued from itself'.

As Dowden went on to note, however, 'there were certain awkward facts which did not fit this picture'. For one thing, as several commentators have observed, the worst of the famine was actually over by the time the US deployed its forces in Operation Restore Hope. Michael Maren (1997: 204), for instance, notes that: 'the problem that supposedly required military intervention was becoming less of one every day'. Critics have also pointed out that the problems of conflict and disorder were localised, affecting only about a quarter of the country (Drysdale 2001: 56–7, 104), and that the extent of looting of food aid had been exaggerated. Describing the US operation as 'very well stage-managed', a senior UN official in Somalia dismissed as 'bullshit' State Department claims that 80 per cent of aid was being looted (*The Guardian*, 9 December 1992); while the Red Cross and other charities estimated that 'a maximum of 20 to 30 per cent' had been lost through looting, an unexceptional figure (*The Independent*, 10 December 1992). Perhaps most importantly, the heroic image of the US saving Somalia from itself tended to obscure the fact that it was previous US policies which were largely responsible for creating the country's problems in the first place. From the late 1970s, America took over from the Soviet Union as the sponsor of General Mohammed Siad Barre's regime, giving him arms and aid in return for the use of military facilities. The US food aid undermined the domestic economy, and encouraged division and political corruption as Barre used it to favour his allies and weaken his enemies. After the Cold War, Barre became expendable, the military facilities were abandoned and aid was cut off. Not surprisingly, since it had become a society dependent on, and divided by, foreign sponsorship, Somalia rapidly descended into civil conflict. Somalis' problem was international interference rather than themselves.

The discrepancies between the media image and the reality of the situation beg the question of why the West intervened. Somalia held no economic or geo-strategic significance for the US – which was why, after all, America had only recently withdrawn its troops. From a realist perspective, the intervention made little sense. Former US diplomat George Kennan, for example, argued that undertaking an 'immensely expensive' and protracted mission in a country where there was 'no defensive American interest' was irrational. He concluded that the decision to launch Operation Restore Hope must have been driven by media coverage of suffering and the consequent public pressure for action: policy had been 'controlled by popular emotional impulses ... provoked by the commercial television industry' (*The Guardian*, 7 October 1993). Kennan's argument was an influential formulation of the concept of the 'CNN effect': the notion that the crises spotlighted by real-time global television news dominate the foreign-policy agenda of Western states. The idea has commonsense appeal as an explanation for the apparent arbitrariness of Western actions: why target Somalia, for instance, when the suffering in neighbouring Sudan was just as bad (Livingston 1996)? However, subsequent studies have mostly failed to substantiate the existence of the CNN effect (Livingston 1997; Livingston and Eachus 1995; Mermin 1999; Robinson 2002). In the case of Somalia, coverage followed the agenda of US policy-makers, rather than preceding and causing elite interest. As Jonathan Mermin (1999: 137) concludes, the intervention was not 'evidence of the power of television to move governments' but of 'the power of governments to move television'.

Although critics have found little evidence of the media's capacity to determine foreign-policy priorities or to influence decision-making directly, some have drawn attention to what Piers Robinson (2002: 40) calls a 'potential CNN effect', whereby the likely tone of future coverage is taken into account in formulating present policy.[4] It is not so much that the media independently exercise any direct influence over policy decisions, but that the need to produce feel-good soundbites and images becomes acutely felt when policy itself is oriented toward generating a sense of purpose and meaning. As Ben Macintyre suggested at the time of Operation Restore Hope, 'The troops ... have already restored hope in the United States: in the capacity of a government taking a moral stance, after an election season of deep cynicism' (*The Times*, 9 December 1992). This is much closer to the mark than Kennan's idea of elite policy being led by popular emotions. While the 'CNN effect' thesis points to the elite's lack of self-belief and vision, this has not arisen in relation to intense public pressure for action. Rather, the problem has been one of public disengagement and cynicism. It is for this reason that humanitarian intervention in the 1990s may be understood as a media spectacle: it was the creation of an image of purposefulness which mattered.

What was new?

Of course, the importance of drama, myth and spectacle in the public presentation of military action is hardly a new phenomenon, and neither is the use of militarism as a political resource. But whereas in the past propaganda generally played a secondary role, aimed at securing public support for a military venture, in more recent years the point of the missions undertaken by the Western military has often seemed to be primarily their propaganda value rather than, say, the acquisition of territory or the achievement of some strategic goal. Indeed, such goals have been conspicuous by their absence: as Richard Keeble (1997: 5–6) argues, 'major wars are now fought as media spectacles for largely non-strategic purposes'. Following James Combs (1993), Keeble suggests that this trend developed in the 1980s, with Britain's Falklands conflict and US interventions in Grenada, Libya and Panama, culminating in the 1991 Gulf War. As the credibility of the Soviet threat declined, there was a search for new enemies against whom the West could wage a form of 'unreal warfare' in which military action became 'essentially a media event: an entertainment, a spectacle' (Keeble 1997: 8).

The valuable insight of Keeble's analysis of what he calls 'new militarism' is his recognition that: 'the causes of the conflicts lie more in the (unspoken) dynamics of US/UK domestic and foreign politics than in any credible external threats' (1997: 11). In explaining the Gulf War, Keeble firstly notes the need of 'the US elite … [to] eradicate the trauma of the Vietnam defeat from their collective memory'. The meaning of the 'Vietnam syndrome' is discussed further in Chapter 4, but clearly President Bush's 1991 declaration that America had 'kicked the Vietnam syndrome' by bombing Iraq suggested that the war was intended to overcome the elite's lack of confidence and self-belief. Secondly, Keeble argues that the war served, 'to bring some sense of unity to deeply fractured societies … and legitimise the media/military/civilian elites in the eyes of the public'; and thirdly it was 'needed by the US … to assert its primacy' against powerful rival states.[5] Keeble has extended his analysis to interventions such as those in Somalia, Bosnia and Kosovo, but has emphasised what he sees as the 'contradictions of the new militarism post 1991', and the ways in which later military spectacles did not quite fit the pattern (Keeble 1997: 198; 2000: 66–8). Intervention in Bosnia did not meet the new militarist requirement that actions be quick, easy and 'controllable as media spectacles'; while Somalia was 'a total disaster' (1997: 198).

We need to be clear about what has changed in the post-Cold War era. Focusing on the Gulf War and viewing it against the background of the 1980s points up some interesting continuities, but the post-Cold War political landscape is quite different from the past. The 1982 Falklands conflict, for example, emphasised traditional themes of British nationalism and the defence of sovereign territory. The Conservative government of the day had a relatively clear political project, albeit one which tended to be defined negatively against state socialism and organised labour, and it was in this context that the 'Falklands factor' was mobilised as a domestic political weapon: during the 1984–1985 miners' strike Mrs. Thatcher characterised militant workers as 'the enemy within', to be defeated like the Argentine 'enemy without'. In the 1990s, by contrast, the political life of Western states was characterised by the absence of any ideological contest, and rather than pursuing a definite political vision parties found it increasingly difficult to say what they stood for. This domestic political malaise is examined in greater detail in the chapters which follow, but for now it can be argued that the salience of the factors highlighted in Keeble's account is even greater in relation to the 'humanitarian' military operations of the 1990s, particularly the elite's own sense of incoherence and its lack of wider public legitimacy.

Keeble's third point – the need to assert US hegemony over powerful rivals – was also more important in the 1990s, but although there were significant divisions and rivalries among Western powers, at the same time humanitarianism offered a framework for mutual cooperation and consensus. Some French politicians denounced the arrival of US troops in Somalia as a 'repulsive American media show', for example, but the French government had supported the operation, reportedly at the instigation of Minister of Health and Humanitarian Action Bernard Kouchner, and Paris was as eager as Washington for a good photo-opportunity. As a British report on the French debate noted tartly: 'On Sunday Dr. Kouchner could be seen wading ashore in Mogadishu harbour with a sack of French rice over his shoulder. Yesterday he was reporting live from Bosnia' (*The Times*, 10 December 1992). Earlier the same year, Kouchner had accompanied President François Mitterrand on a dramatic personal visit to Sarajevo, and a week after that he had escorted the president's wife on a trip to Kurdish 'safe areas' in Iraq. The media show was presumably felt to be less repulsive when it was French. Germany's decision to join the operation in Somalia seems to have been driven by similar considerations. Justifying the landmark decision to deploy Bundeswehr troops outside the NATO area for the first time since the Second World War, Chancellor Helmut Kohl argued that: 'This is hugely important for Germany's image in the world' (*The Independent*, 18 December 1992). As Gérard Prunier notes, 'the motivations for joining Operation Restore Hope had little to do with Somalia itself and everything to do with a variety of domestic political and diplomatic concerns':

> Each involved European country had a prudent desire for 'solidarity' with the US giant, a need to appear 'caring' in the eyes of ... domestic public opinion ... a preoccupation ... with displaying its armed forces in an attractively humanitarian role, and a feeling that its rank as a 'power' (even secondary) was linked with membership of the Restore Hope club.
> (Prunier 1997: 136–7)

As the mission ran into trouble Europeans distanced themselves from the failure and became critical of how the US had handled the operation, but this did not imply that they were about to abandon the overall orientation toward 'ethical' intervention. Oftentimes competition and rivalry between Western states took the form of leaders trying to outdo each other in the grandness of their moral poses and humanitarian gestures. In Bosnia, after Major announced he would evacuate 'Little Irma', the Irish government offered to take five injured children from Sarajevo. In a bizarre bidding war, the Swedes said they would take 16, whereupon the British, having initially insisted that Irma was a unique case, decided they could actually accommodate 20 children. Within days, the Italians made it known that they too were trying to evacuate Bosnian children, but the Dutch topped everyone else with an offer to save 30, at an estimated cost of £5 million (*The Guardian*, 12 August 1993).[6]

Looking for continuities with the past runs the risk of missing what is distinctive about the more recent period. Keeble's account is somewhat misled by a preoccupation with the 'secret state' and its covert role in manipulating the media: he tends to overemphasise the extent of elite control through the 'media-military-industrial complex' (1997: 25–6). Similarly, Combs (1993: 277–8) argues that:

> With their political and military power to command, coerce and co-opt the mass media the national security elite can make the military event go according to script, omit bad scenes and discouraging words and bring about a military performance that is both spectacular and satisfying.

In the Gulf War the media were indeed tightly controlled and censored, as they had been in the Falklands, Grenada and Panama (Knightley 2000: 484–5; MacArthur 1993: 138–45). However, this was not the overall pattern in the 1990s. From Vietnam to the Gulf War the relationship between the media and the military was widely understood as one of irreconcilable antagonism, but in the 1990s a more cooperative relationship developed between Western journalists and the Western military; they saw themselves as working toward common goals. Nik Gowing (1994: 15) describes how in Bosnia Western reporters 'willingly submitted to a UN pool system', in contrast to the 'principled complaints by journalists of pool arrangements and news management during the Gulf war'. In fact the change began at the end of the Gulf War itself: from the April 1991 Kurdish refugee crisis onwards, the Western military acted in concert with the media and also with international agencies and NGOs. As noted in Chapter 1, theorists of 'global civil society' such as Kaldor and Shaw commend such organisations as encouraging the spread of 'cosmopolitan' values. It is argued here that what might be called 'freelance interventionists'[7] in the media and elsewhere did play an important, but somewhat different, role: while they did not dictate Western policy, and indeed were often critical of the actual policies adopted, they helped to create a climate in which humanitarianism could be used as a potential new source of meaning for the Western elite.

Freelance interventionists

This is how contemporary humanitarian justifications for military intervention developed: partly through initiatives by politicians seeking to make their actions meaningful; and partly through a critique of Western policy. At the end of the Gulf War America's intention was to withdraw after achieving the stated aim of expelling Iraqi forces from Kuwait. In response to criticism that, by leaving Saddam in power, the US had not 'finished the job', President Bush said it was up to Iraqis to overthrow their government. When they attempted to do so, and were crushed by Saddam's forces, the moral claims made by the US looked hollow. Had not this war been fought in the name of liberation? Had not Saddam been denounced as a tyrant, as worse than Hitler? The compromise solution of setting up 'safe areas' and 'no-fly zones' offered a way to avoid the risks of further direct military engagement while attempting to retain some claim to the moral high ground. The extent to which this was a direct response to pressure from the media is open to doubt: Robinson (2002: 69–71) suggests that the key factor in the US decision was the desire to allow Turkey, a NATO ally which had supported the Gulf War, to contain the problem of Kurdish refugees who laid claim to Turkish territory as well as to part of Iraq. In any event, with the spectacular Gulf victory already beginning to lose its lustre, political leaders saw the opportunity and claimed to be moved by humanitarian concern.

Though they still faced criticism, the main complaint was that they had not gone far enough. During the 1992 US presidential election campaign Clinton's foreign policy advisor, Strobe Talbot, argued that Bush's policy in the Gulf had been insufficiently moral:

> when Americans fight, they want to see not just victory but virtue. ... In mobilizing his fellow citizens to go to war against Saddam Hussein, Bush had suggested that what was at stake were standards, championed by the United States but applicable to all humanity, about how governments should govern. But in the way he ended the war, he repudiated that principle.
>
> (Quoted in Roper 1995: 39)

Talbot, a former *Time* journalist who went on to be Deputy Secretary of State under Clinton, stretched the point in arguing that the Gulf War had been fought over 'how governments should govern'. Criticism of Saddam may have implied this, but the war was ostensibly fought in defence of Kuwaiti sovereignty, and it ended with official protests that any attempt to overthrow the Iraqi regime would violate the prohibition on interference in a state's internal affairs. It was only in the aftermath that, to allow the setting up 'safe areas', it was claimed that such considerations were no longer so important. As British Foreign Secretary Douglas Hurd reportedly argued:

> the international community must be free to act in Iraq to relieve the Kurds' suffering. It could not allow the UN charter's ban on intervention in the internal affairs of member countries to become a straight-jacket.
>
> (*The Guardian*, 11 April 1991)

The critique offered by Talbot and many others was essentially that Western governments ought to be even freer to act.

Intervention in Somalia took the idea a stage further: it was the country's lack of proper statehood that was said to allow international action to relieve suffering (Lewis and Mayall 1996: 94). By all accounts, this policy also seems to have emerged in an *ad hoc* manner. If military humanitarianism had provided a way to avoid embarrassment at the end of the Gulf War, it was now reinforced by the lack of any strategic vision. Operation Restore Hope seemed to offer a way to demonstrate American leadership while avoiding the risks that would be encountered in more difficult situations, particularly Bosnia (Maren 1997: 219–20). Yet the fact that it was driven, not by a commitment to a clear strategy underpinned by agreed values, but by the felt need to discover some purpose and 'values', produced only incoherence and failure. Prunier (1997: 136, 145) describes the operation as a 'rudderless ship' and as 'a case of the blind leading the blind'. According to former aid worker Tony Vaux, it was plagued by divisions at all levels:

> The NGOs ... were engaged in fierce competition. ... Within the military contingent there was competition between units from different countries. In the US government there was competition between the various departments concerned with aid.
>
> (Vaux 2001: 145)

Vaux argues that this petty infighting resulted from the 'lack of policy about humanitarian intervention in the new world order'. According to a study by two members of the Congressional Subcommittee for Africa at the time of the operation, 'The debate in Congress did not suggest the evolution of a new foreign policy doctrine but reflected uncertainty among policymakers about the US role in the post-Cold War world' (Johnston and Dagne 1997: 191).

James Woods, then US Deputy Assistant Secretary of Defence for African Affairs, describes both US and UN policy as 'drifting without apparent cohesion' (1997: 163). Within the US administration, Vaux recounts, 'Everyone wanted his or her say, but no one knew what to do':

> With the US president unsure of what to do, different government departments sensed the need to push themselves forward to secure advantage in the new world order. Much of the debate was about position rather than humanitarian response.
>
> (Vaux 2001: 141–2)

The muddle in Washington had disastrous effects as 'Leaders on the ground in Somalia felt increasingly betrayed by uncertainties back at home' (2001: 141). With no clear overall strategy, the main preoccupation became keeping Western forces out of harm's way. Walter Clarke, the Deputy Chief of Mission at the US Embassy in Somalia in 1993, comments that: 'Lacking political purpose, [the US-led UN force] focused its tactics on force protection rather than the achievement of strategic goals' (Clarke 1997: 4). Unsure of their mission and fearful for their own safety, troops began to lash out, attacking a hospital and opening fire on civilian demonstrations. Thousands of Somalis were killed, and many others were abused and tortured by UN forces (African Rights 1993; de Waal 1997, 1998). Attempts to look tough, such as the decision to put a price on the head of Somali leader General Mohammed Farah Aidid, simply escalated the fighting between the international forces and local militiamen. According to Woods (1997: 163), Aidid 'emerged as a mocking and elusive media personality, visibly twisting the UN and US tails on the world's stage'. Attempting to save face, the US tried to kill him. But the pursuit of Aidid led instead to the deaths of 18 US soldiers and the decision to pull out as America 'lost the will and therefore the capacity to lead internationally' (Woods 1997: 167).

As the US government extemporised on the theme of humanitarian military action in Somalia, it was joined by a chorus of freelance interventionists. Many individuals within the UN and in NGOs were highly critical of the conduct of the US-led intervention in Somalia, but in general these organisations were pushing in the same direction as America and other Western powers. In June 1992 UN Secretary-General Boutros Boutros-Ghali outlined his 'Agenda for Peace', calling for wide-ranging international action in preventive diplomacy, peace-keeping, peace-making and post-conflict peace-building. Noting that his recommendations drew on: 'ideas and proposals transmitted ... by Governments, regional agencies, non-governmental organizations, and institutions and individuals from many countries', he claimed that: 'It is possible to discern an increasingly common moral perception that spans the world's nations and peoples' (Boutros-Ghali 1992: paras. 4 and 15). The essence of this 'moral perception' was that the UN Security Council should take on a more activist role. Most significantly, while he formally acknowledged the principle of non-interference in the internal affairs of sovereign states, Boutros-Ghali argued that: 'The time of absolute and exclusive sovereignty ... has passed' (para. 17). The following month, the Secretary-General urged the Security Council to pay more attention to Somalia instead of focusing only on the 'war of the rich' in former Yugoslavia. According to John Drysdale, who worked in Somalia as an adviser to UN Special Representative Admiral Jonathan Howe, Boutros-Ghali's 'ambition was to use chaotic Somalia as an experiment to prove the viability of his new doctrine: that the absolute sovereignty of nations, in the post-Cold War era, was over' (Drysdale 2001: 1). By August, as the Bush administration announced an airlift of food to Somalia, relief agencies were demanding that the US and UN go further. Save the Children's director called for 'armed intervention' (*The Times*, 14 August 1992), and Rakiya Omaar of the human rights NGO Africa Watch advocated 'dramatic gestures' in the form of 'a relief operation unprecedented in scale' accompanied by 'armed escorts' (*The Guardian*, 14 August 1992).[8]

Despite issuing strident calls for action, the UN and many NGOs were as strategically clueless as the US. As with the competition among different branches of the US administration, judgements tended to be clouded by concern with self-promotion. While his representative, Mohamed Sahnoun, was engaged in delicate negotiations with Somali leaders about how many UN troops might be appropriate, for example, Boutros-Ghali announced to the media that 3,000 would be sent. As Vaux (2001: 144) comments: 'Perhaps Boutros-Ghali was keen to assert a sense of strong leadership but the result was the opposite. He undermined both himself and his envoy and reflected the overall lack of strategy'. Sahnoun himself noted that Boutros-Ghali's announcement 'led to a rapid deterioration of the security situation in Mogadishu' (Sahnoun 1994: 53). Vaux (2001: 151) also recounts how 'aid agencies kept secret their information about areas of need' in case a rival agency got there first.[9] Regarding his own organisation, Oxfam, he describes internal squabbling over turf: 'There was no sense of an agreed organizational purpose. Order had collapsed. ... The organization found itself without a firm base in agreed policy to cope with a changing world' (Vaux 2001: 152). One of Oxfam's managers acknowledged that the decision to go to Somalia was 'largely a result of media pressure and the need for Oxfam to raise its profile'. But when it got there, an internal assessment concluded, 'There was no clear work and Oxfam was "scrabbling about" trying to find a role for itself. There was no team spirit' (2001: 153). 'Trying to find a role': this effectively describes not just the activities of many NGOs, but also what the UN and Western governments were doing in Somalia.

The media were also generally supportive of the idea of stronger interventionism. In a series of reports from Somalia in May 1992, for example, one CNN correspondent accused the US of having ignored starving children who 'want the world to see ... and to forcefully act'; another said the West would be 'neither forgiven nor forgotten' if it did not mount 'a massive, coordinated rescue mission' (quoted in Mermin 1999: 132). As Mermin demonstrates, these explicit calls for action had no discernible impact on public opinion or government policy at the time. But they may well have suggested to political leaders that the media would respond favourably to an initiative on Somalia. Media advocacy may also have been viewed as a barometer of public opinion since, as Robinson (2002: 3) points out: 'available evidence indicates that policy-makers and elite groups ... rely on "perceived public opinion" ... that in turn is largely formed via the media'. That is to say, elite assessments of public opinion are largely derived from a reading of news reports and commentaries.[10]

Journalists were not hapless dupes of official misinformation about Somalia. All the points noted above – about the relatively limited extent of famine and conflict, the exaggeration of looting, and the dismal US record of past interference in the country – were known at the time and, though they were not particularly prominent, they were reported. Media commentators were not so much in ignorance as in denial over the realities of Operation Restore Hope.

Dowden (1995: 95), for example, says he was a 'prophet of doom', constantly pointing out problems and forecasting disaster. Yet the leader columns of his newspaper, *The Independent*, were highly supportive of the intervention, advocating the establishment of a 'benign imperium' (1 December 1992). What tended to excite leader-writers and columnists was not the details of the situation in Somalia but the opportunities it offered for recasting international relationships and endowing the projection of Western power with meaning. For *The Independent*, Somalia showed the US and UN 'moving towards a new role', which it described as 'noble': 'guarding innocent civilians from the grossest abuses of criminal governments and warlords' (23 December). For *The Times*, intervention in Somalia had a 'broader purpose': demonstrating that 'force can be used, under the UN umbrella, to help non-white, Muslim people, and not just where vital American interests are at stake' (9 December). Editorialists were clear-sighted about the fact that the intervention overturned the principle of non-interference in a state's internal affairs, marking 'a radical departure in international law' (*The Times*, 1 December) and setting 'an important precedent' (*The Independent*, 23 December). The response of both newspapers was to urge the maximum interference possible, by 'putting Somalia under temporary trusteeship' (*The Times*) or 'imposing formal and continuing UN mandates on once-sovereign states' (*The Independent*, both 1 December 1992).

If Western governments had little strategic interest in Somalia, news editors surely had none. But in a sense they too were trying to find a role for themselves in the new post-Cold War landscape: as professional mediators charged with the task of explaining the world to their audiences, journalists were also responding to the crisis of meaning. In all cases – from governments, through the UN and NGOs, to media commentators – while there were no doubt many well-meaning and altruistic individuals involved, the overall approach to international intervention was essentially narcissistic. The sudden interest in 'rescuing' Somalia had less to do with the country's actual problems than with the opportunities it seemed to offer for Western societies.

Western narcissism and the search for meaning

The pattern described above was repeated a number of times over the 1990s as Western governments, claiming to be acting on the basis of humanitarian and human rights concerns, interfered directly in weak states while critics in the media and elsewhere urged them to go further. The narcissistic approach to international affairs reached a climax in relation to the break-up of Yugoslavia as saving Bosnia became the favourite cause of Western intellectuals.

'I have never been to Sarajevo', wrote the novelist Salman Rushdie in 1994, 'but I feel that I belong to it, in a way'. Ordinarily, claiming to be 'an exile' from somewhere one has never visited might sound pretentious. But the city of which Rushdie declared himself to be 'an imaginary citizen' was not so much the actual place as 'a Sarajevo of the mind, an imagined Sarajevo':

> That Sarajevo represents something like an ideal; a city in which the values of pluralism, tolerance and coexistence have created a unique and resilient culture. ... If the culture of Sarajevo dies, then we are all its orphans.
>
> (*The Guardian*, 25 April 1994)

The culture and values which appealed to Western liberals apparently had less resonance among the leaders of the Bosnian Muslims themselves, however. Within days of Rushdie's article appearing he was denounced by Bosnian government minister Rusimir Mahmud Cehajić as: 'one of the advocates of Satanic forces that turn to dust and ashes all they can in this country' (*Times Literary Supplement*, 14 October 1994). What outraged Cehajić was Rushdie's idea of a secular, multicultural Bosnia, as opposed to the Islamic state he wished to promote. The fantasy Sarajevo may have borne little resemblance to the reality, but in a sense Rushdie was correct to argue that 'the fight for the survival of the unique culture of Sarajevo is a fight for what matters most to us about our own'. He was right, not because wartime Sarajevo really did embody the secular multiculturalism he wanted to defend, but because outsiders' professions of support for the Bosnian cause were animated by a desire to define what the West stood for.

Unlike Rushdie, others were able to travel to Sarajevo. Aspiring authors hung out with the journalists at the Holiday Inn, Joan Baez gave concerts, Susan Sontag staged *Waiting for Godot*. One visiting American writer described Sarajevo as 'the coolest city in Europe' (*The Independent*, 12 April 1993). Commenting on a December 1993 Strasbourg–Sarajevo television broadcast titled 'A Corridor for Free Speech', and on recent visits by intellectuals such as Sontag, Baudrillard ridiculed the 'false apostles and voluntary martyrs' who went to Bosnia for a spot of 'cultural soul-boosting':

> It is us who are weak and who go there to make good for our loss of strength and sense of reality. ... [We] feel the need to salvage the reality of war in our own eyes ....
>
> Susan Sontag ... must know better than them what reality is, since she has chosen them to incarnate it. Or maybe it is simply because reality is what she, and with her all the Western world, is lacking the most. ... All these 'corridors', opened by us to funnel our foodstuffs and our 'culture' are in fact our lifelines along which we suck their moral strength and the energy of their distress. ... Susan Sontag comes to convince them of the 'reality' of their suffering, by making something cultural and something theatrical out of it, so that it can be useful as a referent within the theatre of Western values, including 'solidarity'.
>
> (Baudrillard 1994)

Characteristically, Baudrillard couched his argument in terms of a loss of 'reality', but this should be understood in the same way as his doubts about the reality of the Gulf War. That is to say, it was not existential angst so much as the political exhaustion of Western societies which sent intellectuals and adventurers to Sarajevo. Bosnia was interesting to them because of what it could be made to mean in the 'theatre of Western values'.

One such figure, Michael Ignatieff, later acknowledged that 'when policy was driven by moral motives, it was often driven by narcissism':

> We intervened not only to save others, but to save ourselves, or rather an image of ourselves as defenders of universal decencies. We wanted to know that the West 'meant' something. This imaginary West, this narcissistic image of ourselves, we believed was incarnated in the myth of a multiethnic, multiconfessional Bosnia. The desire to intervene may have caused us to rewrite the history of Bosnia to make it conform to our ideal of a redeemable place. ... Bosnia became the latest *bel espoir* of a generation that had tried ecology, socialism, and civil rights only to watch all these lose their romantic momentum.
>
> (Ignatieff 1998: 95)

From these comments it rather sounds as if Ignatieff came to think that Bosnia had never been 'redeemable' to begin with: the consistent failure of Western 'humanitarian' intervention is often blamed on those it was ostensibly designed to help. His main point stands, however: that the West's narcissistic preoccupation with its own self-image led to a distorted perception of Bosnia. As Lene Hansen's (1998: 172) analysis of official and media discourse about the war suggests, Bosnia came to be seen as an 'ideal Western self' – a romanticised embodiment of the values of the West. Visiting intellectuals projected onto Bosnia their own notions of 'multiculturalism', variously understood to be an American or a European ideal. David Rieff, for example, says he went to Bosnia in search of the '"Americanization" of the European future', convinced that the US was 'the most successful multicultural society in history' and that 'Western European countries [were] becoming multiracial and multiethnic' (1995: 35, 10). For Europeans, who already saw themselves as multiculturalists, 'Bosnia became a "little Europe" which must be saved from the evils of nationalism' (Johnstone 2000: 143–4).

Many of the Western journalists who covered the Bosnian war came to think that their role was not simply to observe and report, but to become advocates on behalf of victims, calling on the West to act against the abusers. His experiences in Bosnia famously led former BBC correspondent Martin Bell to coin the phrase 'journalism of attachment' to describe this new style of reporting which would be openly partisan and engaged. Rejecting the 'dispassionate practices of the past', Bell argued instead for a journalism which 'cares as well as knows' and which does not 'stand neutrally between good and evil, right and wrong, the victim and the oppressor' (1998: 16). Similarly, CNN's Christiane Amanpour warned that adopting a stance of objectivity and neutrality would make the reporter into 'an accomplice to all sorts of evil' (quoted in Ricchiardi 1996). This simplistic good-versus-evil approach inevitably resulted in distortion as reporters shoehorned events into a preconceived moral framework, omitting 'inconvenient' facts which might throw doubt on the clear-cut delineation of villains and victims, and minimising or excusing violence against those groups considered unworthy of sympathy (Hammond 2002). The main point to note here is that the distortion resulted, not from censorship or from slavish reliance on official sources, but from journalists' own efforts to make Bosnia into a meaningful cause. For many, Bosnia was not so much a war to be reported as a morality play about good and evil; not a cruel local conflict but a titanic struggle on a par with the Second World War, in which the Serbs were the new Nazis.

The equation between Serbs and Nazis suggested by journalists – and by the Western PR firm employed by the Bosnian government – did not aid public understanding of the conflict. As BBC correspondent John Simpson (1998: 444–5) subsequently wrote, 'a climate was created in which it was very hard to understand what was really going on, because everything came to be seen through the filter of the Holocaust'. What it did do, however, was offer a moral anchor in a meaningless world. As Mick Hume (1997: 18) suggests, the Bosnian war thereby provided: 'a twisted sort of therapy, through which foreign reporters [could] discover some sense of purpose – first for themselves, and then for their audience back home', as journalists undertook a 'moral mission on behalf of a demoralised society'. For Western societies in which past political allegiances and values no longer made much sense, the Holocaust offered a still-plausible way of invoking moral absolutes. Hume's idea of war-as-therapy echoes Combs's perceptive description of the 1991 Gulf conflict as 'therapeutic war'. Noting then Secretary of Defence Dick Cheney's suggestion that the Gulf War had been a 'catharsis … that sort of lifted the burden that the country had borne, almost without being aware of it, since the war in Vietnam', Combs (1993: 280) argues that: 'The new mass-mediated performance art of warshow can be expanded to include the lack of political morale, serving a therapeutic function'. The context was different – in Bosnia it was intervention in somebody else's war that was now supposed provide catharsis; and it was freelance interventionists who continually sought to raise the stakes, calling for ever-tougher action by Western governments, rather than, as in the Gulf, politicians leading the way – but the dynamic was similar. In both cases, military action was supposed to provide moral clarity.

Advocacy journalists in Bosnia and elsewhere usually presented themselves as critics of Western foreign policy, battling against the indifference or hostility of their own governments. Bell, for instance, recounts how the British government dismissed him and his colleagues as 'the something-must-be-done club' (1996: 138). Yet while media coverage was often critical of particular policy choices, the point of the criticism was invariably to urge earlier, more comprehensive and longer-term intervention, usually involving military action rather than only neutral aid-giving or peace-keeping. Not unlike those who called for further intervention to 'finish the job' at the end of the Gulf War, or those who warned that the US might lack 'staying power' in Somalia, in Bosnia the call was always for more, rather than less, Western interference. By the end of the decade, the moralistic approach to international affairs elaborated by journalists had become the official policy of Western states, as exemplified in the 1999 Kosovo conflict. Bell's refusal to 'stand neutrally between good and evil, right and wrong, the victim and the oppressor', had become Blair's explanation of NATO bombing as 'a battle between good and evil; between civilisation and barbarity; between democracy and dictatorship' (*The Sunday Telegraph*, 4 April 1999). Yet the underlying problems which this approach was designed to address remained unresolved: ultimately, humanitarianism and human rights have proved inadequate responses to the crisis of meaning.

The disappointments of therapeutic war

Kosovo was the highpoint of 'ethical' interventionism and, at least in the short term, drew forth an ecstatic response from those who had championed such action over the previous decade. Observing that the war had 'blooded Tony Blair', *The Independent* said it proved he was 'developing into a national leader of stature' (editorial, 12 June 1999), for example; while *The Guardian*'s Martin Walker hailed the 'potent generation of leaders' who had 'lost their military virginity' (7 June). As these comments suggest, the war was understood as marking some sort of rite of passage. No doubt some commentators were genuinely concerned about Kosovo's ethnic-Albanians, but it appeared that for many NATO bombing was most significant for what it said about the virility of West. Explaining 'Why Kosovo matters', *The Guardian* said it was 'a test for our generation' (editorial, 26 March), for example; and *The Independent*, recalling how Western troops in Bosnia had been 'forced … to scuttle around in armoured personnel carriers, dealing out charity', hoped that: 'Now that humiliation may be over' (editorial, 25 March).

As suggested earlier, the complaint that Western governments had failed to act more decisively in Bosnia was not a criticism of militarism as such, since it presumed the right, indeed the duty, of powerful states to interfere in weaker countries. Nevertheless, criticism of Western pusillanimity had a corrosive effect. Throughout the Bosnian war, a key concern was that Western prestige was threatened by the weakness of politicians who failed to give a moral lead (see further Hammond 2007: Chapter 3). According to *The Independent*, for example, the failure to take a tougher stance was a 'betrayal of everything the West claims to stand for', and threatened the 'credibility' of Western governments and the entire 'international order' (13 and 23 April 1993 editorials). The prevalent idea that the West was shamed and humiliated by its inability to impose order in the Balkans indicated its lack of self-belief. As James Gow (1997) puts it, policy in Bosnia could be described as the 'triumph of the lack of will'. Such critics had a point: there really was a reluctance to take political and military risks in Bosnia and elsewhere in the name of 'ethical' human rights concerns; policy was for the most part *ad hoc*, reactive and inconsistent. NATO's Kosovo campaign was initially welcomed because it promised to break with this dishonourable past, but in the long run it became obvious that it had failed.

For political leaders, of course, the idea was to use Kosovo to demonstrate their sense of moral purpose and 'values'. In a series of speeches President Clinton explained that 'it's about our values', making it clear that these were specifically 'American values'.[11] Yet, as Ben Macintyre reported in *The Times* (12 June), 'Americans never became engaged with the conflict': opinion polls suggested that people remained 'distanced' from it throughout. Pro-war commentators praised Clinton for skilfully managing public opinion, rather than for inspiring genuine support. Even frontline US military personnel reportedly experienced 'feelings of "profound disconnect"' (*The Guardian*, 12 April). 'We're over here doing our job, fighting for the cause', said one, 'Whatever that cause is'. For Europeans, meanwhile, the war was about European values. British Foreign Secretary Robin Cook described the conflict as a battle between 'two Europes competing for the soul of our continent' (*The Guardian*, 5 May 1999), while NATO Secretary-General Javier Solana said it was 'a defining moment not only for NATO, but for the kind of Europe we wish to live in at the beginning of the 21st century' (*Mail*, 14 April). As the bombs rained down, Blair said he felt that 'Europe is … a better place than it was before the military action began' (*The Times*, 5 June); and when it ended he announced that: 'We intend to start building [the] new Europe in Kosovo' (*Mirror*, 11 June). Journalists sometimes joined in with this celebration of the reinvigorated European identity supposedly delivered by the US-led bombing. *The Guardian*'s Hugo Young predicted that: 'the value of "Europe" will be proved more decisively by the Balkan outcome than by the hardness of the euro' (3 June); and Martin Walker declared that in the wake of the conflict: 'The solidarity of the Europeans … will have a potent legacy' (7 June). A week later, however, Walker was reporting the results of elections to the European Parliament and already the potency had turned flaccid. 'Apathy reigned everywhere', he said, with voter turnout so low that 'Europe was facing a crisis of political legitimacy' (*The Guardian*, 14 June).

As Combs (1993: 281) observes in relation to the 1991 Gulf War, the effects of therapeutic war on the body politic soon wear off. In the case of Kosovo, the disappointment was sometimes expressed in terms which recalled Baudrillard's doubts about the 'reality' of the Gulf conflict. *The Independent*, for example, asked 'was it a "war" at all?' (editorial, 10 June 1999); and Ignatieff (2000) described it as only a 'virtual war'. The victory was soured by the fact that, for the time being, Yugoslav President Slobodan Milošević was still in power and Kosovo's future status remained uncertain, but the main reason the war was thought to lack 'reality' was that no Western troops were killed. Complaining that the war left a 'bitter taste', *The Independent* said there was 'no sense of triumph, or of virtue rewarded', though there 'might have been, had NATO suffered some casualties' (editorial, 10 June). Similarly, in *The Guardian* Isabel Hilton objected that 'we are in a war that has no storyline we can believe in':

> Like the Gulf war, it is described as a war of good against evil, of the nations of the light against the forces of darkness, an affirmation of civilisation against barbarism. But we are not convinced enough by abstract notions of civilisation and internationalism to die for them. ... In the absence of the hero-warrior and the shared values he would embody, television, the consumer society's storyteller supreme, has been floundering in the attempt to construct a narrative that makes sense to us.
>
> (*The Guardian*, 5 April 1999)

As with Baudrillard's comments on the Gulf, so too in Kosovo the war's lack of 'reality' was essentially a lack of meaning. The grand values proclaimed by political leaders seemed to be undermined by their unwillingness to risk the lives of their own troops to defend them. Since the Bosnian war had already been understood in the same way, in 1999 this problem was highlighted by some right from the start. On the day the bombing began, Mary Kaldor was already bemoaning the fact that 'Western leaders still privilege the lives of their own nationals', arguing that 'What went wrong in Bosnia was the reluctance to risk the lives of peace-keepers' and identifying 'the same syndrome in Kosovo' (*The Guardian*, 25 March). Similarly, Hugo Young wondered whether, if NATO forces were 'not prepared to match their enemy's risk with their own', they 'cannot expect to win, and maybe don't deserve to?' (*The Guardian*, 1 April). In part, such arguments were about how best to safeguard the lives of Kosovo Albanians: high-altitude bombing seemed less effective than ground troops and inevitably involved 'collateral damage' – though a full-scale ground invasion would undoubtedly have been much more bloody. But the underlying concern was not so much the facts on the ground in Kosovo as the self-image of the West. Kaldor was worried about 'NATO credibility'; while Young feared that without ground troops risking their lives 'all this passionate rhetoric of human solidarity will turn to ashes, and NATO, quite possibly, will be ruined'.

That some Western commentators should have supported the war while wishing for more casualties on their own side is frankly perverse and irrational. What bothered them was the nagging suspicion that the framework of 'ethical' foreign policy and humanitarian military intervention had failed to offer a new source of meaning for the post-Cold War world. This, after all, was always the point. Ignatieff, for example, complains that with the collapse of the Cold War framework 'the absence of narratives of explanation is eroding the ethics of engagement':

> If we could see a pattern in the chaos, or a chance of bringing some order here or there, the rationale for intervention and long-term ethical

engagement would become plausible again. We forget that the Cold War made sense of the world for us: it gave an apparent rationale to the wars of the Third World; it explained the sides; it identified whose side we should be on. We have lost our narrative, and with it, the rationale for engagement.

(1998: 98)

People dying for the cause would prove it was 'real'; that it was viable as a new basis for political engagement. Instead, NATO's 'virtual war' showed the triumph of the rhetoric but with no wider significance. As Ignatieff (2000: 3) explained, 'citizens of NATO countries ... were mobilized, not as combatants but as spectators. ... [The war] aroused emotions in the intense but shallow way that sports do'. Like the Gulf, politically it was only the spectacle of war, not the real thing.

'Sacrifice in battle has become implausible or ironic', says Ignatieff (2000: 186), but he is something of an ironist himself. A vociferous and prominent supporter of the 1999 NATO bombing, even as it was in progress Ignatieff could not help raising an ironical eyebrow at the fact that: 'we are more anxious to save our souls than to save Kosovo' (*Time*, 12 April 1999). Describing the campaign as a 'post-modern war', he maintained that NATO was 'bombing to enforce a moral conviction, not to defend a vital national interest', but acknowledged that 'when conviction is severed from interest, doubt steps in and the rhetoric becomes strident. The people we need to convince are ourselves'. Evidently, even Ignatieff was having a hard time doing so. Others in the media also sometimes put themselves at an ironic distance from the most obviously manufactured propaganda stunts. Reports of Blair's visit to a refugee camp in Albania, for example, analysed his carefully-constructed image, including the fact that: 'a great deal of thought went into what he should wear ... even down to the red and black of the prime minister's clothes which are the colours of the Albanian national flag' (*The Guardian*, 20 May). Similarly, the fact that the entry of NATO ground forces into Kosovo was delayed until US troops were in place to lead the advance drew hoots of derision from journalists, who knew a managed photo-opportunity when they saw one. *Mail* correspondent Ross Benson, for instance, described the Americans as fighting 'for control of the public relations high ground' in a 'cynical game of media manipulation' (12 June). Such media self-consciousness rarely implied criticism of the war: it simply registered the fact that, as Baudrillard might have put it, it was difficult to believe fully in its reality.

In the wake of Kosovo, some commentators started to worry that perhaps the humanitarian rhetoric which justified war in moral terms was insufficient. Having spent the 1990s agitating for military intervention in the Balkans, after Kosovo David Rieff came to see humanitarian justifications as too glib. He argued that failing to emphasise 'the horror of what such an intervention will involve, *assuming* it is justified, is the gravest mystification' (2002: 284).

His objection was not that military intervention in Kosovo had been wrong but that, since the 'recourse to a moral imperative like humanitarianism puts war beyond debate', the arguments had not been properly had out (2002: 218). This meant that Western publics had only 'lethargically assented' to the Kosovo campaign, and even then with the proviso that 'there were no casualties on our side' (quoted in Chandler 2003). Rieff understood that the moralistic language of humanitarian intervention was an evasion of politics (2002: 330). Similarly, Ignatieff criticised the way that human rights had been turned into a 'secular religion', calling instead for a political rationale for human rights action (Ignatieff 2001: 53). To his credit, Rieff has continued to reassess and revise many of his previous opinions (Rieff 2005), but if either he or Ignatieff or anyone else has devised an alternative, political justification for the interventions which were promoted in the name of morality, humanitarianism and human rights, they have yet to share it with the world.

The preference for moralism over politics is hardly accidental: the rise of the doctrine of humanitarian military intervention was premised on the collapse of the political sphere. It is notable that such justifications for military action cut across Left/Right divisions, mooted by Reagan and Bush and then presented as a fresh departure by Clinton; drafted in to serve John Major's lacklustre Conservative administration and then offered as a novel turn toward 'ethical foreign policy' by Blair's New Labour. It was precisely because the old framework of Left and Right no longer made sense, either in domestic politics or as a justification for international action, that humanitarianism and human rights were called on to provide a new sense of purpose. Indeed, to a great extent the attraction of this discourse lay in the fact that it was anti-political. Putting morality above *realpolitik* and vested interests, it appealed directly to no interest, and addressed itself to no particular constituency.

The underlying problem revealed by Kosovo has little to do with the fact that the Western military now has such high-tech hardware at its disposal that it can wage 'risk-free' wars against weaker states, nor with the distancing effect of experiencing war via television and other media. Nineteenth century wars of empire were fought with an even greater disparity in military technology, and today's electronic media surely make war closer, more vivid and more immediate than a newspaper dispatch. The problem lay with the project of humanitarian militarism itself. As Baudrillard observed, the ideology of humanitarianism holds out no greater prospect than mere survival:

> This is the difference between humanitarianism and humanism. The latter was a system of strong values, related to the concept of humankind, with its philosophy and its morals, and characteristic of a history in the making. Humanitarianism, on the other hand, is a system of weak values, linked to salvaging a threatened human species, and characteristic of an unravelling history.
>
> (Baudrillard 1996: 89)

The humanitarian spectacle, in other words, was a symptom of the crisis of meaning, not a solution to it.

Conclusion

According to Luc Boltanski (1999: 191–2), humanitarianism is a 'politics of the present', but while he takes this as a strength, it is actually a weakness. Repudiating the amorality of the bad old days, the humanitarian discourse severs connections with the past; preoccupied with the management of current crises, it offers no viable vision of the future. For Boltanksi, the 'overwhelming' advantage of being focused on the present is that it is 'real' – a statement as banal as it is literally true. Politically, as we have seen, it is difficult for even its most zealous advocates to believe fully in the reality of the humanitarian spectacle. Of course, short of a perpetual all-out war against human rights abusers the world over, it is impossible to imagine circumstances in which the practice of humanitarian militarism would ever match the rhetoric. More fundamentally, the attempt to use it as a source of meaning presupposed the inadequacy and bad conscience of the West – what Baudrillard (1994) described as 'an immense feeling of guilt, shared by intellectuals and politicians alike … which is linked to the end of history and the downfall of values'.

Paradoxically, in the 1990s there was little external constraint on the global projection of Western power and virtually no domestic opposition to its use, and yet the humanitarian cause seized on by political leaders and freelance interventionists did not speak of a confident and positive West. Rather, the overwhelming impression was of a weak and fearful society which failed to live up to its proclaimed principles, bold in its talk but unwilling to die for its 'values'. Baudrillard's (1994) remark at the time of the Bosnian war that the West was 'merely expressing its own disappointment and longing for an impossible violence against itself' was borne out by the Kosovo conflict when commentators explicitly wished that their own soldiers would die in order to make the war 'real'. Such sentiments suggest that by the end of the decade, at the moment of its apparent triumph, humanitarian militarism had turned into decadent self-loathing. Unfortunately, despite its failure as a new source of meaning, it has not been subjected to sufficient critique that it cannot be reused, and it is likely to be drawn on again in the future. Soon after the Kosovo conflict, however, the discourse of humanitarian intervention was overtaken by and – as we shall see in Chapter 3 – incorporated into the 'War on Terror'.

Chapter 3

The media war on terrorism

The War on Terrorism launched in 2001 is another attempt to resolve the crisis of meaning. It has been offered by neo-conservatives as a kind of long-term replacement for the Cold War, and seen by many critics in the same light. Yet if the War on Terrorism can be compared to the Cold War as a new justification for US foreign policy, it has been a signally unsuccessful and unconvincing replacement. Baudrillard's sarcastic descriptions of the first 'non-war' on Iraq sound even more applicable to the 2003 sequel. He observed, for example, that Saddam Hussein's military strength was exaggerated in 1991 by:

> brandishing the threat of a chemical war, a bloody war, a world war – everyone had their say – as though it were necessary to give ourselves a fright, to maintain everyone in a state of erection for fear of seeing the flaccid member of war fall down.
>
> (Baudrillard 1995: 74)

His account of this 'futile masturbation' might just as well have been written about the talking up of Iraq's non-existent WMD capability in 2003, or about the West's exaggerated fear of al-Qaeda. Similarly, Baudrillard's remark that: 'the war ended in general boredom, or worse in the feeling of being duped .... It is as though there were a virus infecting this war from the beginning which emptied it of all credibility' (1995: 62) now calls to mind the efforts to build public support for the 2003 invasion with dubious dossiers of 'evidence', and the seemingly endless enquires and post-mortems which followed.

This chapter explores the reasons why the War on Terrorism has been an ideological failure. Like the doctrine of 'humanitarian military intervention', the War on Terrorism is also narcissistic in the sense that it is primarily concerned with attempting to create an image of purposefulness. Indeed, the preoccupation with image and presentation reached new heights in the 2003 Iraq war, yet the effectiveness of the propaganda was undermined by the way that the news media self-consciously drew attention to its deliberately manufactured quality. This is not to say that the media are to blame for the war's lack of success. Rather, the problem is that not only the propaganda but the conduct of and justifications for military action are also shaped by the crisis of meaning. War itself is driven by the felt need to create the 'right' image. The emphasis on spectacle, a surprise return to 'humanitarian' themes and an aversion to risk all betray the lack of confidence beneath the often bold rhetoric.

Virtual victories and media cynicism

'You stand for nothing, you support nothing, you criticise, you drip. It's a spectator sport to criticise anybody or anything'. So said Air Marshal Brian Burridge, the commander of British forces in the Iraq war, complaining about the media (*The Telegraph*, 7 April 2003). His comments accurately described much of the coverage. In most cases it was not a question of outright opposition, nor even of sceptical and critical analysis, but a more insidious cynicism, manifested through an acute self-consciousness about the media's role in constructing 'reality'. Rather than simply reporting events, journalists often discussed them in terms of news management and image projection, such as when one BBC presenter contrasted pictures of angry Iraqis protesting against the shooting of demonstrators with the day's 'intended message' delivered by Defense Secretary Donald Rumsfeld (*Newsnight*, 29 April 2003). On a day when the most significant weapons find was a factory making bullets, another BBC journalist noted that 'the Americans very deliberately drove captured Iraqi missiles past the media hotel in Baghdad' (BBC1, 17 April). 'The day's big message was Saddam's neglect of the Iraqi people', said Quentin Letts in *The Mail* (26 March), subverting the impact of the message by noting how Blair's delivery of it seemed stagy and contrived: 'At this point, to accentuate his sincerity, he put on his reading glasses'. Reporting the same press conference for *The Times*, Ben Macintyre pretended that Blair was using a body double like Saddam was thought to have done in recent television appearances, and remarked that: 'The session might even have been pre-recorded, for we had heard much of it before'. Macintyre rendered Blair's attempted message ineffective by mocking its attempted sincerity:

> Some elements of the Iraqi Army would fight to the death, said the Blair-figure, 'because they know when the regime falls ... (pause, one, two, lower voice) ... and it will fall ... (pause, one, two, grave expression) ... they will have nowhere to go'.
>
> (*The Times*, 26 March 2003)

Bush received similar treatment: Alex Brummer noted in *The Mail* that the president's 'public appearances are choreographed to make him look like the commander-in-chief without placing [him] in harm's way', for example, reporting Bush's most recent speech as a 'stage-managed event' (4 April). These sorts of comments rarely implied opposition to the war. Rather, they indicated that the media often had trouble taking it entirely seriously.

'Is it all a photo-op?', asked Mark Borkowski in *The Guardian*, comparing the propaganda campaign to a 'corporate-style PR, advertising and marketing strategy' (27 March). The paper also ran a series of articles by Michael Wolff of *New York* magazine describing the surreal atmosphere at the coalition media centre in the Qatari capital Doha, where coalition spokesmen held forth from a 'podium of truth' designed by Hollywood art director George Allison. Wolff ridiculed the pretence that reporters were being given the 'big picture' at Doha:

> Eventually you realise that you know significantly less than when you arrived, and that you are losing more sense of the larger picture by the hour. At some point you will know nothing.
>
> (*The Guardian*, 31 March 2003)

The media centre, he said, was a 'theatre of the absurd', where journalists interviewed other journalists and watched television news reports to find out what was going on (14 April). Back home, jaded reporters were on their guard for political spin and military PR, frequently drawing attention to the language used by the coalition leaders. One BBC Radio programme instituted a 'Rumsfeld Soundbite of the Week' feature; *The Independent* ran a 'lexicon of war' series, satirising jargon such as 'Revised battle plan' (definition: 'What you issue after cock-up'); and *The Guardian* carried three regular series highlighting the propaganda claims made by the coalition: a 'language of war' feature which aimed to 'decode' official terminology, a column titled 'Behind the lines: Footnotes to a war' which often included comments on media coverage, and a feature on 'The first casualty', which investigated 'the way the war is being spun and reported'. This type of coverage sometimes explicitly challenged coalition claims, but perhaps its most important effect was to add to the media's self-consciousness about their own role.

Press commentators often compared television coverage of the war with reality TV shows and sporting events, underlining the war's perceived lack of 'reality'. In *The Mail*, for instance, Sky News was criticised for resembling 'the tackiest reality TV show', with reporters asking questions such as 'Hi guys, you're live on TV. How's the fight been?' (10 April). In *The Times*, TV journalist Nick Robinson acknowledged that coverage had been described as 'Big Brother Iraq', but claimed that it was therefore compulsive viewing: 'This is what the controllers of 24-hour news channels dream of – it's news, it's live, it develops as you watch, the pictures are dramatic and, boy, does it fill time' (28 March). In *The Guardian*, satirist Armando Iannucci argued, with a nod to Baudrillard, that 'The first Gulf war was a video game. This one was reality TV' (28 April); and Gareth McLean described the war as 'the mother of all reality-TV shows' (26 March). *The Independent*'s Terence Blacker also said the war was 'the ultimate reality show', but observed that newspapers too were 'playing up the spectacle, borrowing images from Hollywood to describe the action' (25 March). Perhaps, he mused, papers could provide 'pull-out sections rather as they do for the World Cup so that viewers can read about the teams – sorry, armies – and key matches – sorry, battles – as they take place'; and in the same day's edition of *The Mail* Stephen Glover said the war was 'a spectator sport, a bizarre form of entertainment, a sort of deadly World Cup carried on by other means'. This self-consciousness put journalists at an ironic distance from the war even when, like Glover, they supported it.

The high point of media cynicism was coverage of Bush's 1 May 2003 speech announcing the 'end of major combat operations'. In what *The New York Times* (15 May) called 'one of the most audacious moments of presidential theater in American history', Bush co-piloted a fighter jet (renamed 'Navy One' for the occasion), which landed on an aircraft carrier returning from the Gulf. He then strode around the deck wearing a military flight suit before making the speech in front of an enormous banner bearing the slogan 'Mission Accomplished'. The elaborate performance, which reportedly cost around $1 million, was trailed for 24 hours in advance and positively invited a cynical response. BBC reporters described it as 'carefully choreographed', 'stage-managed', 'made for American TV' and 'pure Hollywood'. The BBC's diplomatic correspondent even suggested that the war itself had merely provided a 'useful prop' for Bush's re-election campaign (BBC Radio 4, 3 May; BBC1, 2 May 2003). The cynicism deepened when it was revealed that the official rationale for the flying stunt – that the carrier was too far out to sea for Bush to travel there in his helicopter – was bogus. As *The Times* later reported, in order for the president to stage his 'Top Gun moment' the ship actually had to slow down 'lest views of the shoreline spoilt pictures of Mr Bush at sea' (3 May). Yet, strikingly, the tone of press coverage was similar even before Bush made the speech. It would be 'staged with rich symbolism' predicted Roland Watson in *The Times*, while *The Independent*'s Rupert Cornwell described it in advance as 'a production the White House might have borrowed from Hollywood' and as a 'media spectacular' which was being 'scheduled for … prime time' (both 1 May).

Such coverage was not welcomed. The media were encouraged to undertake rigorous analysis of Osama bin Laden's or Saddam's video- and audio-tape releases, with much official speculation about their authenticity. As Mark Lawson noted in *The Guardian* (31 March), 'the CIA is effectively employing a television criticism unit, replaying Saddam Hussein's broadcasts to ascertain if they were live or taped'. But when it came to coalition leaders the media were not supposed to shatter the illusion. At the start of the Iraq campaign, when the BBC went live to the Oval Office a few minutes early and showed Bush rehearsing his lines and having his hair done, the White House was reportedly furious, threatening a 'strong retaliatory response' – against the BBC, that is, not a belligerent state (*Washington Post*, 20 March). Yet coalition leaders really only had themselves to blame: it was their own image-conscious conduct of the war which encouraged media cynicism.

The media and the problem of trust

As argued in Chapter 2, the constructed spectacle of humanitarianism in the 1990s was a symptom of the political crisis of meaning. It should be emphasised that it is not the growth of the media themselves nor even the logic of what Guy Debord (1967) famously dubbed 'the society of the spectacle' which has led to an emphasis on image and presentation. Rather, it is the insubstantial and vacuous character of contemporary politics which is the root of the problem. Analysts such as Douglas Kellner who take their lead from Debord are in danger of explaining everything and nothing through the concept of 'spectacle', offering elections and wars alongside developments in film, TV, music, sports, advertising, shopping, fashion, food and celebrity, as examples of the way that 'Political and social life is ... shaped more and more by media spectacle' (Kellner 2004). While there are some interesting connections to be made, there is also a need to prioritise if we are to make sense of patterns of cause and effect. Furthermore, the passivity and conformity of the spectator is generally assumed in the Debordian approach, where the accent is usually on the 'triumph of the spectacle'. This makes it difficult to explain the sort of media cynicism and self-consciousness discussed above. Kellner (2005: 77–83) notes that the spectacle of victory in Iraq was subsequently overturned as, at least for a time, negative images of occupation and torture came to dominate news coverage, but the premise of his analysis is that, due to the 'overwhelming power of media spectacle disseminated from an ever-proliferating culture industry', people are 'Lost in the diversions of entertainment ... becoming less informed and more misinformed' (2005: xvi).[1]

Yet contemporary media developments could more plausibly be interpreted in the opposite way. As Phillip Knightley observed at the time of the Iraq war, 'out there in Britain is a new, informed section of the population: young computer-literate people who are scornful of spin and the traditional media' (*The Guardian*, 2 April 2003). Today's media culture is one in which there is an acute awareness of image manipulation. School students practice deconstructing television programmes for their Media Studies GCSEs, advertisers frequently appeal to us on the basis of our awareness of advertising techniques, and Hollywood films such as *The Truman Show*, *The Matrix* and *Wag the Dog* play with the idea that the media produce illusions of reality. The War on Terrorism is not immune from this culture. Digitalisation, the Internet, and the growth of global media audiences all play a role in promoting a greater self-consciousness about image construction. Crucially, they do so in a context of popular political disengagement. This is the problem which official image-making is designed to address, but which it cannot overcome.

Photographs have always been posed, cropped, staged and altered, but digitalisation not only makes manipulation much easier, it severs the indexical bond between the photographic image and reality. The London *Evening Standard* was accused of having digitally altered the picture of joyous Iraqis which featured on its 9 April 2003 front page, in order to create a bigger crowd than there actually was – an allegation denied by the newspaper.[2] A front-page photo in the *Los Angeles Times* was a combination of two images, merged to produce a more appealing composition of a soldier near Basra directing a group of civilians to take cover.[3] The photographer, Brian Walski, was instantly sacked. In a sense, however, it is the possibility of manipulation which is important, rather than any particular deception. Most newspapers now feel obliged to have policies on the honest use of digital images, and the very fact that the press have to promise not to use digitally-altered pictures indicates that they know their readers have less confidence in the photograph as a reliable record of reality.

Another story of image manipulation, of the more conventional sort, circulated on the Internet, where wide-angle shots of the fall of Saddam's statue in Baghdad on 9 April were contrasted with the more tightly-framed versions more usually featured in mainstream news, making it clear that the number of Iraqis participating in the event was much smaller than had appeared.[4] The Internet also undermines trust in mainstream news. It is now easy to compare different versions of the same news story, to look at contrasting national perspectives on an event, to seek out alternative sources of information and commentary, or to compare official statements and press releases with what appears in our newspapers. Even if most people still rely on television for their news, the proliferation of available news and comment means that we are less likely simply to accept the truthfulness of any single account. The culture of 'blogging', which centrally involves challenging, satirising and criticising mainstream news, exemplifies this distrust, and it was no surprise that many rumours were disseminated via the Internet immediately after 9/11. Some of the various conspiracy theories concerned not only the event itself but also the media coverage, such as the tale circulated by a Brazilian university student about CNN using old footage from 1991 to suggest that Palestinians were celebrating the World Trade Center attacks. CNN rebutted the story,[5] but whether such rumours are false or true is perhaps less significant than the fact that they quickly gain currency. There is almost an expectation that we will be manipulated and lied to.

The Internet, along with satellite and cable television channels, creates a global audience for news, and this too exacerbates problems of trust. American news audiences reportedly turned to British sites in much greater numbers after 9/11,[6] and disapora communities in Britain and elsewhere have access to Arab satellite channels. A study of audience reactions to news of 9/11 uncovered a 'deep lack of trust in British and American TV news' among UK Muslims, and argued that: 'The existence of non-Western transnational satellite TV news stations, providing alternative accounts of events, directly feeds scepticism and cynicism about "western news"' (Michalski *et al.* 2002: 6). In a global media environment, identifying closely with one's government or with the Western coalition may play well with some sections of the audience, but risks alienating others. BBC Director-General Greg Dyke recognised this problem when, in a 24 April 2003 speech, he attacked the 'gung-ho patriotism' of Fox News and other US networks. Claiming that 'we are here for everyone in the UK', Dyke argued that the BBC 'cannot afford to mix patriotism and journalism', since this would undermine its credibility.[7] In fact the BBC's Deputy Head of News, Mark Damazer, later admitted that the Corporation's coverage had been 'too conservative': 'We've been too static and our credibility with international audiences is on the line. BBC World is showing one thing and other channels around the world are showing something different' (*The Guardian*, 25 June 2003). Again, the number of people in Western countries who actually watch Arab satellite channels is less important than the fact that it is possible to do so. In order to retain credibility with audiences who potentially have access to such alternative sources, editorial decisions about what to report have to take into account the diversity of available views.

For similar reasons, video cassettes released to the media by Osama or Saddam seemed to send the US and UK authorities into a panic. Following the first al-Qaeda video release in October 2001, then national security adviser Condoleezza Rice asked American television networks not to show bin Laden's messages live and unedited, and then Secretary of State Colin Powell asked the Emir of Qatar to 'restrain' the Arab satellite channel al-Jazeera, which had aired the tape. During the bombing of Afghanistan the US and UK set up 'Coalition Information Centres' in Washington, London and Islamabad, tasked with refuting reports of civilian casualties by using press conferences, speeches and Internet reports timed to meet morning and evening news deadlines in different time zones (*Washington Post*, 1 November 2001). The US bought up all commercial satellite imagery of the region, bombed Afghan radio stations, and strictly controlled the movements of Western reporters in order to prevent information coming out of the country (Mahajan 2002: 87–9). The US also bombed al-Jazeera's offices in Kabul, and hackers tried to disable its English-language website. In Iraq, journalists again became targets: the coalition again bombed al-Jazeera, killing one of its journalists; opened fire on the Palestine Hotel which housed the international media, killing two Western journalists; and attacked the Baghdad offices of Abu Dhabi TV. Knightley (2003) argues that these attacks were part of a deliberate attempt to deter reporting from the enemy side. Yet in an era of global information flows it is not easy to restrict unwanted images, and even these extreme measures did not prevent al-Jazeera and Abu Dhabi TV from screening pictures of civilian casualties and captured US servicemen, nor from airing footage which exposed the falsehood of coalition claims about an 'uprising' in Basra.[8]

While developments in media technology and the globalisation of news are important, however, they do not take place in a vacuum. The mainstream Western media's own cynicism and the audience's lack of trust are symptoms of a broader problem of political culture. When British government adviser Jo Moore described 9/11 as 'a good day to bury bad news', she only confirmed what everyone already knew: that the political class are obsessed with news management (B. Franklin 2003). Coalition leaders managed to score some dazzling own goals in this respect. Within just a few days of the start of the Iraq war, enough Western claims had already proven false that newspapers started carrying the sort of retrospective accounts of distorted and misleading coverage which usually only appear after a conflict is finished. Both *The Guardian* and *The Independent* featured articles on 29 March dissecting half a dozen coalition-inspired news stories which had turned out to be untrue. In the longer term, the phantom Weapons of Mass Destruction (WMD) probably did most damage to coalition credibility: trumpeting dossiers of 'evidence' which turn out to be phoney hardly helps to inspire public confidence. As *Sunday Telegraph* editor Dominic Lawson later commented, 'If you feel you have been duped, then you are more cynical' (*The Independent on Sunday*, 5 December 2004). Even before the war had been declared over, calls for UN weapons inspectors to verify any finds of Iraqi WMD reflected the wide assumption that coalition governments were likely to lie and to plant evidence. As one BBC reporter asked of the hunt for weapons materiel: 'If they [the US and UK] find it, who'll believe them?' (BBC1, 17 April 2003).

Though the propaganda may have been uncommonly clumsy, there was a more fundamental problem: the coalition's obvious intention to generate good PR simply confirmed the perception that the war's presentation was carefully calculated and manipulative. The coalition announced in advance, for instance, that it was planning to fly journalists in to Iraq to film the desired 'scenes of liberation' because, as one US Marines spokesman put it: 'The first image of this war will define the conflict' (*The Independent*, 19 March). It was therefore hardly surprising that a few days later, when the first shipment of humanitarian aid was delivered with a fanfare of publicity, reporters noted the fact that it was part of a deliberate propaganda effort. The ship had been met by a 'reception party of journalists' who had been 'bussed in ... by the military's press handlers', said one BBC reporter (*Newsnight*, 28 March), commenting that 'like many of the events of recent days laid on by the coalition, there was a very clear message they wanted to get across'. The event was 'choreographed', and designed to 'send a message to the world', wrote *The Independent*'s correspondent Andrew Buncombe (29 March). He quoted a British officer as saying 'This is a story we are trying to direct to the international media and the regional media', and noted that the British and American authorities were 'desperate' to see the image 'beam around the world'. In *The Times* (28 March), David Sharrock observed that while the quantity of aid was 'negligible in real terms', the coalition had 'invested heavily in its symbolism'. In confirmation, he quoted a British soldier explaining: 'The sooner we help the Iraqis the better, so the message spreads that we are the good guys'. The very fact that a delivery of aid was treated as a media opportunity by the coalition led to it being reported in this self-conscious fashion, reinforcing a view of political leaders as calculating and image-obsessed.

Image-mongering

Mohammad Said al-Sahaf, Saddam's Information Minister during the 2003 invasion, became a figure of fun in the West, inspiring both a website devoted to an ironic appreciation of his sayings, and a talking action figure. The cause of the merriment was the ever-widening gap between his rhetoric of victory and the certainty of his defeat. 'God will roast their stomachs in hell' he proclaimed as coalition forces advanced; adding, as they began occupying the capital, 'there are no American soldiers in Baghdad'.[9] Yet in asserting the primacy of image over reality al-Sahaf was only trying, with more limited resources, to do precisely what the coalition did. It was telling, for example, that Bush's 1 May 'mission accomplished' speech stopped short of declaring the conflict over. Instead, he emphasised the image, rather than the fact, of victory, claiming that: 'In the images of falling statues, we have witnessed the arrival of a new era'; and that 'In the images of celebrating Iraqis, we have also seen the ageless appeal of human freedom'. Al-Sahaf's loud and colourful protestations of success in the face of disaster struck many as comical, but he nevertheless had a point when he accused the coalition of producing misleading images:

> This is an illusion .... They are trying to fool you. They are showing any old pictures of buildings .... Some of their acts that took place at dawn yesterday and today are similar to what happened in *Wag the Dog* ... they are pretending things which have never taken place.

The fact that, within a few months of Bush's speech, more US soldiers had been killed since the end of 'major combat operations' than had died during the invasion, suggested that Bush's priorities were similar to al-Sahaf's: achieving the impression of victory and liberation rather than the substance.[10]

In line with Bush's proclamation of an image of victory, coalition forces in Iraq spent some time literally attacking enemy images. Troops encountered more difficulty than they had anticipated in securing control of towns, claiming to have 'taken' the port of Umm Qasr several times before actually doing so, for example. Far easier, however, was to create the impression of control by rolling tanks and armoured vehicles over shrines to Saddam, painting over his murals, and ripping up his pictures. As Jonathan Glancey noted in *The Guardian* (10 April 2003), this was 'not ... a knee-jerk reaction by angry soldiers .... The photographs are too many, press coverage too knowing for that'. While still hunting for the real Saddam, troops simulated his defeat by defacing his image and pulling down his statues, and when they did finally catch him the coalition released humiliating pictures of him having his teeth examined by Western medics. The climax of the image-war was the toppling of Saddam's statue in Baghdad on 9 April 2003. The first, instinctive reaction of most Western journalists was to hail this obvious stunt as an 'historic' moment.

BBC reporters enthused that it was a 'momentous event', 'a vindication of the strategy' of the coalition, proving that: 'This war has been a major success'. The BBC's political editor, Andrew Marr, said that Blair had been 'proved conclusively right' and that he was 'a larger man and a stronger prime minister as a result'.[11] Yet the tone of celebration lasted less than 48 hours before this event too fell prey to the prevailing cynicism. As Sheldon Rampton and John Stauber (2003: 3) note, amid the media jubilation in the US, the *Boston Globe* observed that the image had a 'self-conscious and forced quality'. In Britain, *The Independent*'s Kim Sengupta put ironic quotes around 'spontaneously' in describing how the statue fell, raising the possibility that the event may have been 'stage-managed'; while on the front page Robert Fisk said it was 'the most staged photo-opportunity since Iwo Jima' (11 April). The head of BBC television news, writing in *The Sunday Business* (13 April), seemed unsure if it had been 'a moment of history' or 'a piece of drama', remarking that it was 'odd' that the marines had pulled down the statue 'right outside the city's media hotel'. In *The Telegraph* (11 April), Iannucci wrote that: 'with Saddam's whereabouts still unknown, President Bush has now re-stated his war aim, which is "to capture the statue of Saddam Hussein, dead or alive"', adding that 'in northern Afghanistan, the CIA says it is closing in on the statue of Osama bin Laden'. The very importance attached to image-making called forth a cynical response.

The media were hardly innocent, sometimes staging events and faking images themselves. Sky News reporter James Forlong resigned from his job and later committed suicide after it was revealed that he had faked a report from a submarine apparently firing a cruise missile in the Persian Gulf. In fact the submarine was in dock, the crew were rehearsing a drill, and the picture of the missile launch was library footage (*The Guardian*, 17 July 2003). Although Forlong's falsification was treated as exceptionally unethical it was not so unusual. Vaughn Smith, a freelance photographer and cameraman who covered the Afghan war for the BBC, complained about the artificial nature of much of the coverage (*The Guardian*, 26 April 2002). While journalists were confined to an area of the Panshir valley, ostensibly awaiting helicopter transport, in order to fill the hours of airtime they got the Northern Alliance to become actors, firing off rounds for the cameras in return for hard currency. In many instances, journalists were acting too: doing reports which were based, not on any actual newsgathering, but on press releases and agency stories which had been read to them down the satellite phone from studios in London or Washington prior to their live pieces to camera. Yet if the media were guilty, as Air Marshal Burridge suggested, of turning war into 'reality TV' and 'infotainment' (*The Telegraph*, 7 April 2003), so too were the military. As Janine di Giovanni observed of the fighting in Afghanistan, military action had a 'bizarre, staged effect', with 'front lines, ceasefires and surrenders all ... "managed" as though they were taking place on Broadway' (*The Times*, 22 December 2001).

Burridge complained that journalists in Iraq wanted a 'Hollywood block-buster', but as *The Telegraph*'s interviewer, Rachel Sylvester, pointed out: 'it was soldiers who named the battle for Basra Operation James Bond (complete with targets Pussy and Galore)'. Notwithstanding Burridge's criticisms, the military are usually more than willing to help reporters to spin a good yarn. One of the first actions of troops arriving in Umm Qasr at the start of the Iraq conflict, for example, was to provide innumerable photo-opportunities with lovable dolphins which seemed to have been deployed on both mine-clearance and heart-warming duties; and the military were happy to mobilise in support of media campaigns to help individual Iraqi children, such as Ali Abbas, who had his arms blown off by the coalition missile which killed his family. Moreover, the military themselves proved adept at producing infotainment in both Iraq and Afghanistan. The US Marines hired a professional production company to help their efforts to make films of both conflicts: shot using high-definition digital video cameras, the style was a pastiche of 1940s Movietone newsreels.[12]

Astoninshingly, the military sometimes carried out entire operations specifically in order to film themselves. The US special forces who went into Kandahar in October 2001, for example, were essentially actors, staging a stunt and videotaping their exploits for the world's media. The operation was of dubious military value since, as Seymour Hersh reported in *The New Yorker* (5 November 2001), army pathfinders had already gone in beforehand to make sure the area was secure. Similarly, when US forces rescued a captured solider, private Jessica Lynch, from al-Nasiriyah in Iraq, they again took their video cameras, producing something so closely resembling fictional drama that Lynch's story immediately attracted interest from film studios, while headline-writers *en masse* composed variations on the title of the movie *Saving Private Ryan*. Two weeks later, Richard Lloyd-Parry revealed in *The Times* that it had not been 'the heroic Hollywood story told by the US military, but a staged operation that terrified patients and victimised the doctors who had struggled to save her life' (16 April 2003). Like the Kandahar raid, it was of questionable military value. Local Baath Party officials and Iraqi troops had left the city the day before, so the only available 'targets' were doctors and patients – including one who was paralysed and on an intravenous drip – who were handcuffed and interrogated by the soldiers. Indeed, it turned out that the only reason Lynch needed to be 'rescued' at all was that nervous troops had previously fired on an ambulance attempting to deliver her to an American checkpoint. John Kampfner reported that the Pentagon produced the Lynch story in the style of a television series about US troops in Afghanistan, *Profiles from the Front Line*, devised by Hollywood producer Jerry Bruckheimer.[13] It was therefore fitting that, when screening the video of the rescue, spokesman General Vincent Brooks began to mimic the script of Bruckheimer's film about a 1993 military rescue mission in Somalia, *Black Hawk Down* (hook-line: 'leave no man behind'), declaring that 'they'll never leave a fallen comrade'. Appropriately enough, the photogenic

Lynch was in fact rescued in a Black Hawk helicopter, with an American flag draped artistically over her stretcher by the design-conscious commandos who carried her.

Not just particular episodes like 'Saving Private Lynch', but the whole invasion was conducted as a propaganda exercise. As Roland Watson noted in *The Times* (21 March 2003), the name of the campaign – Operation Iraqi Freedom – had been chosen 'with an eye to public relations', 'crafted' and 'designed' in order to 'massage world opinion about America's war aim'. The conduct of the war reflected these priorities. The US announced that it would use 'shock and awe' bombing and 'effects-based' warfare, designed to win by demoralising the enemy rather than killing them. It was as if Pentagon planners had read their Baudrillard and resolved that this time it really would be a 'bloodless' war-show. As Philip Hensher remarked in *The Independent* (26 March), 'the plan is to stage a war that will look good on television'. In a triumph of media-military synergy, the military campaign was propaganda and the propaganda was part of the military strategy. So, for example, reporters were embedded with the coalition forces in order to produce dramatic footage of the front-line advance which, it was hoped, would cheer domestic audiences while intimidating Iraqi leaders, who were known to be watching the same images. Senior Iraqi figures were then contacted directly by US officials via phone and email to reinforce the message that they should give up. Similarly, the widely-publicised Massive Ordnance Air Blast Bomb (MOAB) – or 'Mother Of All Bombs' – was deployed, but only propagandistically. The US released footage of a test drop and briefed journalists about its possible use in Iraq. As Stuart Millar reported in *The Guardian* (11 April) its utility was primarily psychological, in that it was hoped that the MOAB would 'terrify enemy forces into submission by its presence alone'. The weapon, or rather the publicity surrounding it, was also directed at Western audiences: it was claimed that the MOAB might be needed to deal with underground bunkers containing bio-chemical weapons. It was, in other words, a propaganda weapon, not used in combat but ostensibly available to take out a target which did not exist. No wonder that film-maker Michael Moore used his acceptance speech at the 2003 Oscars ceremony to denounce Bush as a 'fictitious president' who was 'sending us to war for fictitious reasons'. If coalition leaders had deliberately set out to destroy their own credibility they could hardly have done a better job.

The War on Terrorism was initially supposed to be a largely covert effort rather than a television war conducted in a blaze of publicity; an untold story of anonymous heroes rather than a series of human-interest mini-dramas. Unable to inspire and engage the public in the domestic political sphere, leaders have found in the War on Terror an opportunity to create the impression of purpose and mission, though ironically, the greater the emphasis on image and spectacle, the more self-conscious and cynical the media's response tended to be. The root of the problem was the hollowness of contemporary politics, despite the attempt by neoconservatives to promote an explicitly ideological agenda.

The neocons' blurred vision

A few weeks after 9/11, the American Enterprise Institute (AEI) held a public meeting, hosted by then Pentagon advisor Richard Perle, about 'The Battle for Ideas in the US War on Terrorism'.[14] The most forceful speaker was the AEI's Michael Ledeen, who attempted to set out 'a kind of global vision of what this war is about and how we should wage it'. The 'war against terrorism is simply the latest form', he suggested, of the 'conflict between dictatorship and democracy' which the US had fought in the Second World War and in the Cold War. Ledeen's main historical reference point, however, was the eighteenth century American War of Independence: the current struggle, he suggested, was a continuation of 'the oldest kind of war in which we have engaged'. In his mind, at least, the War on Terror harked back to the revolutionary 'war against tyranny' fought by Enlightenment America against the *ancien régime* of British and European colonialism. Ledeen thus sought to present the War on Terror as embodying a 'winning Messianic vision' which was both quintessentially American – the love of freedom, he said, was 'built into our national DNA' – and also universal, since this 'vision of human freedom is not limited to one culture or another'. In this sense, Ledeen portrayed the US as the universal nation: the people whose national character embodies the aspirations of humanity; the state whose national interest coincides with the universal interest.

In a post-ideological era, the neocons often seem to cut against the grain, offering the kind of grand narrative of History which is otherwise absent from contemporary politics. In practice, however, this vision has been blurred because, notwithstanding their occasional bursts of bold rhetoric, neoconservatives have adapted to the prevailing political climate rather than challenging and transforming it. At the same AEI debate, leading Republican politician Newt Gingrich worried that there might be a 'lack of clarity … lack of moral purpose … lack of seriousness on our part'. As it turned out, his concerns were well-founded: the elite were unable to overcome their lack of clarity and purpose through the War on Terror. Three things gave the game away. First, while they could talk a good war, in reality the War on Terror exemplified contemporary risk consciousness: it rested on fear rather than any more positive vision. Secondly, although the Bush administration's tone was quite different from the 'feel-your-pain' empathy of the Clinton years, when political leaders attempted to explain the supposedly positive political content of the War on Terror they tended to reach for the same sorts of humanitarian and human rights-based justifications which had been developed in the 1990s, suggesting that they had little new to say. Thirdly, despite the attempt, discussed in the Introduction, to use 9/11 as a weapon in the culture wars, the War on Terror fell prey to the very political correctness so despised by the neocons, exposing their inability to rally people round a set of agreed values. The sections below examine each of these problems in turn.

Risk-averse War on Terror

As a presidential candidate in May 2000, George W. Bush set out his view of America's place in the world:

> This is a world that is much more uncertain than the past. In the past we were certain, we were certain it was us versus the Russians in the past. We were certain, and therefore we had huge nuclear arsenals aimed at each other to keep the peace. That's what we were certain of .... You see, even though it's an uncertain world, we're certain of some things. We're certain that even though the 'evil empire' may have passed, evil still remains. We're certain there are people that can't stand what America stands for .... We're certain there are madmen in the world, and there's terror, and there's missiles and I'm certain of this, too: I'm certain to maintain the peace, we better have a military of high morale.
>
> (Quoted in Miller 2001: 261)

It is striking how much of the post-9/11 outlook – evil, madmen, terror, missiles, threatened American values – was already in place in this speech, delivered while Bush was campaigning for the presidency. Critics have made much of the fact that US actions after 9/11 seemed to follow neoconservative thinking on foreign and security policy formulated before Bush took office, though this is surely not very surprising. In particular, *Rebuilding America's Defences*, a September 2000 report by The Project for the New American Century (PNAC), a right-wing think-tank whose affiliates and founders were promoted to positions of influence by Bush, is often cited as evidence that a blueprint for American domination of the world was implemented under cover of the War on Terrorism. Yet *Rebuilding America's Defences* is unexceptional. It calls for increased defence spending, proposes reform of the armed forces, and argues emphatically that military power is the key to continued US hegemony or 'global leadership' (PNAC 2000: 51, 76). This is, in fact, exactly what one would generally expect neoconservatives to say, and it is no great revelation that they said it in publicly-available documents prior to September 2001. What set conspiracy theorists off was the remark that the desired military reforms were unlikely to happen quickly, 'absent some catastrophic and catalyzing event – like a new Pearl Harbor' (PNAC 2000: 51). This is an indication of the desire, discussed further in Chapter 6, to overcome internal problems through confronting an external enemy who could be thought to embody them, rather than a sign of some dark conspiracy.

Focusing on the alleged neoconservative conspiracy has prevented many critics from noticing the lack of substance of the neocon 'vision'. What is equally striking about Bush's campaign speech quoted above is the sense of fearfulness in the face of an 'uncertain' and dangerous world. Far from evincing a world-beating confidence, this suggests a view of the US as – to borrow the title of another 2000 report co-authored by one of the PNAC chairmen – 'America the Vulnerable' (Lehman and Sicherman 2000). This sense of vulnerability was not the product of any specific threat, but rather expressed a general feeling of being 'at risk'. As Bush put it in another pre-election speech:

> When I was coming up, it was a dangerous world, and you knew exactly who they were .... It was us vs. them, and it was clear who them was. Today, we are not so sure who they are, but we know they're there.
>
> (Quoted in Miller 2001: 260–1)

September 11, one might imagine, gave these fears more a concrete focus: now we knew who them was. Yet the War on Terror was less a focused campaign than an expression of generalised and diffuse fearfulness. The failure to capture bin Laden meant that the danger posed by terrorism simply added to the sum of formless fears: a constant and ubiquitous source of menace rather than an identifiable enemy who could be engaged and defeated. Here was America, the most powerful state on earth, reduced to bombing empty caves in remote areas of Afghanistan in an effort to allay its dread that who-knows-what might happen.

As discussed further in Chapter 5, in taking the War on Terror to Iraq political leaders sought to win support by playing up threats and dangers. According to US Deputy Defense Secretary Paul Wolfowitz, the issue of WMD was chosen as the justification for the invasion because it appeared to be 'the one issue that everyone could agree on'.[15] This pragmatic, lowest-common-denominator approach betrayed an inability to win support for anything more positive or forward-looking. Moreover, it backfired as the attempt to create a convincing image of purpose was let down by the failure to construct a credible threat. The assertion of the 'reality' of Iraq's WMD was doomed from the start. In a 24 September 2002 speech Tony Blair claimed:

> The threat ... is not imagined. The history of Saddam and the WMD is not American or British propaganda. The history and the present threat are real ... there are many acts of this drama still to be played out.
>
> (Quoted in Brown 2003: 60)

Similarly, in March 2004 he maintained his 'fervent view that the nature of the global threat we face in Britain and round the world is real and existential'.[16] The Prime Minister protested too much: the more he asserted the 'reality' of the threat, the more illusory it seemed.

The emptiness of the justifications for war produced an impoverished and barren public debate as heated but superficial disagreements masked the absence of any more principled clash between supporters and opponents of the war. Blair set the tone for the discussion in his October 2001 speech to the Labour Party conference, arguing that: 'Whatever the dangers of the action we take, the dangers of inaction are far, far greater'.[17] Explaining his reasons for invading Iraq in another speech to Labour activists in February 2003 he said:

> I know many of you find it hard to understand why I care so deeply about this. I tell you: it is fear ... the fear that one day these new threats of weapons of mass destruction, rogue states and international terrorism combine to deliver a catastrophe to our world.[18]

With political leaders trying to exploit people's fears and insecurities instead of making a political argument, it was not surprising that the debate over whether to go to war often degenerated into a quarrel over which course of action would be least scary. Supporting the war, *Guardian* columnist Martin Woollacott suggested that 'action is risky, but turning away could be even riskier' (*The Guardian*, 7 February 2003); while David Aaronovitch parroted Blair's line that 'the dangers of inaction are probably greater than the dangers of action' (*Iraq: A Just War?* Channel Four, 28 February 2003); and Johann Hari argued that 'this war is going to be terrible – but leaving Saddam in place would be even more terrible .... there will be horrible deaths either way we leap' (*The Independent*, 15 February). Meanwhile, on the anti-war side Timothy Garton Ash argued that 'an American-British "imperial" invasion of Iraq will increase the chances of Arab terror attacks in Europe and America' (*The Guardian*, 6 February); and Jonathan Freedland worried that 'a war against Iraq is not just a foolish diversion from fighting terror, it is a sure-fire way to fuel it' (*The Guardian*, 22 January). If the advocates of war were motivated by fear, then so were their critics, and despite the appearance of a polarised political debate there rarely seemed to be any substantive issue of principle at stake.

Humanitarian War on Terror

As James Der Derian (1992: 73) observes, a shift of emphasis from 'human rights' to 'terrorism' as America's top foreign policy priority was instituted in 1981 by the Reagan administration, and was continued by George Bush Snr., who as Vice-President had headed the Task Force on Combating Terrorism. It is tempting to see a similar shift in the changeover from Clinton to Bush Jnr. – a switch from a liberal, 'ethical', multilateralist approach which justified international action on the grounds of human rights and humanitarian concern, to an America-first unilateralism in which aggressive 'War on Terror' was the overriding priority of US policy. However, as we saw in Chapter 2, the idea of using humanitarianism as a new source of meaning originated with the Republicans, as did the notion of an ethical New World Order. In the 1990s, the idea of 'ethical' foreign policy became associated with left-of-centre politicians such as Clinton and Blair, but the continuities are much more striking than relatively superficial changes of tone and style. A collection of essays expounding the ideas of neoconservatism, for example, includes as an exemplar of the outlook a speech Blair gave during the 1999 Kosovo conflict setting out his 'doctrine of international community' (Stelzer 2004). Accusations that Blair supported Bush because of British subservience to the US were misplaced and misleading: there was a genuine continuity between New Labour's 'ethical foreign policy' interventionism and the War on Terror.

By the time the invasion of Iraq started in March 2003 political leaders seemed to have all but forgotten about searching for WMD, let alone combating international terrorism, instead promising to 'liberate' the Iraqi people. 'The tyrant will soon be gone', Bush told the Iraqis, 'The day of your liberation is near' (*The Times*, 18 March 2003). In part, the emphasis on what Blair called 'the moral case for removing Saddam' was a response to continuing public opposition to the war and the shakiness of the evidence on WMD (Kampfner 2003: 273). Yet similar themes had already been developed in the first 'War on Terror' campaign in Afghanistan. Recalling the rhetoric he had used during the Kosovo war, Blair maintained in his October 2001 Labour conference speech that the bombing of Afghanistan was 'not a conventional conflict' and 'not a battle for territory', but 'a battle to allow the Afghans themselves to retake control of their country'. Similarly, at a March 2002 press conference US Secretary of State Colin Powell claimed the bombing was 'a triumph for human rights', citing the removal of the Taliban and the appointment of two women to the country's interim government as evidence.[19]

Washington reportedly spent hundreds of thousands of dollars hiring advertising and PR consultants to 'humanise the war' in Afghanistan (Channel Four News, 6 November 2001), but the attempt to turn it into some kind of humanitarian mission produced bizarre results. While Bush appealed to American children to donate a dollar to the Red Cross his airforce repeatedly and deliberately bombed the organisation's facilities in Kabul and Kandahar (Mahajan 2002: 38). US planes dropped aid as well as cluster bombs, both in bright yellow packaging, in an effort to rescue some Afghans from starvation while killing others. These aerial food drops were hopelessly impractical, but being seen to care was what counted. In an article incongruously titled 'Give 'em Hell ... and Food', *The Sun* newspaper portrayed the deployment of US and British special forces to help the Northern Alliance take the city of Mazar-i-Sharif as having the goal of setting up a 'sanctuary' for refugees. It quoted a military source describing this as 'good perception management' and explaining that the anticipated 'bitter and bloody' battle would 'demonstrate that we are not only bombing but using military action to bring emergency help for millions who need it' (5 November 2001). The pattern was repeated in Iraq: the BBC reported that British forces hoped to win the 'battle for Basra' quickly in order to enable the delivery of humanitarian aid. This, we were told, would 'prove that they come in peace' (26 March 2003). On the same day, a coalition missile killed at least 15 civilians in a Baghdad marketplace. After the war, practical measures to solve chronic problems with water, food, medicine and electricity supplies took second place to the production of scenes of simulated humanitarianism for the cameras. As James Meek reported from Baghdad, there was 'a sense that US efforts to restore essential services are more about self-boosting short-term fixes' than about getting the city functioning again (*The Guardian*, 16 April).

Critics have understood the 'humanitarian' claims made for the War on Terror as simply propaganda. As Rieff (2002: 236) notes, for example, Secretary of State Powell's description of NGOs in Afghanistan as 'an important part of our combat team' betrayed a cynical and instrumentalist view of humanitarianism. Yet there is more to it than that. The attempt to invest the War on Terror with some higher 'moral' purpose results from what David Chandler (2006: 71) calls the 'Other-regarding ethics' of Western foreign policy. That is to say, even with such a catalyst as 9/11, popular disengagement from politics cannot be overcome through the flag-waving pursuit of national interests: such traditional ideas no longer provide a meaningful framework for the projection of power. Instead, power is wielded apologetically, justified on the basis that it will benefit someone else. Hence, the millions who marched in Western capitals to protest against the planned invasion of Iraq accused their leaders of acting from self-interest – for example, to secure access to Middle Eastern oil or to dole out lucrative reconstruction contracts to Western corporations. Meanwhile, politicians insisted that they had no interests in Iraq but had to act in order not to disappoint the Iraqi people. Despite the sometimes grating incompatibility of the humanitarian discourse with the War on Terror, there was no other available moral vocabulary.

Inoffensive War on Terror

According to AEI Fellow William Schneider, after 9/11 President Bush argued 'Clearly and nondefensively' for 'the superiority of our values over those of others' (*Los Angeles Times*, 9 June 2002). 'No postmodernist relativism here', declared Schneider with satisfaction, citing as evidence Bush's statement that in the twenty-first century there was 'a single surviving model of human progress', based on 'non-negotiable demands of human dignity, the rule of law, limits on the power of the state, respect for women and private property and free speech and equal justice and religious tolerance'. On any honest assessment, the War on Terror can hardly be said to have confirmed these values. Where was the 'non-negotiable' respect for human dignity in coalition mistreatment of prisoners in Iraq, for example? How did the assault on civil liberties in the PATRIOT Act and other 'homeland security' measures set limits on the power of the state? Even if we set aside such awkward questions, it stretches credibility to suggest that political leaders were arguing unapologetically for the superiority of Western values.

Today, traditional ideological standbys – celebrating a martial, national or Western identity – seem to cause disquiet instead of cohering support. This was why news audiences witnessed the Stars and Stripes being proudly hoisted in

Iraq one minute, only to see it hauled down in embarrassment the next. When US Marines raised the flag at Umm Qasr at the start of the war, British MPs condemned it as 'crass', and the Defence Secretary promised to raise British 'concerns' with his American counterparts. UK troops had been instructed not to 'wave the union flag' because of Britain's 'determination to respect Iraqi sovereignty' (*The Guardian*, 22 March 2003). For their part, US military officials were reportedly 'stunned' by flag-related incidents involving their troops. One US spokesperson said that commanders had been told not even to fly the American flag from their own vehicles: to do so would be 'inappropriate' and might 'send the wrong message', since it could 'give the impression of conquering the Iraqi people' (*The Times*, 22 March). The absurdity of invading and occupying a country while professing respect for its sovereignty and denying any desire to conquer it illustrated the difficulties the coalition encountered in trying to craft the right image of victory. When the Stars and Stripes was draped over the face of Saddam's falling statue on 9 April 2003 it seemed in danger of ruining the occasion – the image reportedly caused 'a moment of concern' in Washington before the flag was hastily removed (BBC News 24, 9 April 2003).

Similar worries about appearing too militaristic were voiced in the British debate about whether to hold a victory parade, a 'cavalcade' or a church service after the Iraq campaign. In the event, a 'multi-faith service of remembrance' was held at St. Paul's Cathedral, designed to be 'sensitive to other traditions, other experiences and other faiths', including Islam. The service commemorated Iraqi military and civilian dead as well as British losses. As the Dean of St. Paul's explained: 'I don't believe in today's world we can have a national service behaving like little Brits' (*The Independent*, 11 October 2003). Similar considerations applied beforehand, one journalist revealed:

> We were not allowed to take any pictures or describe British soldiers carrying guns. I was told that there was ... a decision made by Downing Street that the military minders of the journalists down there were to go to any lengths ... to not portray ... the British fighting men and women as fighters.[20]

An inability to celebrate victory or to portray soldiers as soldiers is symptomatic of the elite's lack of confidence. Insisting that the War on Terror should not be understood as a 'clash of civilisations', coalition leaders made a great show of 'respect' for Islam.[21] Bush visited a mosque in the wake of 9/11, for instance, and Blair claimed to be reading the Koran. Even the name of the attack on Afghanistan was changed when it was found that calling it 'Operation Infinite Justice' could be offensive to Muslims. It was as if during the Cold War Western leaders were accused of being anti-communist and responded by making repeated public statements praising the 'great ideology' of Marxism and announcing their admiration for the works of Lenin. Discussion about promoting 'our' values was defensive and apologetic in the extreme. Indeed, the Italian Prime Minister, Silvio Berlusconi, literally apologised for saying that Western civilisation was superior to Islam. After his remarks provoked a 'storm of condemnation from the European Union and the US', Berlusconi said Islam was a 'great' religion for which he had 'deep respect'.[22]

After 9/11, the US government consulted marketing and PR companies and swore in a former advertising executive, Charlotte Beers, as the Under Secretary of State for Public Diplomacy and Public Affairs. Her brief was to 're-brand' US foreign policy. Some critics have suggested that Beers's efforts were 'an abject failure' because they did not address the underlying causes of resentment of the US in the Muslim world (Rampton and Stauber 2003: 34). A more fundamental problem, however, was the uncertain nature of the 'brand' itself. Beers's 'Shared Values' advertising campaign was bound to fail precisely because of the lack of agreed values in Western societies. While politicians drafted in the branding gurus of Madison Avenue, the military turned to Hollywood filmmakers for advice on how to handle terrorist threats. Top advisors reportedly included action specialists such as the writer of *Die Hard* and the director of *Delta Force One*, but also left-field choices such as Randal Kleiser, the director of *Grease* and *Honey, I Blew Up the Kid* (*The Independent*, 10 October 2001). The US Army asked the Institute for Creative Technologies (ICT) to 'create a group from the entertainment industry' to help them 'think outside the box'. The ICT, established at the University of Southern California in 2000 with a $45m US Army contract, was set up to conduct computer modelling and simulation research with applications for the media, film, games, theme park and IT industries as well as the military. Extending this cooperation from technical research to policy brainstorming smacked of desperation.[23]

As discussed in Chapter 1, the military are keenly aware of the erosion of traditional values. As the authors of an article in the US Army's *Parameters* journal observe:

> militaries now lack a shared interpretative framework with their publics. As a result, postmodernist and anti-institutionalist cultural shifts in public attitudes and opinion further devalue the military institution and its absolutist ethos.
>
> (Snider and Watkins 2000)

Also writing in *Parameters*, Charles Moskos illustrates the 'absence of absolute values' in the military with a number of anecdotes of political correctness run amok:

> In 1997, the Secretary of the Army hired as a temporary consultant an advocate of replacing a 'masculinist' with an 'ungendered vision' of military culture.

[In] ... 1999, the US Army chaplaincy recognized the neo-pagan Wicca as a legitimate faith. More than 40 active-duty 'witches', male and female, celebrated the Rite of Spring at Fort Hood, Texas.

The American Federation of Government Employees filed a complaint after a squadron commander ordered a male civilian Air Force employee to change his attire. The man had been wearing a dress, bra, and makeup.

(Moskos 2001)

Even under the pressures of war, such trends continued to assert themselves. After a row about airmen scrawling offensive slogans, such as 'High jack this, fags', on bombs dropped in the 2001 Afghan war, the US Navy instructed commanders to 'keep the messages positive', and US troops sent to Iraq had to go through a 'cultural boot camp' to educate them about Arab culture.[24] A culturally-sensitive army of non-masculinist, cross-dressing Wicca sending 'positive messages' to the enemy while killing them from afar is an absurd but telling symptom of the West's ideological incoherence.

Conclusion

'I think that the American people will sustain casualties. The American people will do what is necessary', ventured Gingrich at the AEI's October 2001 Battle for Ideas debate. 'But', he added, 'it requires communicating clearly what this is about, and nothing will lose the will of the American people faster than a chaotic, confused, morally uncertain and internally contradictory campaign'. How prescient his remarks now seem. Neoconservatives attempted to invest the War on Terror – and particularly their war of choice against Iraq – with a larger meaning, claiming that it served the broader purpose of promoting freedom and democracy around the globe. In practice, like the humanitarian interventionists of the 1990s, they violated and retarded these ideals. In Iraq, the coalition became Saddam, killing civilians in battles against 'insurgents' and torturing suspects in the former dictator's prisons. Ideologically, too, the outcome was more or less the opposite of that intended: instead of uniting people around the neocons' ideas, the war sharpened divisions within and between Western societies, further exposing the lack of shared values and the lack of any future-oriented project which can inspire.

Press commentators frequently compared the 'shock and awe' bombing and the 'fast and light' tactics favoured by Defense Secretary Rumsfeld in the Iraq invasion with the Nazi Blitzkrieg (*The Guardian* carried 10 articles making the comparison in the 21 days from the start of invasion until the fall of Saddam's statue, for example). The parallel was an apt one – not only because of the rapidity of the ground assault but also because the Nazis too placed great importance on propaganda, including the psychological value of particular military tactics designed to sap the enemy's morale.[25] This is not to suggest, of course, that the neocons were somehow 'like the Nazis', but there is one aspect of the comparison which seems illuminating. Historian Wolfgang Schivelbusch (2003: 288) suggests that the concept of Blitzkrieg was part of a broader set of cultural developments in inter-war Germany which sought to recapture a sense of forward momentum for a society that had suffered a demoralising defeat. Without wishing to exaggerate the similarity, there was an analogous dynamic at work in 2003, as US leaders attempted to galvanise popular support through a swift, overwhelming and propagandistically-impressive military assault. America had not suffered a direct military defeat like Germany had in the First World War, of course, but military action in the post-Cold War era was about restoring a sense of purpose and meaning for societies which had lost their grand narrative. It is to the circumstances and implications of that loss which we turn next.

Chapter 4

Culture wars and the post-Vietnam condition

The Vietnam war, argues Michael Bibby, 'can be seen as foundational to the emergence of postmodernity', since: 'It took the Vietnam War to give rise in the United States to the notion that the Enlightenment project of modernity and humanism could have its own horrors' (1999: 167, n15; 162). Douglas Kellner agrees, arguing that 'the Vietnam War was a highly modern war that showed the pretensions and flaws of the project of modernity'. Vietnam, he says, 'revealed the limitations of the modern paradigm of technocratic domination of nature and other people through the use of science, technology, and cybernetic control systems' (1999: 200, 216). Similarly, noting Henry Kissinger's claim that 'A scientific revolution has, for all practical purposes, removed technical limits from the exercise of power in foreign policy', Chris Hables Gray sees in Vietnam the failure of 'the systems analysis war, the electronic war, the computer war, the technological war' (1999: 183, 185). Although these writers emphasise the failure of hi-tech, 'scientific' warfare against a less sophisticated opponent, there must surely be more going on. It is not immediately apparent why a particular defeat for US military technology should have led to a more fundamental questioning of the whole 'project of modernity and humanism'.

When President Bush exclaimed excitedly in 1991, 'By God, we've kicked the Vietnam Syndrome once and for all', he did not mean only that the US had fought a successful hi-tech war in the Gulf. Rather, he was expressing the hope that the war had overcome the political divisions and doubts associated with Vietnam, and that the projection of US power was again 'meaningful'. The concept of the 'Vietnam Syndrome' refers not simply to the legacy of a traumatic military defeat, but to the way that the war became, as Simon Chesterman (1998) puts it, 'a defeat on both military and moral fronts'. In this respect, the 1991 Gulf War was not so successful. A decade later, as the US again prepared to attack Iraq, Bush Jnr. was still trying to overcome the 'Vietnam Syndrome'. Anticipating a 'Culture War with B-2s', *New York Times* columnist Maureen Dowd perceptively described the proposed invasion as an attempt to lay the ghost of Vietnam to rest. It was, she said, 'the latest chapter in the culture wars, the conservative dream of restoring America's sense of Manifest Destiny' (22 September 2002). As this suggests, the 'Vietnam Syndrome' is another name for the elite's ongoing crisis of meaning. In Christopher Coker's words, after Vietnam 'America is no longer engaged in great projects', but is instead 'reduced to managing the present' (2001: 157).

We have so far followed Zaki Laïdi in emphasising the importance of the end of the Cold War in precipitating a 'crisis of meaning'. Yet this crisis did not emerge overnight. Rather, the fall of the Berlin Wall brought to a head trends which had been developing for many years, and made manifest a crisis of politics which was formerly, if not exactly latent, then at least less obvious. This chapter sketches out the historical background to the contemporary crisis of meaning, seeking to explain how it came about. The strength of Laïdi's analysis is that he understands this crisis as a problem for the elite, but we begin by examining the development of postmodernism on the Left, asking why left-wing thinkers abandoned the Enlightenment tradition. In this respect it might seem curious to take Vietnam as 'foundational to the emergence of postmodernity'. After all, the Vietnam era is usually understood as a high point of left-wing politics in the West, characterised by student radicalism, popular anti-war protest and the rise of the feminist and anti-racist movements. Why should this moment be associated with a postmodernist abandonment of the 'grand narratives' of the Left?

The 'death of the subject'

Over a year before the fall of the Berlin Wall, the leading exponent of British Cultural Studies, Stuart Hall, was already arguing that 'we live in an era when the old political identities are collapsing'. In particular, he announced the collapse of 'that single, singular subject we used to call Socialist Man':

> Socialist Man, with one mind, one set of interests, one project, is dead. And good riddance. Who needs 'him' now, with his investment in a particular historical period, with 'his' particular sense of masculinity, shoring 'his' identity up in a particular set of familial relations, a particular kind of sexual identity? Who needs 'him' as the singular identity through which the great diversity of human beings and ethnic cultures in our world must enter the twenty-first century? This 'he' is dead: finished.
>
> (1988a: 169–70)

Yet this was not a prescient anticipation of the coming fall of communism but simply a restatement of themes which had been unfolding for 30 years. Hall had written in 1958 that the consumerism of the post-war economic boom had resulted in a new 'sense of classlessness' and was leading to 'changing pattern of life, attitudes and values', thereby undermining the claims of 'vulgar-Marxist' determinism (quoted in Kenny 1995: 58–9). The context and terms of the debate were different, but the underlying analysis was strikingly similar. In the 1950s it was expressed in more measured terms as a need to engage with new conditions, while in the late 1980s clearly the knives were out for the white working-class male, but in both cases new developments were held to have confounded expectations that the working class could change society. The 1988 volume in which Hall signed the death certificate of Socialist Man was a collection of essays that he had mostly published in *Marxism Today*, the journal of the Communist Party of Great Britain (CPGB), while his 1958 article was written for *Universities and Left Review*, one of the forerunners of *New Left Review*. From the Stalinist CPGB to the 'New Left' which, in Britain, defined itself largely through its attempted break with Stalinism, the shared perception was that the working class was unlikely to be the agency of historic change identified by Marxism. This is what gave rise to the idea of the 'death of the subject' – a concept through which leftist intellectuals theorised their own doubts about the potential of the working class. On the Left, the emergence of a postmodernist sensibility was driven by such doubts, and was often expressed in terms of the multiplication of plural 'identities', in contrast to the universalism of Marxism. Yet the underlying problem was not so much changing circumstances as the Left's own political weakness.

The emergence of postmodernism

James Heartfield's outstanding study of postmodernist thought traces its emergence to France's brutal war in Algeria in the late 1950s, when the country was 'occupied in the name of humanism and universalism' (2002: 118). Arguing that they knew what was best for the Algerians, the French government invoked the Enlightenment tradition to justify colonial domination. Freedom and equality were denied to Algeria in the name of the universalism which French rule supposedly embodied; humanism was invoked to justify the repression, torture and inhumane treatment of the colonised. Former Second World War Resistance leader Georges Bidault, for example, defended colonial rule in Algeria by claiming that it exemplified 'the Rights of Man', describing the French Establishment as 'humanists, universalists to the end' (quoted in Heartfield 2002: 118). Of course, this was not the first time that Enlightenment values had been debased by the real denial of equality and freedom. What was new was the reaction of those who might have been expected to defend Enlightenment humanism. Previously, leftist thinkers had criticised capitalism for failing to live up to its own high ideals. The aspiration for human emancipation was seen as an entirely positive one, but the present form of society was understood as inadequate and oppressive because it failed to deliver on its promises. The corollary was that a better form of social organisation would allow the Enlightenment project to be fulfilled.

This time, however, a very different criticism was voiced. Instead of simply rejecting the way that claimed values of universalism and humanism were being used as an ideological cover for inequality, the values themselves were called into question. Jean-Paul Sartre, the leading intellectual of the day, anticipated the perspective that was to become postmodernism when he wrote that: 'there is nothing more consistent than a racist humanism since the European has only been able to become a man through creating slaves' (quoted in Heartfield 2002: 123). The criticism was not that a double standard was being applied, or that positive ideals were being let down in practice, but that the enslavement of others was built in to the values of the West. French Enlightenment, in other words, depended on Algerian oppression; European humanism could only be bought at the price of denying the common humanity of the colonised; the Western Subject existed only through denying subjectivity to the Other. Sartre's condemnation of Enlightenment humanism might be seen as a rhetorical flourish; a way to drive home the angry reaction of the moment. After all, as a supporter of the Algerian struggle, Sartre did want equality and freedom to be extended to the Other. Yet the terms of his rejection were taken up and elaborated into a more widespread and thoroughgoing scepticism toward grand narratives of liberation.

In seeking to understand why this was so, two things stand out from the story of Algeria: the baleful influence of Stalinism, and the Left's tendency to explain its own compromises by pointing to the presumed inadequacies of the people it was supposed to represent. The government which denied Algeria its freedom was led by the Socialists and supported by the French Communist Party (PCF). These official organisations of the Left laid claim to a future of freedom and equality in a way that the parties of the Right, committed to defending the status quo, could not. They could point to their recent record in leading the Resistance against the Nazi occupation as evidence of their moral authority. Yet in Algeria they betrayed everything they stood for. Denouncing the Algerian uprising as 'fascist', the PCF voted in favour of special powers for the Socialist government to suppress the insurrection (Heartfield 2002: 120–1). When they were criticised for their failure to support Algerian independence, the PCF blamed the working class. The Party's spokesman pointed to the 'spontaneous attitude of the French popular masses' as the reason why the PCF failed to challenge colonial rule in Algeria, privately describing French workers as 'racist, colonialist and imperialist' (quoted in Heartfield 2002: 121). Strikingly, Jean-François Lyotard, who had worked in Algeria and who supported the cause of independence, took a similarly dim view of the French working class even though his position on the war was very different. Observing at the time that 'the French working class has not in all honesty fought against the war in Algeria', Lyotard forlornly described the supposed 'solidarity between the proletariat and the colonised' as a 'sacred cow', an article of faith which had been exposed as false (quoted in Heartfield 2002: 125).

The PCF's betrayal over Algeria was part of a larger moment of disillusion, the latest of a series of blows to the credibility of the Left's grand narrative. At the height of the Algerian war, Soviet tanks invaded Hungary to suppress the October 1956 revolution, an event which prompted mass resignations from Western communist parties. Many members had already resigned earlier the same year, after Russian leader Nikita Khrushchev criticised the crimes of Stalin in a sensational 'secret' speech. These disappointments were all the more crushing because just a few years earlier the Left had emerged from the Second World War believing itself to be in a relatively strong position. In Britain, for example, the experience of wartime controls in industrial production seemed to have vindicated the superiority of Soviet-style planning over the free market, while Labour's 1945 election victory and reforms in education and health provision seemed to confirm that the tide of history was in the Left's favour. Yet within a few years this apparently promising situation had gone awry, with the onset of the Cold War and a rightward drift in domestic politics. The crude 'orthodox Marxism' of the USSR and its affiliate parties in the West forecast the immiseration of the proletariat leading inevitably to revolution, yet the post-war phenomenon of the 'affluent worker' confounded such predictions. Leftist thinkers were disheartened by the exposure of Soviet brutality and disorientated by the fact that the effect of the Second World War was to reinvigorate capitalism rather than throwing it into crisis. In such circumstances, the official organisations of the Left did indeed seem to be telling stories which were unbelievable.

The widespread assumption that the Western Left had been strengthened by the Second World War was mistaken: in reality, they had compromised with their own national ruling elites in the name of fighting the common enemy of fascism. After the war they continued in the same vein, developing 'national roads to socialism' which emphasised their patriotic credentials. As Heartfield (2002: 121) notes, although the PCF excused its own political betrayal by complaining about the chauvinism of the French working class, the PCF had itself played the leading role in promoting such chauvinism, having long assumed France's right to rule in the face of Algerian demands for self-determination. A national and patriotic orientation was rarely challenged even by those who sought to break with Stalinism. Leading British New Left intellectual E. P. Thompson, for example, complained while still a member of the CPGB that the Party's 1951 programme, *The British Road to Socialism*, did not go far enough in this respect, and might be 'better entitled *The Russian Road to Socialism Done into English*'; and after leaving the party he became involved with the Campaign for Nuclear Disarmament, which, as Perry Anderson observes, 'insisted on Britain's ability to "lead the world" … by setting a moral example' (1980: 188, 146). It never occurred to such critics to examine the conservative influence of Stalinist politics in promoting nationalist prejudices: they simply did not see it as a problem. Instead, they advocated a more 'moral' international role for their national ruling class. The *British Road to Socialism* also declared explicitly that this would be a road that led through the British parliament, acknowledging the *de facto* compromise with Labour Party reformism which had been implicit in the CPGB's approach since the 1930s. Like other Western European communist parties, the CPGB had been established as a revolutionary organisation inspired by the Bolsheviks at the end of the First World War, but by the end of the Second World War it had become as conservative an influence as the Labour Party in constraining and containing working-class militancy within the bounds of mainstream parliamentary politics.

The 'cultural turn'

This political decline was rarely challenged by the Left. Instead, the post-war intellectuals who sought new directions in left-wing thought tended to mis-diagnose the problem, constructing novel explanations for what they took to be the conservatism of the working class. One prominent theme was the role of ideology. In retrospect it seems astonishing how much intellectual effort went into finessing ever-more complicated models of ideology in the three decades before 1989, producing hundreds of books and thousands of papers. The (usually unspoken) motivation for this enduring fascination with arcane debates about the so-called 'base-and-superstructure metaphor' was a felt need to explain the Left's own isolation but without decisively confronting the influ-ence of Stalinist and Labourist ideas among the working class. When radical intellectuals and 'academic Marxists' took up the question of ideology, they were usually less interested in challenging the contemporary influence of par-ticular ideas than with devising models to explain why 'ideology in general' was so powerful and with exploring the minutiae of its operation in the media and popular culture. Theoretically, this 'cultural turn' was heavily influenced by structuralism and treated ideology as operating 'like a language', generally emphasising the 'autonomy' of ideology and its overwhelming power to define or construct reality.

The constant target of theoretical critique was economic determinism, since the absence of social and political change despite the fact of capitalist exploitation was the problem to be explained. Yet the outcome of the enquiry was curiously deterministic: the scope for human agency was understood as strictly circum-scribed by the power of ideology or discourse. Again it is striking how much common ground there was between apparently different schools of thought. Michel Foucault's work, for example, might be understood as a coded cri-tique of Stalinism in that it emphasised the way that all forms of knowledge involved 'regimes of truth' through which power operated. Another highly influential French theorist, Louis Althusser, seems quite different from Foucault in many respects. Where Foucault resigned from the PCF and looked to Nietzsche for theoretical inspiration, Althusser remained loyal to the Party and retained an avowedly Marxist orientation. Where Foucault doubted the possi-bility of any objective viewpoint outside the paradigms of 'power/knowledge', Althusser emphasised the 'scientific' status of his own brand of Marxist the-ory. Yet the two converged in questioning the category of the Subject, seeing it as an effect produced by our 'interpellation' by 'ideological state appara-tuses' (Althusser), or as being constructed by discourses of power/knowledge (Foucault). Indeed, a distinctive feature of both approaches was to equate subjectivity with subjection. For Althusser (1984: 48–9), we become subjects when we recognise ourselves as being addressed by, and subjected to, ideology; while Foucault insists that it is misleading to think of the subject as 'repressed' by power, arguing instead that individuals are created as subjects through the application of technologies of discipline and knowledge (Foucault 1991: 194; Rabinow 1984: 7–11). There is no subject of history, said these theorists; the working class cannot be the agency of historical change.

While these explicitly anti-humanist ideas reduced the subject to a mere 'effect' of ideology, discourse and power, a second key strand of post-war Left thought seemed more dynamic, celebrating alternative sources of political agency such as Third World nationalists or so-called 'new social movements'. Politically, however, this implied the same disillusion with the working class. As former 1960s student leader Todd Gitlin recalls, the rise of identity politics was predicated on the weakness of what he terms 'commonality politics' (1994: 157). That is to say, the search for a host of 'little subjects' was prompted by the rejection of the idea that the working class could be understood as the universal subject. Despite the appearance of dynamism, this too was an evasion – an attempt to discover a ready-made revolutionary vanguard, avoiding the slog of building support and winning people over. The degeneration of 1960s radicalism into terrorist groups like the Weathermen, the Red Brigades or the Baader-Meinhof gang expressed the same logic at work – these were also attempts to find a short-cut, a way to avoid the difficult business of politics. Over time, it was not only increasingly difficult to sustain claims about the newness of the 'new social movements', it was also painfully obvious that they were not moving very much. In truth, the idea that women, blacks, gays, students and others constituted 'new social movements' was wishful thinking. As David Steigerwald's (1995: 148–53) history of 1960s America shows, initiatives such as radical feminism and gay liberation were more a product of the Left's own fragmentation than important new sources of political agency. Although activists often strove to 'connect the issues' and to construct alliances and coalitions, the logic was in the opposite direction, since this approach began from a questioning of universals.

In classical Marxist thought, the working class was understood as having the potential to act as the 'universal class' because its revolution could represent the interests of the whole of society in a way that the bourgeois revolution could not. The truly admirable ideals of the capitalist class, as embodied in the US *Declaration of Independence*, or in France's *Declaration of the Rights of Man and of the Citizen*, would always be let down in practice under a system in which the wealth created by the many is owned by the few, because of capitalism's inability to develop society's productive capacity fully and consistently. Excuses would always have to be found to explain away the resulting social inequalities – for instance through inventing ideas about 'natural' differences, such as the notion that women were 'naturally' more suited to the domestic sphere than to full participation on equal terms in public life; or that blacks were 'naturally' inferior to whites and therefore incapable of self-government. In this respect, the New Left's interest in identity and difference presented itself as a challenge to the false universalism of Western culture. It aimed at the deconstruction of what Raymond Williams (1980: 39) called 'the *selective* tradition: that which, within the terms of an effective dominant culture, is always passed off as "*the* tradition", "*the* significant past"'. New efforts to write people's history, black history or women's history reassessed the past from the perspective of those who had been marginalised or ignored in mainstream accounts, while the voice of the excluded 'Other' began to be listened to attentively in literary and cultural studies.

Yet the demand that other voices be heard was not an attempt to construct a truer universalism, but a plea for pluralism. This was most obvious in the US, where there was less tradition of working-class organisation and politics; elsewhere the underlying trend took longer to work through. In Britain, it was the labour movement which was usually seen as providing the overarching framework that could unite different issues and interest groups, and for many years this meant that the demand for inclusion appeared to have some broader progressive significance. In fact, however, this approach was never oriented toward developing human agency and subjectivity which could actively change society. Despite the intentions of those who undertook such work, the approach was essentially conservative: instead of an active orientation toward the future, the attempt to recover forgotten traditions sought the authority of the past. As Anderson notes, it echoed the romantic nationalism of the nineteenth century, treating history as 'essentially a pattern-book of moral examples' or an 'album of values' (1980: 85, 87). The values recovered from the past might be radical rather than conservative, but in the absence of a universalist vision the assertion of alternative traditions, cultures, histories and identities could not really challenge the status quo, only demand to be included in it. With the decline of the labour movement, this became increasingly obvious: it turned out that the 'new social movements' were not so much a force for social transformation as a springboard for a new would-be cultural and political elite demanding admission to the institutions of society as it exists.

In tacit recognition of the declining credibility of claims about uniting 'new social movements', leftist thinkers began to deconstruct the identities they had once promoted. In line with the critique of economic determinism in theorising about ideology, identity too was understood in a 'non-essentialist' fashion. In this perspective there could be no 'authentic' identities since, as Hall (1996: 4) puts it, 'Identities are ... constituted within, not outside representation'. There is no pre-existing 'essential self' which is then represented or expressed; rather, subjectivity and identity are 'constructed within discourse'. The main target for deconstruction was the working class: if universalism was oppressive, perhaps the working class was another exclusivist idea masquerading as a universal. Looking increasingly out of place in the Holy Trinity of 'race, class and gender', from this perspective the working class started to seem like just another

Dead White Male – the sort of figure reviled by Hall as 'Socialist Man'. The category of the universal class had to be deconstructed because it elided differences between men and women, for example. But then 'women' too appeared as an excessively broad category, obliterating differences of, say, ethnicity or sexual orientation. It had to be picked apart in turn. Theorised by Jacques Derrida (1982: 11–12; 1987: 28–9) as the infinite play of *différance*, this self-consuming process, once unleashed, seemed unstoppable. The theoretical mistake was to confuse a critique of natural essence (as in the concept of 'race') with a critique of social essence (as in the concept of class). Since, in the anti-essentialist, post-structuralist perspective, identity was not given by *any* essence, either natural or social, there could be no political subjects who pre-existed their constitution as such in the field of discourse (Laclau and Mouffe 1985). Rather, there were only different ways of 'articulating' or 'constituting' people as different sorts of subjects. As Hall (1988a: 180) put it, in place of the politics of class – the transformation of a class 'in itself' to a class 'for itself' – the goal was a 'politics for itself'. This meant that people were free to construct their own identities, but it also meant that the Left spoke to no particular constituency.

As far as the Left is concerned, then, the Vietnam era might be seen as foundational to postmodernity in so far as it is from this period onwards that we see the development of a brand of radical politics which either rejected or debased the Left's universalist and humanist orientation. Retrospectively interpreting the Vietnam war itself as having called the ideas of modernity and humanism into question is an evasion of the fact that it was the Left's failure to capitalise on the real political energies of 1960s radicalism – or indeed, on the upsurge of industrial militancy in the late 1960s and early 1970s – that was the problem. If one wanted to pick an aspect of the politics of the era which sums up its significance, a better candidate than the war might be the interest in consumption. From early worries about the supposed *embourgeoisement* of the working class, through the hippy counter-culture, the rise of environmentalism since the 1970s and moralistic denunciations of the 'greedy' 1980s, this sentiment has long expressed the Left's disillusion with modernity. It marks the distance travelled in left-wing thought, away from an approach which criticised capitalism for its failure to develop society's productive capacity, to one which views industrial development as a problem. The anti-consumerism sentiment also expresses the Left's disillusion with the working class, seen as having been seduced by the charms of post-war affluence. As Steigerwald (1995: 127) notes, the US New Left rejected the 'long-held faith in an insurgent working class' because this was understood as 'a product of the age of scarcity that ignored how conservative workers had become'. The downbeat critique of capitalist society as too affluent is also a critique of the Left's own former identification with the cause of progress, and broadens out to a more general sense that the goal of human progress is no longer tenable. Baudrillard's writing is typical in this respect, although he moved faster and further than other thinkers heading in the same direction. In a kind of French high-theory version of the worries about the 'affluent worker', his earliest works, *The System of Objects* (published in 1968) and *Consumer Society* (1970), grapple with the problem of consumerism, drawing on structuralist linguistics to deal with a phenomenon that does not seem to Baudrillard to be addressed adequately by Marxism. In *The Mirror of Production* (1973) he then rejected Marxism because it seemed stuck in the old world of production and labour rather than addressing the new world of desires and signs, advertising and consumption. Drawing out the logic more quickly than most, by 1976 Baudrillard was arguing that the only possible escape from the system of signs was death (Poster 1988: 5).

In one sense, Gitlin (1994: 164) is correct to say that 1960s radicalism was not a straightforward repudiation of universalism, but entailed 'a search for a substitute universalism' – except that the implicit universal was not the fantasy assemblage of 'new social movements' but the state. In Britain the lobbying for recognition was channelled through the state socialism of the Labour Party, while in the US activists took their cases to the Supreme Court; but in both cases it was the state which was called on to meet the demand for inclusion. It was the state which radicals hoped would grant them a place at the table, on the basis that they hailed from, or could otherwise invoke the moral authority of, the marginal, the excluded and the voiceless. Ironically, this underling faith in the state has led the heirs of the New Left back to the place they were trying to escape to begin with. In a chilling echo of the French Left's 'humanist' support for colonial rule in Algeria, many former 1960s radicals now enthuse over what Gitlin (2003) calls 'not empire, but human rights with guns'. As Heartfield (2002: 151) observes, the generation that once looked, through rose-tinted spectacles, to Third World nationalists as the *deus ex machina* that would lead the revolution, now demands that Western governments invade other people's countries for 'humanitarian' reasons or to uphold universal standards of human rights. It is instructive to note here that Lyotard looked back on his own involvement with the Algerian struggle as a moral gesture, rather than a political act, arguing that it was possible to relate to 'Third World struggles' only on 'an *ethical* basis, not a political one' (Lyotard 1989: 26). The pseudo-universalism of 1990s 'ethical' interventionism was also anticipated by the New Left idea of influencing Western governments to 'give a moral lead' on apartheid or nuclear weapons. Tracing it back, it is obvious that this 'ethical' orientation expressed a growing disillusionment with working-class political agency.

It is also not quite correct, however, to say that there is no conception of agency in New Left and postmodernist thought, despite the 'death of the subject'. With identity understood as a matter of discursive construction rather than as determined by natural or social factors, identity-creation seems to be a highly fluid and creative process. David Morley and Kevin Robins (1995: 46), for example, hope to 'develop a dynamic view of identity, focusing on the ability of social groups continually to recompose and redefine their boundaries'. The appearance of agency is deceptive, however. This is so in two senses. Firstly, it is evident that activity, agency and creativity are sometimes understood to be the preserve of the elite few, while the majority remain passive. Hall, for instance, argues that the challenge is to seize the means of 'making new human subjects and shove them in the direction of a new culture' (1988a: 173). In this scenario, agency is abrogated to the intellectuals who devise 'counter-hegemonic projects'. The rest of us are the raw material to be shoved hither and thither. In similar vein, Homi Bhabha argues that: "'The people" always exist as a multiple form of identification, waiting to be created and constructed' (Rutherford 1990: 220). Secondly, even when agency and creativity are seen as more generalised qualities, they are understood in a highly restricted fashion. Much as the anti-determinist theory of ideology ended up with a deterministic view of ideology as an autonomous power standing above society, so anti-essentialist thinking about identity narrowed the scope for agency. In Hall's analysis of 'post-Fordism', for example, there is a conception of agency, but one centred around the act of consumption. He argues that:

> in the modern world, objects are also signs, and we relate to the world of things in both an instrumental and a symbolic mode. In a world tyrannised by scarcity, men and women nevertheless express in their practical lives not only what they need for material existence but some sense of their symbolic place in the world, of who they are, their identities.
>
> (Hall 1989: 130)

A diversity of lifestyle choices is said to 'allow the individual some space in which to reassert a measure of choice and control over everyday life and to "play" with its more expressive dimensions' (Hall 1988b: 28). In plain terms, this means shopping. Shopping is the sphere in which agency is exercised. It is ironic that the outcome of the concern with consumerism is to discover the sphere of freedom in the shopping mall, but perhaps it is not so surprising. The conviction that the post-war boom confounded the possibilities of social change meant that critique was about inclusion rather than revolution, always on the verge of tipping over into a celebration of the *jouissance* of consumption rather than challenging the exploitation of capitalist production (see further Heartfield 1998).

The postmodern elite

So far in this chapter we have examined how postmodernism became influential among a Left which had grown disillusioned with universalism and humanism, become sceptical of any 'grand narrative', and effectively abandoned the goal of progress. What remains to be explained is the way that an outlook formerly associated with disappointed leftists has become mainstream. Peter van Ham (2001: 7), for example, says that 'Postmodernism is the social, cultural and political air we breathe', adding that it 'permeates virtually all facets of contemporary life in the West'. Cultural conservatives tend to understand this development in terms of a 'war' against the insidious influence of relativistic leftists in the intellectual and cultural sphere. Yet although it is no doubt true that the 1960s generation has now risen to senior positions in academia and the cultural industries, there is surely more at stake than simply a turnover of personnel within particular institutions. As Christopher Lasch (1995: 192–3) points out, for example, the allegation that universities are dominated by 'tenured radicals' exaggerates both the extent of the latter's influence and their supposedly 'subversive' qualities. There has certainly been a cultural shift, but it affects all sorts of institutions, most of which seem unlikely to be packed with radical intellectuals. The language used by mainstream politicians and other public figures now routinely adopts the idiom of radical feminism, using his/her, he/she formulations to avoid the problem of gender bias; the police force now speaks the language of multiculturalism, promoting diversity and working to attract more recruits from ethnic minorities; the military attends gay pride events in the hope of boosting the number of enlisted homosexuals.

None of this can be understood as reflecting the influence of the Left. Indeed, it is ironic that the Right should get so worked up about the supposedly pervasive influence of leftists and radicals when the postmodern relativism they complain of was the product of the Left's defeat. This stab-in-the-back theory is analogous to the way that, for many years, the media were blamed for the military defeat in Vietnam. Yet as Daniel Hallin (1986) and others have shown, the idea that media scepticism about the war undermined morale and provoked public opposition is a myth. In fact media coverage reflected elite dissensus. It was the growing doubts among the elite themselves – over the way the war was being conducted, about whether it was wise to have embarked on it, and about whether it should continue – which encouraged critique and opposition in the media and the wider public sphere. Similarly, it is argued here, the post-Vietnam 'culture wars', in which every aspect of Western history, society and values was questioned and contested, were a product of the elite's own self-doubt rather than of the influence of the Left. It is the mutual incoherence of both Right and Left that has led to the postmodern sensibility becoming mainstream. This development represents, not a victory for academic postmodernists or anyone else, but society's generalised uncertainty about values; its lack of a shared moral vocabulary.

Culture wars

Public discussion of the 'culture wars' took off in the early 1990s, following the publication of James Davison Hunter's (1991) sociological analysis of the phenomenon and, more prominently, right-winger Pat Buchanan's reference, in a speech to the 1992 Republican Party convention, to 'a cultural war' for the 'soul of America' (Guth 2000: 204). Highlighting issues such as abortion ('the Bosnia of the culture war'), same-sex marriage, a general rise in secularism and a decline in moral and cultural standards, Buchanan argued that the forthcoming

US presidential election would be 'about who we are ... what we believe ... what we stand for as Americans'.[1] The curious thing about this speech, and the heated debate which ensued, is the timing. Buchanan presented conservative values as under threat, yet conservatives had been in power for a decade. Under Reagan, as Buchanan reminded his audience, America had recently 'won' the Cold War, and under Bush the US had just fought a successful hot war in the Gulf. This should have been a moment of triumph for American conservatives; a point at which, if they were ever going to achieve their desired definition of America, that vision should have been clear and unambiguous. Yet they instead gave the impression of being an endangered species. Lashing out, conservatives blamed their old ideological adversaries on the Left, yet the Left was in terminal crisis at the end of the Cold War. The real problem that confronted the Right was that, without any credible enemy at home or abroad, the emptiness of their own ideas was exposed.

Conservatives in the US and Britain had been on the offensive throughout the 1980s. The governments of Ronald Reagan and Margaret Thatcher both presented themselves as overturning a previously established left-liberal consensus, opposing 'big government' or the 'Nanny State', seeking to curtail welfare spending and promote individualism. As noted in Chapter 2, both governments used military campaigns against weaker opponents to demonstrate their strength and to restore a sense of national pride (Keeble 1997). The issues highlighted by Buchanan, such as abortion and gay rights, had been the focus of controversies in both Britain and the US during the 1980s, when traditional 'family values' had been promoted as part of a package of social conservatism. Yet by the end of the decade, as historian Robert Jensen (1998) suggests, US conservatives had 'become postmodern, and began representing themselves as a persecuted minority whose rights were trampled upon by a cultural elite that controlled Washington, the media and the universities'. That is, rather than claiming absolute authority for their own values, conservatives were pleading to be part of the pluralist diversity of voices. Paradoxically, after ten years in government conservatives seemed to think of themselves as the marginalised Other whose values were being ignored under a new politically-correct orthodoxy.

Conservatives became conscious of the 'culture wars' when they had already lost. The complaint that traditional values were under threat was a tacit admission that conservatives had not been able to establish any new sense of purpose or unity around such values. Attempts in the early 1990s by the successors to Reagan and Thatcher to rally support for 'traditional' values were like an absurd parody of the assertive conservatism of the 1980s. The 'back to basics' campaign that Prime Minister John Major launched at the Conservative Party's 1993 conference, for example, was a pale imitation of Thatcher's promotion of 'Victorian values', and backfired when several prominent Tory politicians became involved in high-profile sex or corruption scandals. Major's whimsical nostalgia, in another speech the same year, for 'the country of long shadows on cricket grounds, warm beer, invincible green suburbs, dog lovers and pools fillers', fell well short of Mrs. Thatcher's combative rhetoric; while the more stridently jingoistic, anti-EU stance taken by some Conservative politicians became a source of embarrassment and division instead of inspiring national unity. Similar attempts by Bush Snr. and his vice-president, Dan Quayle, to raise moral issues rebounded to their disadvantage because their arguments appeared both trivial and out-of-touch. Seeking to promote 'family values', Bush wished in a 1992 speech, for instance, that Americans would emulate the fictional 1930s family from the long-running TV drama *The Waltons*, rather than the less edifying cartoon family in *The Simpsons*. The same year, Quayle famously attacked another popular television show, disparaging sit-com character Murphy Brown who, as an unmarried mother, sent the wrong moral message. The fact that both Bush and Quayle fastened on television representations as the target of criticism was not only tactically obtuse, showing them to be out of step with popular taste, it also suggested that moral indignation was being worked up out of anything available, rather than being a serious response to real-world problems or events.

Both Reagan and Thatcher put a high premium on image and presentation, while Bush and Major seemed stiff and lifeless, lacking in charisma and charm. Yet the problems ran deeper than the personalities of particular individuals. By the start of the 1990s the conservative programme of the previous decade had run out of steam. In Britain, grand schemes for the privatisation of nationalised industries had been reduced, by 1992, to proposals for enhanced 'competition and diversity' in the provision of motorway service stations and toilet facilities. The guiding theme of Major's government was the introduction of 'Citizen's Charters', which would supposedly empower the users of services and extend personal choice. In retrospect, this was clearly the precursor of New Labour's practice of introducing targets and increasing the bureaucratic control of areas such as health and education. Where the Thatcher government had attempted to deregulate and to 'roll back' the state, its successors promoted pettifogging regulation. Mrs. Thatcher's ambition had been, in her words, to 'kill socialism', but once socialism was dead the conservatives' project had to stand on its own merits and it was found to be wanting.

If it was not the influence of the Left that was the problem, then what was? Intellectually, the conservative offensive of the 1980s was an attempt to overturn a compromise made in an earlier era. This offensive was directed against the labour movement and the Left, but it was the Left's relative weakness at the end of the 1970s which allowed the Right to go on the attack. This weakness provided an opening for the Right to attempt a more forthright assertion of pro-capitalist ideas than had seemed possible at any time since the 1930s.

The elite's postmodern moment

To understand this it is useful to recall Stephen Toulmin's account of 'humanising modernity' discussed in Chapter 1. The key turning points for

Toulmin – the periods following the two world wars – are presented positively in his telling, as moments when a mature reassessment of the negative aspects of modernity began to take hold. Yet these were moments, not of quiet reflection but of intellectual crisis, when, as Frank Furedi suggests, elite thinkers were forced on to the defensive. Arguing that 'the reaction to the Great War anticipated the Vietnam syndrome', Furedi observes that, at the level of ideas, 'the real 1960s took place between the wars', in the sense that this was when 'the legitimacy of bourgeois thought was put on trial' (1992: 166, 162). Discussing works such as Oswald Spengler's 1926 book *Decline of the West*, Furedi describes the intellectual life of the inter-war period as dominated by an overwhelming sense of terminus as a generation of intellectuals lost belief in their own societies. Others have noted the similarity with the 1930s. Andrew Williams (2003: 12–13), for example, remarks on the parallel between the intellectual crisis of the inter-war period and the contemporary crisis of meaning discussed by Laïdi, but simply comments that: 'what comes around goes around'. Yet what if the relationship is not one of coincidental similarity but of continuity?

The experience of the First World War, coupled with the destabilising impact of the Bolshevik revolution, meant that it was difficult to associate capitalism with progress. Suffering what Furedi (1992: 166–7) characterises as a 'moral collapse', the European elite instead abandoned the idea of progress 'in case it became a weapon in the hands of its opponents'. That is to say, at a point when belief in historical progress was more likely to motivate support for communism than for crisis-ridden capitalism, 'progress' became a dangerous idea. In the 1930s, a 'lost generation' of young Western intellectuals found Stalin's Soviet Union more attractive than their own societies, while even pro-capitalist thinkers such as Friedrich Hayek felt unable to mount a full-blooded defence of the free market: the consensus was that some form of planned economy was inevitable (Furedi 1992: 173). World war, economic crisis, class conflict and colonial unrest, followed by another world war, shattered elite confidence. Plagued by doubt, establishment thinkers were horrified to find that ideas of race and empire which had previously been a source of ideological strength were now tainted by their association with Nazi barbarism. The response, after the Second World War, was typified by the 'end of ideology' thesis developed by Daniel Bell, Raymond Aron and others. With the traditional vocabulary of bourgeois values now discredited, these thinkers responded by condemning belief in any system of values, any vision of historical progress, as 'ideological': as both dangerous and as lacking credibility. In practical terms, this compromise was expressed in the 'corporatist' approach to industrial relations, incorporating the trades union bureaucracy into a tripartite management structure in nationalised industries; in reforms in education and social welfare provision; and in the convergence of mainstream parties around the centre ground of consensus politics.

As a damage-limitation exercise, the end of ideology thesis had some success. The theory of 'totalitarianism' severed any connection between fascism and its capitalist socio-economic context, instead associating Nazism with Stalinism; while Western capitalism was justified as the moderate, pluralist alternative to 'ideology' of any sort (Aron 1968). The Cold War itself also served to rally defenders of the West. Yet there was a price to be paid for the defensive, compromise solution of post-war pluralism: it implied that there were no absolute values, no overall meaning to history. The scepticism toward any 'ideological' system of values might be directed at belief in communism, but it might equally be turned inward, as a questioning of capitalist society. This is what happened in the 1960s. Critics have sometimes seen Bell's thesis on 'the exhaustion of political ideas in the fifties' as having been disproved by the upsurge of 1960s radicalism, but in fact Bell understood that the problem with the 'non-ideological' West was that it was unable to engage the passion and enthusiasm of the younger generation. 'The young intellectual is unhappy', he wrote, 'because the "middle way" is for the middle-aged, not for him; it is without passion and is deadening' (2000: 404). Similarly, Aron tried to circumvent the problem of values by arguing that while there was no single big meaning to history, little meanings were still possible (Furedi 1992: 172).

The idea that there are no big truths, no grand narrative, no plausible systems of belief, bears a striking similarity to what would become known as postmodernism. In effect, the elite had its own postmodern moment *avant la lettre*, defending capitalism on the grounds that belief in 'ideology' and progress led to totalitarianism. Instead, the emphasis was on consensus, moderation and political centrism. Not only was this a rather uninspiring political credo, it also invited postmodern scepticism. The 'tenuous unity' of capitalist society had 'withered', Bell later observed (1976: xxi). If the justification for Western capitalism was not belief in a definite set of values but a repudiation of the 'chiliastic passions' aroused by any strong beliefs, then clearly Western values were also open to scepticism. As several critics have pointed out, Bell's work in the 1970s echoed some key themes of postmodernism, particularly his prediction of 'the coming of post-industrial society' (Kumar 1995, Rose 1991). Yet the far more significant parallel lay in the earlier 'end of ideology' thesis.

In his later work, Bell also complained about consumerism, portraying capitalism as the victim of its own success. Mass production and mass consumption, he argued, had 'destroyed the Protestant ethic by zealously promoting a hedonistic way of life' (1976: 477). In Bell's reading, the 1960s counter-culture was basically an extension of this hedonism, a search for 'polymorphic pleasure in the name of liberation from restraint' (1976: 479). While for the Left consumerism seemed to undermine the possibility of a revolutionary working-class subject, for Bell and others the hedonistic culture of consumerism led to the permissive '60s and the erosion of bourgeois values. In either perspective, 'hedonism' or 'consumerism' functioned as code words for the lack of agreed values. The complaint about consumerism was an attempt to find an 'objective' explanation for the fact that, as Bell put it, 'society is left with no transparent ethos to provide some appropriate sense of purpose, no anchorages that can provide stable meanings for people' (1976: xxi) – just as, for the Left, it provided an 'objective' rationalisation of subjective political weakness. Yet it seems more likely that the chain of cause and effect worked the other way round: it is the absence of meaning that encourages a narrow preoccupation with personal fulfilment. As van Ham (2001: 11) puts it, 'The erosion of all values has given way to the aestheticization of everyday life in which the (western) Protestant work ethic has been replaced by an all-dominant consumer ethic'. Bell's assessment of the counter-culture is correct, however, in that 1960s radicalism was a response to an invitation: an invitation to claim a place in the pluralist political system, and an invitation to exercise scepticism toward all systems of belief. His own 'end of ideology' thesis found its counterpart in the end of grand narratives. The conservative offensive of the 1980s was directed against the 'permissive' relativism of the 1960s, attempting to re-establish absolute values, but could not overcome the scepticism toward 'ideological' belief-systems and grand narratives. What the Right experienced as the pervasive influence of relativists and radicals in academia and the cultural sphere was its own failure to cohere society around traditional bourgeois values.

None of this is to suggest that it was purely a matter of ideas. The conservative ideological assault accompanied a material attack on the working class, which in Britain involved privatising nationalised industries, creating mass unemployment, confronting organised labour and ending the system of negotiation with trades union leaders which had prevailed in the UK since the 1940s. Seen in this light, the Left's intellectual deconstruction of the subject in theory was a capitulation to the very practical assault on the universal subject by the Right. This is why the postmodernists cannot be said to have been proved right: they simply gave up on the Left's grand narrative early, declaring the theoretical 'death of the subject' before the actual defeat of the working class. The problem for the Right was that, having defeated the collective subject, they had nothing to put in its place. In their own minds, conservatives imagined that, by defeating collectivism, the individual's entrepreneurial energies would be liberated from the deadening influence of the state. What actually emerged was not a robust and confident individualism but an atomised and fragmented society of isolated individuals, disengaged from public life and disenchanted with politics, in which there was no shared web of meaning and values. Žižek's (2000: 373) observation about postmodern identity politics – that 'extreme individualization reverts to its opposite, leading to the ultimate identity crisis: subjects experience themselves as radically unsure, with no "proper face"' – could stand equally well as a description of the individualism promoted by the Right. For the conservatives, for whom there was, in Mrs Thatcher's phrase, 'no such thing as society', collective and individual subjectivity were understood as being antagonistic – as one fell, the other should rise. In reality, our sense of ourselves as individuals is forged through our sense of making connections with society. By the end of the 1980s, the collective institutions through which people had made sense of their social engagement were emptied of meaning, but it was a Pyrrhic victory. The ideological attack of the 1980s gained momentum from the fact that there was a real target, a tangible 'enemy within' against whom it could be directed. Once that target had been defeated, the momentum was lost and conservatives became just another minority interest group contesting the culture wars.

Postmodern politics

The outcome of this history of compromise and defeat is the peculiarly vapid political culture we have today, in which the old labels of Left and Right, though they continue to be used, no longer signify any meaningful and substantial difference. With the defeat of the working class as a political force, we now have something like the 'politics for itself' advocated by Hall: characterised, not by clashing ideologies and polices tied to competing social interests, but by the elevation of image and presentation in the service of the re-election of the political class. Slavoj Žižek's writing on the 'death of the subject' offers one of the most interesting and suggestive guides to thinking through the implications of what he calls 'the end of politics proper' (2000: 209). In particular, he identifies two key themes of contemporary debate which will be explored further in the following two chapters: multiculturalism and 'risk society'. The remainder of this chapter will outline these themes and suggest how they relate to the foregoing historical sketch, as well as indicating the limits of Žižek's critique.

From identity politics to official multiculturalism

Žižek complains of the 'tolerant procedure' and 'suffocating closure' of multiculturalism (2000: 203–4), whereby the elite seem to have taken over the language of the Left:

> the post-political liberal establishment not only fully acknowledges the gap between mere formal equality and its actualization/implementation, it not only acknowledges the exclusionary logic of 'false' ideological universality; it even actively fights it by applying to it a vast legal-psychological-sociological network of measures, from identifying the specific problems of every group and subgroup (not only homosexuals but African-American lesbians, African-American lesbian mothers, African-American unemployed lesbian mothers …) up to proposing a set of measures ('affirmative action', etc.) to rectify the wrong.
>
> (Žižek 2000: 204)

The complaints that radicals used to voice, about the limitations of formal political equality and about the false universalism of Western bourgeois culture, now inform official policy. The result is not equality, however, but a 'disavowed, inverted, self-referential form of racism' which makes a patronising show of 'respect' for the Other's identity (2000: 216).[2]

Žižek makes two points, one of which is stronger than the other, against the politics of multiculturalism. Firstly, he argues that fighting 'PC battles' over difference and identity is a retreat and a distraction from mounting any wider challenge to capitalist social relations: 'critical energy has found a substitute outlet in fighting for cultural differences which leave the basic homogeneity of the capitalist world-system intact' (2000: 218). This is no doubt true, as is his accusation that: 'today's critical theory, in the guise of "cultural studies", is performing the ultimate service for the unrestrained development of capitalism by actively participating in the ideological effort to render its massive presence invisible'. Less persuasive, however, is his conclusion that 'the global capitalist system was able to incorporate the gains of the postmodern politics of identities to the extent that they did not disturb the smooth circulation of Capital' (2000: 21–7). Politically, there were no 'gains' from the 'postmodern politics of identities'. The rise of identity politics did not represent a dangerous challenge which had to be neutralised and 'incorporated', but rather expressed the dissolution and defeat of the Left; its retreat from universalism. This argument has been developed by Kenan Malik (1996), who shows how the demand for equality has now become instead a demand for recognition.[3] The old hierarchy of 'racial' identities has been discredited by the anti-essentialist critique of identity, but in its place is a 'horizontal' scheme of 'equal but different' identities, in which cultural or ethnic differences are fixed just as surely as the imputed biological differences of 'race'. As discussed earlier, this is because the impetus for the celebration of multiple identities, though it appeared as a 'gain', was in fact the product of the Left's anti-universalism. Even when this was extended to deconstructing the particularist identities of the 'new social movements', the bid to reinsert some idea of fluidity and active identity-creation was highly limited.

Secondly, Žižek describes multiculturalism as 'the ideal form of ideology of ... global capitalism' (2000: 216), pointing to the way that multiculturalist 'tolerance' works as a mechanism of social regulation. This implies more than the idea that multiculturalism simply does not 'disturb the smooth circulation of Capital', or that it distracts critics into battles over identity. More than this, the official ideology of multiculturalism entails, as Žižek notes, a 'vast apparatus of experts, social workers and so on', an 'intricate police apparatus' allocating each group its 'proper place within the social structure' (2000: 204, 208–9). Indeed, since the tolerance of difference is the marker of the middle-class liberal's superiority over the lower orders, or of the West's superiority *vis-à-vis* other societies, this vaunted tolerance turns out, in practice, to be all about intolerance. Virtually all aspects of personal behaviour may now be regulated in the name of 'tolerance', from everyday public speech to private sexual behaviour, from the wearing of clothing or jewellery to the expression of political or religious opinions. Most tellingly, Žižek argues that:

> Multiculturalism is racism which empties its own position of all positive content (the multiculturalist is not a direct racist; he or she does not oppose to the Other the *particular* values of his or her own culture); none the less he or she retains this position as the privileged *empty point of universality* from which one is able to appreciate (and depreciate) other particular cultures properly – multiculturalist respect for the Other's specificity is the very form of asserting one's own superiority.
>
> (Žižek 2000: 216)

It is this 'empty' universality, in fact, which makes multiculturalism the 'ideal form of ideology' that Žižek describes. In principle, of course, the toleration of differences or the celebration of diversity is hardly objectionable, but it ought to be seen, in context, for what it is. When political leaders or other public figures define the ethos of Western societies in these terms, they are making a virtue out of the lack of firm values. Unable to assert a common set of values, they instead hold up 'tolerance' as a value in itself. In the postmodern world, argues van Ham (2001: 10), 'The only possible basis for politics is the protection of diversity and the support of universal doubt'. More precisely, it is the doubt which gives rise to the emphasis on diversity. It expresses the absence of shared meanings, rather than a definite set of beliefs.

In the contemporary 'culture of complaint' bottom-up demands for recognition and top-down regulation feed off each other (Žižek 2000: 361, discussing Hughes 1994). The demand for recognition, usually addressed to the state, is a demand that someone else act on our behalf to right a perceived wrong or to curtail 'offensive' speech or behaviour. In this sense, too, the politics of multiculturalism is the logical outcome of the Left's substitution of the state for the universal subject. But we should also recognise that, for the elite, this is hardly a triumph. Although it is a mechanism for regulating and policing behaviour, it is not as if this results from the need to counter some oppositional movement or head off a challenge. Rather, it represents an attempt to find common points of connection with people, a way to negotiate the uncertainties which result from the lack of agreed values. Hence, as Žižek (2000: 361) points out, when the state is called on to 'intervene and put things right … how, exactly, this is done is … a matter for various ethico-legal "committees"'. The proliferation of regulations, ethical bodies and codes of conduct is both a regulatory mechanism and a sign of uncertainty. It is as if we are being policed by a state which is unsure of its own rules.

From anti-consumerism to the risk society

In discussing the currently fashionable idea of 'risk society' Žižek again makes two criticisms, the first of which is that: 'the theory of the risk society …

underestimates the impact of the emerging new societal logic on the very fundamental status of subjectivity' (2000: 341). Against the grain of his own argument
in defence of the subject, he writes of the risk society theorists that:

> they leave intact the subject's fundamental mode of subjectivity: their sub-
> ject remains the modern subject, able to reason and reflect freely, to decide
> on and select his/her set of norms, and so on.
>
> (Žižek 2000: 342)

In one sense, he is right: attempting to evade the consequences of their own
outlook, the risk society theorists call implausibly for new forms of democratic
accountability involving, as the editor of a collection of essays on the politics
of risk society puts it, 'active participation through all layers of social, political
and economic activity':

> In risk society, we need policy initiatives which give space to a new politics,
> still emerging, generated by uncertainty, which insists that decisions which
> affect us are taken in the context of democratic debate.
>
> (J. Franklin 1998: 8)

It is indeed hard to square this idea of unprecedented political engagement
with the radical uncertainty that risk-consciousness entails: uncertainty and fear
seem more likely to result in paralysis than fresh democratic initiatives. Yet
the problem is not that risk theorists have too much confidence in the subject,
remaining wedded to a modern conception of rational subjectivity. Rather,
their understanding of contemporary society in terms of 'manufactured uncertainty' represents an assault on the subject. The modern subject, who thought
she could solve her problems through science and technology, is dismissed
as 'Promethean' (Giddens 1994: 79); the subject who sought to understand
the world through the power of human reason is met with the rejoinder that
'risk' is 'another word for "nobody knows"' (Beck 1998: 12). As Žižek himself
observes:

> The freedom of decision enjoyed by the subject of 'risk society' is not the
> freedom of someone who can freely choose his destiny, but the anxiety-
> provoking freedom of someone who is constantly compelled to make
> decisions without being aware of their consequences.
>
> (Žižek 2000: 338)

In response to this diminished view of the subject, Žižek's peculiar complaint
is that the risk society theorists do not go far enough.[4]

His second argument is that, 'in conceiving of risk and manufactured uncertainty as a universal feature of contemporary life, this theory obfuscates the
concrete socio-economic roots of these risks' (2000: 341). This leads him to

call for 'some kind of radical limitation of Capital's freedom, the subordination of the process of production to social control' (2000: 353). Yet in the context of today's risk-averse culture, urging greater controls on economic production is hardly a challenge to the outlook of 'risk society'. In fact capital is already prone to risk consciousness: it affects not only the anti-development attitude to what used to be called the 'underdeveloped world', but also the conduct of Western financial markets (Ben-Ami 2001). Žižek is right, of course, to point out that the risk society theorists envisage no alternative to capitalism. But when he asks rhetorically whether 'manufactured uncertainty' is not 'rooted in the fact that the logic of market and profitability is driving privately owned corporations to pursue their course and use scientific and technological innovations ... without actually taking account of the long-terms effects of such activity on the environment, as well as the health of humankind itself?' (2000: 350), he is entirely in tune with the outlook of a Beck or a Giddens, rather than offering any challenge to it. Instead of confronting risk-aversion, Žižek's critique joins in the game, offering a different, superficially more radical, way of diagnosing the dangers.

Rather than trying to develop a more anti-capitalist version of risk theory, it would be preferable to ask why society is now so risk-averse. This issue is discussed in Chapter 5, but for now it might be noted that, like multiculturalist 'tolerance', it is also symptomatic of the death of politics; of a society in stalemate, where the working class has been politically defeated and the elite has no purposeful vision of the future. 'Risk society' is a society that is afraid of its own powers and potentialities. The theory has its intellectual roots in anti-consumerism and environmentalism, seeing industrial growth, science and technology as inherently problematic. Where the Left complained of consumerism as eroding working-class consciousness and the Right worried that hedonism would erode the Protestant work ethic, risk society theory links the 'manufactured uncertainty' of a society dominated by 'productivism' and by the consumerism which is its direct expression (Giddens 1994: 168–9) with the erosion of traditional values and a questioning of social institutions such as the family or the nation. In this context, the elevation of 'risk', like 'tolerance', offers a new way of making value judgements for a society unsure of its values. Rather than condemning someone for acting immorally or wrongly, today people are more likely to be denounced for indulging in 'risky' behaviour. The atomisation consequent on the erosion of the collective institutions through which people formerly related to society creates a demand for safety at the same time as the discourse of risk offers the elite new ways to regulate behaviour.

The problem of political disengagement

Children, says Baudrillard, are 'told to constitute themselves as autonomous subjects, responsible, free, and conscious', but are simultaneously required to 'constitute themselves as submissive objects, inert, obedient, and conformist' (1988: 218). As with children, so with 'the masses', he argues, contrasting the 'strategy of the subject' with the approach of 'resistance as object'. Eschewing the political response which asserts a claim to free sovereign subjectivity, Baudrillard instead sees something positive in popular disengagement and inertia, arguing that this is 'a vital reaction', a 'spontaneous, total resistance to the ultimatum of historical and political reason' (1988: 217). Given that 'the present argument of the system is to maximize speech, to maximize the production of meaning, of participation', he says, this is more likely to be the 'winning' strategy (1988: 219). Critics have been understandably dubious about this 'strategy', which looks like a projection onto the silent masses of the theorist's own feelings of irony and antagonism (1988: 208). As is often the way with Baudrillard, however, there is an insight buried under the hyperbole. He describes a real problem here: that the crisis of meaning is a crisis of political disengagement. The suggestion that the inactivity and stupor he describes constitute anything remotely resembling a 'strategy' should not be taken seriously – except as a measure of Baudrillard's own disillusion with the universal subject. Yet while he is unable to identify an alternative, he is right to suggest that popular disconnection from the political and public sphere constitutes a problem for the elite, who find that they have few obvious points of connection with the electorate.

Indeed, it is widely acknowledged that the foremost problem of postmodern politics is that people are basically not interested in or engaged with the public sphere. The leader of the House of Commons and former Foreign Secretary Jack Straw, for instance, observes that the main challenge facing politicians today is the 'problem of declining trust and involvement in the political process', leading to 'lower participation and increasing cynicism'.[5] Noting that membership of political parties halved between 1980 and 2005 while spending by the three main parties trebled over the same period, Straw complains of a 'spectator society' in which people fail to participate. He suggests a number of contributory reasons for this state of affairs, including consumerism ('consumerism which is about me cannot substitute for citizenship which has to be about we'), which, as we have seen, is often blamed by both Right and Left for the decline of shared values. The fact that this 'new' development has been regularly announced since the 1950s rather undermines its credibility as an explanation. Straw also chooses a familiar target when he blames the media, arguing that the 'sheer bulk of information and messages has led to an increasingly passive relationship between those who provide and those who receive'. Somehow, the fragmentation and proliferation of sources of information produces 'an increasing sense of detachment', he claims. Baudrillard similarly argues that the one-way character of media communication makes reciprocal exchange impossible, and contends that 'an *excess* of information' produces a state of 'radical uncertainty' (1988: 209–10). In themselves, however, contemporary communications technologies ought to make for a greater sense of participation and engagement. Compare the distant paternalism of the early BBC monopoly with today's multi-channel, wired world and consider which is most likely to engender popular involvement and interest. The proliferation of sources of information is a positive rather than a negative: the difficulty is that people lack the shared meanings with which to negotiate it.

The real underlying problem is that political and public debate has been emptied of meaning and no longer inspires belief or passion. As Straw puts it, arguments are now more about 'shades of grey', technocratic discussions of means rather than ends. Various remedies have been tried. From time to time, politicians self-consciously set out to find a 'big idea' or a 'vision thing'; they conduct consultative exercises which ask the public for ideas that can then be re-presented back to them; they try technical fixes such as electronic voting; or they focus on educating particular sections of the population, giving citizenship classes to school students and setting citizenship exams for immigrants who want a passport. Most importantly for our purposes, leaders have sought to re-engage the public through foreign wars and interventions. The idea that people had become passive spectators in a 'society of the spectacle' originated as a critique of politics, though one which was also as a condemnation of the apathetic workers bedazzled by consumerism. Yet popular disengagement is also a problem for the elite. This is why it is misleading to suggest, as some critics do, that the spectacle of war is a distraction from politics. Quite the reverse: it is an attempt to forge a connection, to engage and enthuse an otherwise uninterested citizenry and to give the elite themselves a sense of purpose. The idea of war as a distraction from the real business of politics belongs to an earlier era, when the political sphere was one of meaningful engagement and contestation. In that context, in domestic politics militarism was used as a way to neutralise class antagonism by rallying the nation. Today there is no comparable oppositional movement that needs to be diverted or defused. Rather, there is an already distracted and atomised populace with whom political leaders are desperate to connect.

Conclusion

Chapters 2 and 3 looked at how international intervention entails a search for meaning, understood in terms of the difficulty of projecting power internationally in a 'meaningful' way after the end of the Cold War. This chapter has outlined the background to this crisis of meaning, arguing that it is at root a domestic political malaise within Western societies. It is commonplace today to observe that the terms Left and Right no longer define coherent alternative world views: it has been suggested here that this is because the defeat of the universal subject has also proved a problem for the elite. For a society that has grown sceptical of grand narratives, a society that has no vision of the future, politics is meaningless, and there is no obvious way to engage or energise support. As suggested above, key themes of contemporary political discussion – multiculturalism and 'risk' – are a kind of apology for a project, substitute ways to plug the gap of meaning, simultaneously reflecting elite uncertainty and offering new ways to regulate behaviour.

Both of these themes have loomed large in the international interventions discussed earlier. It will be recalled that when intellectuals went to Bosnia in search of a cause, they understood it in terms of 'multiculturalism'. When the British and American military invaded Iraq in 2003 they justified their actions in terms of the alleged risks and threats that would be averted. The following two chapters return to the international arena, examining the interaction between the search for meaning abroad and the crisis of politics at home.

Chapter 5

Security and vulnerability in the 'risk society'

'Life has always been a risky business', says Anthony Giddens (1994: 4), but today 'the sources, and the scope, of risk have altered'. In terms of their scope, what is new is both the large-scale, potentially very far-reaching effects of risks, as in fears about global warming or nuclear catastrophe; and the sense that, in an interconnected, 'globalised' world we can be affected by even relatively small, local events on the other side of the planet. It is change in the source of risk that is most important, however: the argument is that risk is now mainly produced by modernity itself. The claim is that it is this phenomenon – what Giddens and Beck call 'manufactured uncertainty' – that means we are now living in a 'risk society'. Since risks are now understood to be the result of 'human intervention into the conditions of social life and into nature' (Giddens 1994: 4), further development and scientific advance no longer look like a way for humanity to progress but instead appear as the main source of doubt and danger. The old 'notions of progress and benign technological change' (Beck 1998: 17) no longer seem plausible when we are confronted with the dangerous unintended consequences of modern industrial and scientific development.

To put it differently, the emergence of 'manufactured risk' is offered as the explanation for scepticism toward grand narratives of progress. According to Giddens (1994: 79), the 'Promethean outlook which so influenced Marx should be more or less abandoned in the face of the insuperable complexity of society and nature'. The goal is no longer to achieve something positive but simply to avoid bad things happening. As Beck (1992: 49) puts it, 'one is no longer concerned with attaining something "good", but rather with *preventing* the worst'. Moreover, risk society – the sociological theory and the phenomenon it purports to describe – is characterised by a broader questioning of social institutions, roles and mores, a development that Beck and Giddens explain in terms of 'reflexivity' (Beck 1992: 15; Giddens 1994: 5). Established patterns of belief and behaviour in relation to politics, work, social class, the family, are all called into question: they appear outdated, useless and even dangerous when confronted with the 'insuperable complexity' of contemporary risk society.

With no reliable institutional or intellectual framework, society becomes more reflexive and more individualised as people are forced to produce their own meanings and their own rules, critically assessing the claims and counter-claims of expert knowledge.

In its disillusionment with progress and its foregrounding of 'reflexive' questioning of norms, institutions and expert knowledges, the theory of risk society sounds a lot like postmodernism. Indeed, the two are often taken as more or less synonymous: Peter van Ham (2001: 10), for example, quite reasonably lumps Beck together with Lyotard and Baudrillard in suggesting that 'contrary to the modern notion that science can resolve uncertainties and problems of all sorts by the acquisition of knowledge, postmodernism argues that the current accumulation of knowledge actually *produces* uncertainty'. The risk society theorists themselves, however, insist that their outlook is not the same as postmodernism and in fact present their ideas as offering an alternative to it (Beck 1992: 9; Giddens 1990: 2). 'In contrast to postmodern despair', maintains Jane Franklin (1998: 1), for example, the theory of risk society offers the possibility of 'a realistic, yet hopeful politics'. Indeed, Beck even calls for a 'second Enlightenment', a new grand narrative (1998: 21). Perhaps they protest too much: as Žižek (2000: 344) slyly remarks, 'perhaps their overinsistent emphasis on how they are opposed to postmodernism is to be read as a disavowal of their unacknowledged proximity to it'. Ultimately this judgement is correct: the theory of 'risk society' is both a symptom of postmodern scepticism toward grand narratives and an attempt to evade the consequences of this scepticism by turning it into a virtue. Yet the effort to found a new politics on the uncertainties of 'risk society' deserves to be taken seriously, since this is how the contemporary discourse of risk takes on an ideological character, offering political leaders a way to negotiate the crisis of meaning.[1] Sometimes – for example, in relation to domestic terrorism alerts – this has been understood as a conscious and deliberate process, whereby fear is promoted and used by the elite as a social control mechanism, but, it is argued here, this view overestimates the extent of elite command over the politics of fear: political leaders are hardly immune from risk-consciousness themselves.

This chapter assesses the idea that risk offers the basis for a new politics, interrogating this claim both in its own terms and in relation to the War on Terror. The attempt to forge new solidarities on the basis of risk consciousness, it is argued, has had more or less the opposite effect to that suggested by the risk society theorists, fuelling atomisation, distrust and fear instead of producing cohesion. Investigating the problem of trust in relation to the War on Terror, the chapter argues that this can only be understood as a consequence of the lack of political engagement. It then goes on to review attempts to explain the conduct and causes of Western wars in terms of risk. In the international sphere, the content of the 'new' politics espoused by the risk society theorists is cosmopolitanism, yet here too risk-consciousness seems to work against attempts to find new forms of political solidarity.

The ideology of risk

The contemporary discourse of risk should not be taken at face value. As critics have pointed out, the meaning of 'risk' has changed in recent decades. From being a concept with a potentially positive connotation – taking a risk on something could mean anticipating a positive, as well as a negative outcome – the term now 'tends to be used to refer almost exclusively to a threat, hazard, danger or harm' (Lupton 1999: 8). As Deborah Lupton (1999: 60) observes, however, Beck has a 'weak constructionist' view of risk. That is to say, he sometimes acknowledges that it is the changing *perception* of risk that is important, but more usually he and Giddens take it as given that the risks are frighteningly real, and that if there is heightened risk-consciousness today, that is simply a sensible response to the objective existence of 'manufactured uncertainty'. Indeed, it has to be so because, as we shall see, in this perspective it is the risks themselves which are understood to be driving political and social change: if we instead sought to interrogate and problematise the changing consciousness of risk we would have to look for other sources of explanation. Some critics have instead sought to shift the focus on to how risk is constructed as a conceptual framework or discourse, including Foucauldian accounts which understand it as a 'governmental rationality' involving new forms of disciplinary social regulation (Dean 1999), and analyses of the media's role in promoting fears and panics (Altheide 2002: 126–33). Such work usefully draws attention to the way that risk talk seems to be used as a way to regulate people's behaviour. The pitfall, however, is in understanding such regulation as a new form of political contestation, whereby the elite deliberately use risk and fear in order to head off some political challenge. This sort of perspective can produce rather implausible conspiracy theories. Žižek, for example, wondering if terrorism might lead 'the US Government to impose a permanent state of emergency at home', says it is 'hard to resist a slightly paranoid reflection':

> what if the people around Bush know this, what if this 'collateral damage' is the true aim of the entire operation? What if the real target of the 'war on terror' is the disciplining of the emancipatory excesses in American society itself?
>
> (Žižek 2003)

Žižek's assessment points to a real and important issue: the curtailment of civil liberties in the name of the War on Terror. Yet the paranoid suspicion of conspiracy seems far-fetched because it is difficult to see much evidence today of 'emancipatory excesses' that would call forth such an elaborate disciplinary response. It seems more likely that the elite are as prone to exaggerated fears as anyone else: in 2003 the then head of Downing Street's Performance and Innovation Unit, Geoff Mulgan, described the British government's policy on the threat of terrorism as one of 'organised paranoia'[2] – something which cannot be effectively challenged by counter-paranoia. Žižek also says it is 'tempting to consider the hypothesis that the US is deliberately fomenting the fear of impending catastrophe, in order to reap the benefits of the universal relief when it fails to be realised'. Yet, as discussed further below, the evidence to date suggests that governments have not reaped great benefits in this fashion. No doubt Western leaders have deliberately sought to whip up fears and use the risk of terrorism to their advantage, but this is not easily explained within the framework of the conventional political struggle for power. The dynamics of politics in the risk society are better explained by the attenuation of political agency.

The absent subject of risk society

The claims that Beck and Giddens make for a new politics of risk society rest on the idea of shared vulnerability. According to Beck (1992: 29), risk society is 'a social epoch in which *solidarity from anxiety* arises and becomes a political force', while for Giddens (1994: 20) the new politics is driven by fear of 'the collective threats which humanity has created for itself'. This is a weak basis for political action, as Beck acknowledged in his first book on the topic, initially published in 1986, when he wrote that anxiety might be 'a very shaky foundation for political movements' (1992: 50). More than two decades later, the claim is still being made but it looks no sturdier. There have been moments which could be interpreted in terms of 'solidarity from anxiety' – for example, in the reaction to 9/11, when the sentiment that the attack on the US was an attack on the 'whole world' might be understood as expressing this sense of shared victimhood and vulnerability. Yet moments of emotional empathy such as this do not seem to have offered a basis for political action, and the sympathy for the US as a victim turned quite quickly into criticism of the US as a victimiser, killing civilians in Afghanistan and then Iraq. While it is true that public debate is often dominated by issues of risk (and by the 'reflexive' questioning of institutions and knowledges), this cannot overcome the emptiness of politics and take us, in Giddens's phrase, 'beyond Left and Right'. Rather, the discourse of risk re-presents the death of politics in a different form.

The theory of risk society is unable to work as a new grand narrative because it offers no positive vision of the future. Instead of the realisation of human potential, '*self-limitation* is the goal which emerges' (Beck 1992: 49). Leaving aside, for the moment, the question of how far self-limitation can work as a 'goal' with which to motivate change, in Beck's account the contemporary consciousness of limits is not in fact understood as self-imposed. Rather, it is risks themselves which seem to take the active role, allegedly 'forcing' people to think and behave differently.[3] At the same time, Beck and Giddens attempt to avoid the implied determinism of this outlook by invoking a broader social explanation with the idea of 'reflexive modernisation', which involves an apparently more active questioning of norms, institutions and social roles. The risk society theorists are all in favour of the critical, questioning reflexivity: this is what seems to hold out the hope of a radical democratic politics, and they associate it with positive developments such as changing gender roles or the end of traditional forms of deference. Yet there is no political subject, no constituency who is identified as being able to carry this process of change forward. '[W]ho is the *political subject* of risk society?' asks Beck (1998: 19), giving the answer that: 'nobody is the subject and everybody is the subject at the same time'. 'Nobody', because there is no equivalent to the working class, no stand-in to assume the role played by the historical subject in classical Marxist theory; 'everybody', because vulnerability to manufactured risk is supposed to be the universal that unites us. Addressing the same problem, Giddens (1994: 5, 249) describes his approach as 'a critical theory without guarantees': there are no guarantees because there is no social force which is identified as being able to act as the agency of change.[4] To put it another way, 'risk society' is simply a different way of theorising the 'death of the subject'.

There is a stand-in subject of sorts, however. In addition to his 'everyone and no one' formulation, Beck tries a different tack, explaining that: 'To me the hazards themselves are quasi-subjects' (1998: 19). It is the risks which take on what he describes as an 'acting-active quality', forcing change upon us by throwing up problems which have to be faced. It is tempting to see this as something like the Hegelian notion of the Absolute Idea, whereby the cunning of risk drives history forward, but this would be too generous since in the risk society theory there is no real conception of progress. Rather, the idea of risk-as-subject is more akin to the idea of God: an externalisation of humanity's self-imposed sense of limits. These 'quasi-subjects' push us towards the 'goal' of 'self-limitation'. Perhaps surprisingly for a sociological theory, the idea of risk society does have this semi-religious quality. Beck, for example, identifies a 'reversal of the terms secularism and religiosity' in contemporary society: on one hand, given that manufactured risks are understood to be incalculable and uncontrollable, a 'quasi-religious *belief* in the reality of world risk assumes a key significance'; while on the other hand 'religious cultures are marked by a "risk secularism"'.[5] Casting out the false prophets, Beck declares that: 'Whoever believes in God is a risk atheist'. Belief in risk becomes something like a moral imperative, pushing us to 'remoralize our lives' (Giddens 1994: 227), while 'risk atheism' is viewed as dangerous. Similarly, in an echo of Daniel Bell's 'end of ideology' thesis Giddens writes of the challenge risk society presents to 'fundamentalist' beliefs of all sorts: traditional beliefs are 'dangerous', he warns, because they involve 'a refusal of dialogue' (1994: 6). For the risk society theorists, it is not so much a question of believing in this or that specific risk: rather, it is a belief in our own smallness and vulnerability that is key. Belief in risk means emphasising human fallibility, so the 'fundamentalist' who refuses to question his own beliefs seems dangerous because his certainty appears arrogant. We are supposed to humble ourselves before the god of risk, acknowledging the limitations of our own knowledge and capacity for action. In this way, not unlike multiculturalism, risk theory allows judgements to be made but in a 'non-judgemental' way, a way that accommodates postmodern relativism. Behaviour may be condemned as 'risky', attitudes and beliefs reviled as 'fundamentalist', but in the name of a technical concern with safety rather than in accordance with some definite moral code or an alternative set of beliefs.

This is how risk-consciousness works as a regulatory mechanism: the require-ment to behave 'responsibly' and 'ethically' translates risks such as global warming into the micro-management and monitoring of everyday activities like putting out the rubbish, driving the car or choosing a holiday. All sorts of areas of life are now governed by such considerations, not necessarily linked to 'global risks' like climate change. Smoking, for example, is not only a risk to one's own health: it is irresponsible because it poses a danger to others, who must be protected from 'passive smoking', and because it may involve the smoker making extra demands on healthcare resources. Personal choices thereby become hemmed in by 'ethical' considerations. To Foucauldian critics, this sort of thing looks like another 'practice of the self', whereby 'risk discourses contribute to the constitution of a particular type of subject: the autonomous, self-regulating moral agent who voluntarily takes up governmental imperatives' (Lupton 1999: 104). Blinded by their own anti-humanism, such critics simply recycle their habitual complaint that the subject is elevated too much. As we saw in the last chapter, Žižek accommodates to this critique even as he attempts to defend the subject. Yet the discourse of risk does not imply an understanding of the subject as a rational, autonomous agent, or it does so only superficially: the emphasis on vulnerability and uncertainty undercuts any such possibility. Being 'at risk' may sometimes indicate an exposure to a particular danger, but more often today it seems to indicate a general state of vulnerability.[6]

The point about the moralistic regulation of individuals' day-to-day behaviour is not that it serves some ulterior motive, such as finding new ways to raise tax revenue or cut public spending, though it may sometimes do that too. Rather, in an atomised and fragmented society characterised by a general disengagement from established forms of participation in public life, casting issues in terms of risk offers the elite a new way to connect with people. In part this is due to a nervousness about their own lack of purchase on society – the focus on risk is attractive because it enables new forms of intervention and regulation – but it also centrally involves the felt need to give direction and meaning to policy and public debate. This also holds true, as we shall see, of the discussion of risk in relation to the War on Terror.

Fear and mistrust

Logically it might be expected that the fear of terrorism would work to the advantage of political leaders. Scares about possible attacks might be thought likely to produce either the relief that Žižek predicts when an anticipated incident fails to occur, or to prompt people to rally round their leaders if attacks do happen. Actual public reactions have been much less clear-cut, however. In the aftermath of terrorist attacks there has been recrimination and criticism of leaders for not providing safety, most dramatically in the case of the March 2004 Madrid train bombings, when the ruling Popular Party was thrown out of office after protestors took to the streets to condemn their leaders for exposing them to danger by joining the invasion of Iraq. Many US commentators voiced similar complaints about their government's failure to protect them: this was one of the central complaints of Michael Moore's popular film *Fahrenheit 9/11*, for example. In these cases the accusation was that, through general incompetence and/or the pursuit of reckless foreign policies, Western governments had exposed their own citizens to terrorism. In the case of false alarms, however, the opposite accusation has been made: that the authorities have over-reacted to threats or even invented them. In part this has been exacerbated by appalling failures involving the arrest, and in two British cases the shooting, of innocent people.[7] Since a number of false alarms and over-reactions have occurred fairly close together, they have had a cumulative effect, so that by the time of the August 2006 discovery of an alleged plot to plant bombs on passenger planes, described by the British police as threatening 'mass murder on an unimaginable scale', the scepticism was immediate.[8] Yet this trend does not depend on particular mistakes: as suggested in Chapter 3, a degree of cynicism was evident from the beginning.

Much of the cynicism has come from the media, who no doubt worry that their own reliability might be questioned if they report official false alarms too uncritically. Yet the media are also in the business of fear-mongering, producing a number of high-profile programmes simulating terrorist attacks. The BBC, for example, has screened a mock-documentary about a smallpox epidemic, a dramatised 'mock exercise' involving a terrorist attack on London, and a drama about a terrorist 'dirty bomb'.[9] Such programmes have typically involved criticism of the authorities for being unprepared to cope in an emergency: in this respect they are like alternative versions of the official exercises in emergency planning designed to demonstrate that the emergency services are able to deal with 'catastrophic incidents'. Where the authorities have staged mock attacks to prove their ability to cope, the media have done the same thing to make the opposite point. In both cases, the simulations have produced the reality: promoting fear and distrust. If the aim of terrorist attacks is to produce fear and insecurity, then such mock exercises effectively do the terrorists' job for them, inducing fearful reactions and heightening the sense of vulnerability in Western societies.

Politicians have regularly predicted further terrorist attacks against the West, perhaps intending to rally their citizens or to demonstrate official vigilance, but their statements tend instead to be greeted with derision and dismissed as scare-mongering for political advantage. This might seem like a healthy scepticism but it does not represent a rejection of the politics of fear. Though seemingly

contradictory, fearful and cynical reactions to official scares co-exist simultaneously. Writing about a planned rehearsal of how the emergency services would
response to a 'catastrophic incident' in March 2003, for example, *The Guardian*'s
Alexander Chancellor remarked that: 'there is no discernible reason for all this
panic unless it is to terrify us into support for the government in its war on
Iraq'. Having dismissed the scare-mongering as an attempt to create 'a sort of
Second World War atmosphere, but without a convincing enemy at hand', he
then countered with some of his own, wondering if war would make a terrorist
attack more likely and asking: 'what if the government is not being alarmist?
What if it knows things we don't and that we really are threatened by a major
terrorist atrocity?' (*The Guardian*, 15 March 2003). Scares about terrorism do
not seem to have worked to the advantage of the elite, but the cynical reaction
to them also remains trapped within the same risk paradigm. What passes for
political debate is conducted in terms of a trading of worst-case scenarios: very
few commentators are prepared to reject the framework of risk *per se*. As Beck
notes, contemporary politics might be characterised in terms of a clash of 'risk
religions' or 'risk cultures':

> For Europeans risk belief issues like climate change, perhaps even the threats
> which global financial movements pose for individual countries, are much
> more important than the threat of terrorism. While, as far as the Americans
> are concerned, the Europeans are suffering from an environmental hysteria,
> many Europeans see the Americans as struck by a terrorism hysteria.[10]

The debate within individual countries could be characterised in roughly the
same way, with the old divisions of Left and Right sometimes translating into
different risk priorities. As we saw in Chapter 3, the discussion of the invasion
of Iraq worked in just this way: leaders tried to scare people into supporting
war by exaggerating the threat from terrorism and WMD, while the response
of anti-war critics was to counter that an invasion would be even more risky.
This expresses a fundamentally anti-political sentiment, not contesting issues
on grounds of political principle but instead approaching them as a technical
question of risk-management. In this sense, it is the very acceptance of the risk
paradigm that makes it so difficult for leaders to make political capital out of
risk and fear: the fact that belief in the risk religion is so widespread gives rise to
a sense that dealing with risks should be 'above' politics. Attempts to combine
apocalyptic warnings of impending doom with political point-scoring are liable
to look petty and self-serving.

The problems experienced by political leaders in handling the War on Terror
are often discussed in terms of a decline or crisis of *trust*. This is a key issue for the
risk society theorists, especially Giddens. His description of the sorts of debates
about risk which occur in contemporary political life accurately identifies the
'push and pull between accusations of scaremongering on the one hand and of
cover-ups on the other' (Giddens 2002: 29). This was written before 9/11 – he

had in mind things like health scares over contaminated food – but the War on Terror has also been caught up in this mistrustful political culture. The question, however, is why this mistrust has arisen. According to Giddens, it is all to do with the 'new riskiness' of risk: its new sources and scope. In the past, he argues, risks seemed calculable, something that could be managed and predicted; whereas today, in situations of 'manufactured risk', we 'simply don't know what the level of risk is, and in many cases we won't know for sure until it is too late' (Giddens 2002: 28). We are back to the 'insuperable complexity' of risk society: this indeterminacy and uncertainty is what seems to give rise to the 'push and pull' he identifies, since nobody can tell if risks are being exaggerated or underplayed. The example of the 2003 Iraq war shows this to be a false diagnosis, however. At the time, nobody knew for sure whether Iraq possessed WMD or not, so in that sense the risk was indeterminate: the debate was over whether a clear and present danger had to be countered quickly before it could materialise or whether in fact the risk was not so great and was being exaggerated in order to justify a 'rush to war'. But this debate only made sense in the context of the death of politics, where all sides accepted the legitimacy of the West taking action to deal with the threat supposedly posed by Iraq. In Giddens's account, it is the nature of risk itself which transforms politics, whereas in reality it is the emptiness of politics which gives rise to debates about risk – both in the general sense that with no positive vision of progress the future tends to be viewed with fear; and in the sense that, as in the case of the Iraq war, the hollowing out of political life reduces debate to the pragmatic question of how to cope with unknown risks. Hence in 2003 there were different assessments of what the threat level might be, and different views of what was the best method of responding to it – outright invasion or more international weapons inspections – but little sign of any more fundamental disagreement. Only when political debate has been emptied of issues of political principle does this 'push and pull' of risk assessment arise: there is no question of opposing Western intervention as such, the only 'debate' is about how best to manage unknown risks, as if it were merely a technical matter.

Globalisation and trust

There is another dimension to the argument about trust which also needs to be considered here, revolving around the idea of 'globalisation'. According to Giddens (1990), trust has become more important because of the personal insecurity produced by the reorganisation of time and space that globalisation entails. In contrast to the bounded, face-to-face interactions of pre-modern society, in modernity social relations are 'disembedded' and stretched out infinitely in time and space, sustained by 'expert systems' and by 'symbolic tokens' such as money. This 'disembedding' makes trust more important, but also makes it more problematic. We have to rely on expert systems and knowledges, but in reflexive modernity we do not take things on trust (in fact, we do not like being asked to take things on trust, since it smacks of 'tradition' and 'fundamentalism'). As Justin Rosenberg (2000) demonstrates with forensic rigour, Giddens's attempt to explain contemporary social changes in terms of the reorganisation of space and time empties the phenomena he describes of social content. His discussion of money as 'symbolic tokens', for example, is dressed up as cutting-edge social theory but is a step backwards in understanding compared with Marx's treatment of the subject. Whereas, for Giddens, it is the technical properties of money as a 'symbolic token' that seems to 'disembed' exchange from the spatio-temporal constraints of pre-modern barter and direct exchange, for Marx the exchangeability of values via the medium of money was itself interrogated and shown to be, not a property of money, but an expression of underlying social relationships (Rosenberg 2000: 102–6). Ultimately, as Rosenberg (2000: 154) shows, Giddens is unable to sustain his argument that it is the transformation of space and time which is primary, and instead concedes that this is a secondary phenomenon. Yet along the way he has obfuscated the real causes of the changes to which he points, including what Marx described as capital's 'annihilation of space and time' (quoted in Rosenberg 2000: 108).

Rosenberg does a fine job of demolishing the follies built by Giddens and other architects of globalisation theory, contrasting their approach with the explanations offered by classical social theory, especially that of Marx. Persuasive though Rosenberg is, however, we seem to end up caught between emphasising the novelty of the present but explaining it in a superficial and flawed way, or else offering a deeper and more satisfactory explanatory approach but one which seems to downplay everything that appears distinctive about the present. One has the impression that all the really important questions were effectively settled in the 1800s. Rosenberg (2000: 137) notes correctly that in Marx's account it is the fact that our connection with society is mediated through the impersonal mechanism of market exchange, which means that our relationships with other individuals appear to be purely personal, cut free from the forms of direct obligation which prevailed in pre-capitalist societies. Nevertheless, until recently this individuation was mitigated by forms of association and organisation through which people actively made sense of social connections and their place in society, and sought to influence it by exercising collective agency. This is what has broken down today after the political defeat of the working class. It is the end of Left and Right that produces risk-consciousness and reflexivity not the other way round.

In terms of trust, the trouble today is that, as Jack Straw laments, it is a short step 'from not taking things on trust, to not trusting what one is told'.[11] Recognising the problem, Giddens puts forward the idea of 'active trust', whereby institutions and individuals work to gain and maintain trust rather than simply asserting authority in a way that does not engage in dialogue. The idea is explained in terms of intimate personal relationships, whereby trust is established through a process of disclosure, of 'opening up' to the loved one; as well as being explained in terms of public institutions and expert knowledges (for example, Giddens 2002: 62, 75–6). His repeated references to trust in personal relationships indicate that this is not merely an analogy offered by way of illustration but the model on which Giddens understands trust to work in the public sphere. Thus, he advocates a 'democracy of the emotions' (2002: 77–8): an explicitly therapeutic model of governance in which the sociologist takes on the role of counsellor, advising us how to have a 'healthy' democratic relationship. Astonishingly, Giddens takes the insights he has gained from reading self-help literature (for research purposes, that is) and applies them to the relationship troubles that seem to be characteristic of contemporary politics: 'If one looks at how a therapist sees a good relationship', he tells us, 'it is striking how direct a parallel there is with public democracy' (2002: 62). It is worth listening to Giddens's description of the good relationship, particularly his thoughts on that between parent and child:

> Parents must have authority over children, in everyone's interests. Yet they should presume an in principle equality. In a democratic family, the authority of parents should be based upon an implicit contract. The parent in effect says to the child: 'If you were an adult and knew what I know, you would agree that what I ask you to do is good for you'.... [But in] a democracy of the emotions, children can and should be able to answer back.
>
> (2002: 63)

Giddens appears to be discussing the changing patterns of family life, but actually what is at the back of his mind is the changing character of political relationships. The awful truth begins to dawn: citizens and their elected representatives are no longer thought of as bound by a political relationship among equals. Instead, the relationship is understood to be like that between parent and child. The government plays the role of the parents who tell us that if only we knew what they know – if only we were privy to the classified intelligence, perhaps – we would agree that their decisions are for the best. We, the people, are reduced to a child-like state, but are patronisingly told that we are allowed to 'answer back'. Worse than that indeed, we are *required* to answer back and tell mummy and daddy about our emotional inner lives. 'Relationships function best if people don't hide too much from each other', Giddens tells us in full pop-therapy mode (2002: 62). Both sides are required to open up, but of course, we know that there are things that parents don't talk about in front of the offspring, and since it is not a relationship among equals, only a relationship with grown-ups who are condescending to pretend we are equals, it is we who, like good children, must divulge all. As for those sullen and secretive recalcitrants who will not join in, they are the 'fundamentalists', stubbornly refusing to 'engage in dialogue'. This image of the sulky and silent child-masses recalls Baudrillard's suggestion that popular inertia and passivity poses a problem or challenge. As discussed in Chapter 4, this is wishful thinking in so far as it claims to be a political strategy, but it does identify the real problem that popular disengagement presents for the elite: we must be scolded and coaxed into compliance and participation.

Readers may draw their own conclusions as regards child-rearing methods. As far as the therapist's prescription for political relationships is concerned, however, the results have been disappointing. The British government has adopted the policy of 'greater transparency in political affairs' recommended by Giddens (2002: 76), for example in the Freedom of Information Act. Jack Straw, who was Home Secretary when the Act went through Parliament in 1999–2000, hails the reform as bringing about a 'sea change' in British political culture in terms of 'openness and transparency'. Yet, as he concedes, research has suggested that news articles using information obtained through the Act have tended either to reduce trust in government or to make no difference. Similarly, Straw points out that the decision to go to war in 2003 was put to a Parliamentary vote – an unprecedented move which he claims was 'key to establishing the domestic legitimacy of the specific decisions on Iraq'.[12] In reality, of course, it did no such thing: record numbers of people marched in protest against the war. Instituting greater 'transparency' and 'openness' does not resolve the issue of trust; it simply calls forth more questioning. Seeing the problem as one of trust actually misstates the problem, mistaking cause for effect: it is not that distrust causes disengagement but rather the other way about. Accountability has to entail being held to account from below, not assurance procedures from above, if it is to be meaningful. Yet a demand for accountability presupposes the sort of political engagement that simply does not exist today.

To many British observers, the huge protests against the Iraq war suggested that the problem of political disengagement had been overcome, or was at least beginning to change. Equally, for supporters of the war, Blair's unpopular stance seemed to confirm that he was a 'conviction politician' rather than the image-obsessed slave of focus groups that many commentators had taken him to be. Contrary to the arguments developed here, in other words, the heated debate about the war seemed to mark a reinvigoration of politics. This is addressed in the next section, together with the broader claim that today's heightened risk-consciousness may be changing the character of war itself and making it more difficult to justify.

Risk and war

Martin Shaw's *The New Western Way of War* (2005) and Yee-Kuang Heng's *War as Risk Management* (2006) both see the concept of risk as central to contemporary warfare, though in different ways. Shaw concentrates on how war is waged by the Western military, suggesting that it became risk-averse after Vietnam; while Heng focuses more on the rationale for going to war, arguing that since the end of the Cold War military action has been taken for reasons of 'risk management'. Interestingly, both authors also suggest that the trends they identify may be changing or coming to an end. Heng raises the possibility that in future US military action may be presented more as an ideologically-driven project than as pragmatic risk avoidance; while Shaw argues that in the long and bloody aftermath of the 2003 Iraq war the West's risk-averse way of war has run into crisis, possibly even presaging the longer-term de-legitimation of warfare itself. Whereas, for Heng, a heightened sense of risk-awareness has helped to justify recent military interventions, Shaw argues that it helps to turn people away from war. Descriptively, both accounts are broadly accurate in many respects, but – despite the fact that these authors rightly reject a narrow focus on technological change in favour of attempting broader social explanations – are less satisfactory in explaining *why* risk-avoidance should have become such an important consideration in the conduct and causes of war. Shaw's work is most disappointing in this respect, though appearing to offer the more sophisticated theoretical framework.

Modes and ways of war

Shaw (2005: 94) argues that the contemporary Western 'way of war' is one in which the risk to Western troops is transferred – to local allies who act as proxy ground forces (such as the KLA in Kosovo, or the Northern Alliance in Afghanistan); to enemy combatants rather than civilians (using 'smart' weapons, minimising 'collateral damage'); but also to civilians rather than Western troops (for example, via high-altitude bombing which in fact makes 'collateral damage' more likely). While the first and third of these transfers derive from the imperative to reduce the risk to Western troops, the second embodies the West's claim that its 'way of war' has moral legitimacy because it avoids being, in Shaw's terms, 'degenerate' (killing significant numbers of civilians). Shaw gives rather more credence to such moral claims than is justified: they are made propagandistically and are usually misleading. Much was made, for example, of the US military's capacity for 'surgical strikes' and 'precision bombing' in the Gulf in 1991, but it turned out that a mere 7 per cent of bombs were 'smart', and that around 70 per cent of the 88,500 tons of total munitions dropped actually missed their targets (Knightley 2000: 495). Even when greater use has been made of 'smart' weapons, they have sometimes been deliberately deployed against civilian and 'dual-use' targets – in Kosovo, for instance, these included factories, petrochemical plants, power stations and television facilities. Furthermore, the Western military has continued to deploy non-precision weapons in recent conflicts – such as cluster-bombs and 'daisy-cutters' – when it has been thought useful to do so, sometimes killing civilians in the process. Though it is packaged in terms of a desire to spare civilians, the use of precision weapons technologies surely also derives, at least in part, from the need to minimise risks to Western troops: accurate targeting is important if weaponry is to be militarily effective when used from a safe distance (Beier 2006: 276–7).

Still, this is a minor objection. Shaw does acknowledge that the overriding consideration is the safety of Western forces (2005: 79), and as a description of how contemporary Western wars are fought the idea of 'risk transfer' is broadly accurate. The problems really arise when Shaw locates the Western 'way of war' as part of a larger 'mode of warfare', defined by 'global surveillance'. This surveillance, carried out by the media and 'global civil society' institutions such as war crimes courts and NGOs, supposedly constrains the actions of Western governments and their armies in particular conflicts and ultimately, he argues, helps to de-legitimise war in general. Setting aside, for the moment, the problems with the 'mode of warfare' concept, it is not entirely clear how 'surveillance' has this constraining and de-legitimating effect. The core of his argument – already stated before the invasion of Iraq (Shaw 2002) – is that global surveillance institutions encourage and uphold the application of human rights-based moral judgements about war. Thus, even if the West really does minimise the risks to civilians, the deaths of the few who are still 'accidentally' killed are nevertheless seen as highly problematic. The number of civilians who die in 'small massacres' may be low by historical standards, he observes, but it is still much greater than the number of Western troops killed in recent wars. This discrepancy, revealed and analysed by the media and other institutions, undermines the West's claim to fight 'just wars', particularly since the pre-occupation with the safety of Western forces actually leads to more 'accidental' civilian deaths. 'Global surveillance', in other words, is the means by which a demanding normative judgement is passed on Western wars, applying criteria based on 'human rights thinking' according to which every individual life is seen as valuable (2005: 137).

Yet it is hard to find much evidence of 'surveillance' institutions constraining the conduct of war in this way, let alone questioning the legitimacy of Western military action. Perhaps Shaw's most important example is the fact that the International Criminal Tribunal for the former Yugoslavia (ICTY) considered evidence that NATO was guilty of war crimes in the Kosovo conflict. This is evidently supposed to be the clincher: 'what *was* clear', he says, 'is that NATO *could* be held accountable, in principle at least, for the deaths of the civilian victims' (2005: 138). What might have been, however, is surely secondary to what actually happened: the ICTY gave its *approval* to NATO's bombing of Yugoslavia, by charging the country's leaders with war crimes during the Kosovo campaign. When, after the war, the Tribunal's Chief Prosecutor, Carla del Ponte, looked at the evidence against NATO she privately assured the organisation that she 'would not carry this exercise far', according to NATO officials (*Washington Post*, 20 January 2000), and quickly declared that there was no case to answer. Even if 'in principle' the ICTY could have indicted the leaders of the governments which supply it with the bulk of its documentation and evidence, and even if it could have somehow apprehended the heads of the military organisation which acts as its enforcement arm, it would have soon ceased to function had it done so.

With regard to the media, Shaw's argument seems plausible in relation to the controversies surrounding the torture and killing of civilians in Iraq, but in other instances Western journalists have positively welcomed the killing of civilians. Croatia's forcible expulsion of around 200,000 Serbs from the Krajina in August 1995, in the course of which around 2,500 were killed; or the attacks on Hutu refugee camps in Zaire carried out by the Tutsi-led Rwandan government the following year, for example, were both treated as 'good news' stories (Hammond 2002). It is true, of course, that in these examples Western forces were not involved directly, having been largely confined to a 'humanitarian' role (though in both cases the attacks were carried out with US diplomatic approval, air support and military training). Yet as suggested in our discussion of 'freelance interventionists' in Chapter 2, many in the media (and in other 'surveillance' institutions, such as NGOs) campaigned for tougher Western military action in both Bosnia and Rwanda. Indeed, as discussed below, Western 'risk-aversion' in war first emerged as an issue precisely because these so-called 'global surveillance' organisations were demanding more forceful and direct military action.

The 'mode of warfare' concept, which Shaw borrows from Mary Kaldor, is supposed to be the route to the broader, social explanation he seeks. In fact, however, it suggests an essentially asocial understanding, in which 'warfare' is viewed as an autonomous thing which sits alongside society and works according to its own rules. The mode of warfare, we are told, is a 'rational, goal-oriented arena of social action comparable … to the system of production for profit'. Rejecting the '"normal" assumption of the primacy of socio-economic explanation', Shaw maintains that the mode of warfare is 'irreducible' to the mode of production and plays no role for capitalist society. Rather, it is a 'burden on' and is in 'tension' with capitalism, demanding that resources be diverted into a 'permanent arms race' (2005: 41–2, quoting Kaldor). Since the 'mode of warfare' concept is not derived from social relations, its relationship to society is explained inconsistently: sometimes it is understood as dependent on and subordinate to society; at other points it is seen to 'dominate' and 'structure' society (2005: 42–3, 55). These two explanations correspond to the two particular 'modes' which Shaw discusses: the twentieth century mode of 'total warfare' is understood, following Kaldor, to have exercised a profound influence over society, while the new mode of 'global surveillance warfare' is seen as subordinate to it. The fact that the two 'modes' identified are seen as having a diametrically opposite relationship to society rather undermines the coherence of 'mode of warfare' as a general category. Happily for Shaw, however, the inconsistency allows him to argue that the 'world political and economic systems' of capitalism are essentially 'pacific' (2005: 49). Capitalist society does not produce wars, in other words: only the autonomous 'mode of total warfare' did that, by subordinating capitalist social relations to itself. Conversely, in the case of the new 'mode' which is subordinate to society, the allegedly positive characteristics of 'global surveillance' emerge from the operation of capitalism, as: 'More open markets [enable] media and civil society to operate more than ever before in a global context' (2005: 58).

Heng offers a more straightforward account of war's relationship to society, arguing that war 'reflects the ideas, emotions and conditions of particular historical periods' (2006: 144). Today, he suggests, war has become an exercise in risk management, operating according to the precautionary principle. The most obvious example is the Iraq war, which was justified in terms of unfounded worst-case scenarios involving imagined connections between international terrorism and non-existent WMD, and indeed other commentators have made similar points. Writing in mid-2002, for example, science commentator Joe Kaplinsky already noted the surprising convergence between the precautionary outlook of environmentalist campaigners and official US statements about the War on Terror (as in Defence Secretary Donald Rumsfeld's famous remarks on 'unknown unknowns'), and predicted a '"precautionary war" in Iraq'.[13] Similarly, David Runciman (2004) has argued that Blair's use of the precautionary principle in relation to Iraq showed it to be a 'self-contradictory' idea, since 'it purports to be a way of evaluating risk, yet it insists that some risks are simply not worth weighing in the balance' (see further Runciman 2006; Stern and Wiener 2006). Hence Blair could argue simultaneously that that war was necessary to avert the risk posed by Iraq's WMD, and that it was 'not a time to err on the side of caution' and avoid taking the necessary action. As Runciman (2004) remarks 'This, then, is not a time to err on the side of caution and not a time to err on the side of incaution. Such an argument can be used to justify anything'.

The strength of Heng's analysis, however, comes from his comparison of Iraq with the wars in Kosovo and Afghanistan. At first glance, these conflicts look very different – one a 'humanitarian military intervention', the other a direct response to 9/11 – but Heng highlights some striking continuities. In particular, he draws out the way that in both cases arguments for military action exemplified the outlook of 'risk society', summed up in Beck's (1992: 49) idea of 'preventing the worst'. In Kosovo, airstrikes were supposed to avert a humanitarian catastrophe; in Afghanistan, to prevent future terrorist attacks. Military action is now undertaken according to a 'negative dystopian ethos focused on avoiding harm' and is justified on the pragmatic grounds that – as Blair, Clinton and Bush all repeatedly said of the operations in Kosovo, Afghanistan and Iraq – 'the risks of inaction outweigh the risks of action' (Heng 2006: 153, 147). This has proved to be a durable argument: even after Iraq, Blair continued to contrast the certainties of the past with the new and uncertain world in which 'we have to act on the basis of precaution'.[14] As Heng shows, the idea was first formulated in relation to the idea of preventive humanitarian military action: after the Kosovo war the new governor of the province, Bernard Kouchner, argued that 'Now it is necessary to take the further step of using the right to intervention as a preventive measure to stop wars before they start and to stop murderers before they kill' (*Los Angeles Times*, 18 October 1999), apparently oblivious to the fact that calling people 'murderers' before they have killed anyone is nonsensical.

The main limitation of Heng's generally persuasive argument is a certain ambiguity in his attitude to the idea of 'risk society' itself. Early on in the book, drawing on the work of Zaki Laïdi, he recognises that in the post-Cold War era the US has 'wielded power globally without a project or historical purpose and "meaning"', and that it is this absence of a sense of meaning and purpose which has given rise to the risk-averse approach of 'attempting to manage problems with minimal sacrifices' (Heng 2006: 21). Unfortunately, this insight gets rather lost. At times Heng treats the rise of risk consciousness as a given, explaining it as a response to events such as the Chernobyl nuclear disaster, or to the effects of globalisation (2006: 34, 38), and the relationship between the death of politics and risk-averse war is not really explored. As a result, Heng underestimates the extent to which – as well as being an exercise in risk management – war and other forms of military action have also been launched in an attempt to reconstitute some sense of historical project for Western elites. Instead, he suggests that Western leaders face a choice between fighting 'minimalist safety-first wars' and pursuing the sorts of grand ideological claims which have sometimes been made by the Bush administration about transforming the world and 'spreading democracy' (2006: 161). Governments can, as Heng remarks, appear 'schizophrenic' as they switch between the two. The tension identified by Heng is a real one, manifested in the mismatch between the high-flown ideals (whether in terms of spreading freedom and democracy or upholding human rights) proclaimed by political leaders from time to time, and the risk-averse conduct of war. It does not make much sense to risk one's life in combat if war is essentially an exercise in safety; but it looks ignoble not to do so if war is for the sake of some higher purpose or cause. There is not a straight either/or choice here, however. Contemporary war is both a pragmatic exercise in risk management and an attempt to recover a sense of historical purpose.

Risk and cosmopolitanism

The concept of 'risk society' does indeed imply the negative, dystopian, technical-managerial outlook discussed by Heng, but it does not always present itself as such, and in fact a large part of its appeal lies in the claim that it 'opens up individual and political opportunities' (J. Franklin 1998: 1). The content of this new political outlook is cosmopolitanism, the logic being that since 'global risks' cannot be contained or managed within the framework of nation-states, there is a need for a transnational politics of global cosmopolitanism. The model is man-made ecological problems or disasters, the effects of which do not stop at national borders, but Beck extends the same framework to encompass issues of human rights abuse and terrorism (Beck 2000b, 2002). These too may be understood as presenting risks which, since we are all at least indirectly vulnerable to them, supposedly bind us together, thus forming the basis for the 'emergence of universal values' (Giddens 1994: 20) or for a 'cosmopolitan manifesto' (Beck 1999).

The role of the media and civil society in promoting global cosmopolitan norms in situations of crisis and conflict is a long-standing theme in Shaw's work, but in *The New Western Way of War* the accent is on opposition to war. This apparently more critical orientation to Western military intervention is a new departure: like other proponents of 'global civil society', Shaw spent most of the previous decade telling us that 'peace politics can only start now with the use of force' and that 'opposition to western military interventions in the Third World' was 'downright wrong' (Shaw 1993: 16). In the debates of the 1990s, those who argued for a cosmopolitan global order demanded more war, not less. As noted above, it was in this context that the risk-aversion of Western governments and their militaries was first raised as a problem. The US was criticised for intervening in Somalia as a safer alternative to the Balkans in 1992, and then derided because it cut and ran from its 'humanitarian mission' after 18 of its soldiers were killed there in 1993. Even worse, as far as many critics were concerned, was that this led to the codification of new restrictions on the future use of US military force, thereby preventing intervention to avert genocide in Rwanda the following year. The main focus of complaint was Bosnia, where, as we saw in Chapter 2, commentators argued that fear of losing out with the electorate had made Western governments reluctant to risk their own troops: this 'lack of will' meant that the Western military was emasculated and unable to take effective action against the Serbs. Advocates of armed intervention to protect victims of human rights abuse scorned the risk-aversion of the West.

The biggest disappointment of all was Kosovo. NATO leaders enthusiastically adopted the language of cosmopolitan law-enforcement, finally proposing the direct military action in support of human rights norms that the organisations of 'global surveillance' had long demanded. Yet in the event Kosovo was the clearest case to date of the disconnect between grandiose moral rhetoric and the reality of risk-averse war, as the strategy of high-altitude bombing and a refusal to deploy ground troops meant that while there were no Western casualties at all, the initial effect of the campaign was to escalate violence in Kosovo instead of halting it, and 'accidents' were common, including the inadvertent bombing of ethnic-Albanian refugees who NATO was supposed to be protecting. Predictably, the response from more-ethical-than-thou interventionists was to lament the lack of commitment. Mary Kaldor (2000: 61), for example, bemoaned the attempt 'to wage war without risking casualties', wishing that there was more of a 'readiness to die for humanity'; and Michael Ignatieff (2000: 215) yearned for a robust warrior culture in which war was viewed less as a 'surgical scalpel' and more as a 'bloodstained sword'. Yet political leaders showed no lack of zeal in putting their case for intervention in the Kosovo crisis: they did present it as a repetition of the Nazi Holocaust, after all (Hume 2000;

Cica 2001). In fact what Kosovo demonstrated was that the cosmopolitan project was going nowhere.

Against the 'humanitarian' claims made for the bombing of Afghanistan and the invasion of Iraq, some critics have argued that the War on Terrorism has nothing to do with cosmopolitan war (Spence 2005), and Beck himself has expressed some unease that 'The call for justice and human rights is used to legitimate the invasion of other countries', and has insisted that 'It is necessary to make a clear distinction between *true* and *false* cosmopolitanism'.[15] Yet the political limitations of precautionary cosmopolitan war were already apparent before 9/11. The Kosovo campaign was about as perfect an example as one can imagine of a cosmopolitan war, not just because human rights were to the fore, but more precisely because NATO leaders consistently claimed that intervention was driven by a co-incidence of values and interests. As Blair put it in a major speech during the Kosovo conflict setting out his 'doctrine of international community', 'values and interests merge'.[16] 'Interests', in this context, really meant shared risks, invoking exactly the 'solidarity from anxiety' suggested by Beck. As then Secretary of State Madeleine Albright explained in 1998:

> The promotion of human rights is not just a kind of international social work. It is indispensable for our safety and well being because governments which don't respect the rights of their own citizens will in all likelihood not respect the rights of others either.... Such regimes are also more likely to trigger unrest by persecuting minorities, offering a safe haven for terrorists, smuggling drugs or clandestinely manufacturing weapons of mass destruction.
>
> (Quoted in Beck 2000b: 82)

Shared fear of such risks was supposed to provide the basis for a new cosmopolitan global order, in which sovereignty was no barrier to intervention to protect human rights (or indeed to pursue terrorists and halt the manufacture of WMD). Yet while there was little opposition to the war, it also failed to work as the reinvigorated new political project it was supposed to be. Ignatieff worried that 'commitment is intense but also shallow', while David Rieff complained that the public regarded the Kosovo war with 'indifference' and lethargy (quoted in Chandler 2003). The risks highlighted by political leaders in relation to Kosovo – not just a 'genocidal' extermination of Kosovo Albanians, but also waves of asylum seekers flooding Westward, the threat of a wider regional conflict and the collapse of NATO and European security – were just as overblown and hysterical as anything that was claimed about Iraq's WMD and Saddam's links to al-Qaeda. Beck (2002: 114) claims that: 'humanity, expressed through fear, is the last strong resource for making new bonds', yet in the long run the scare mongering did not work any better than the dodgy dossiers and 45-minute warnings did a few years later. It did not work because encouraging a sense of vulnerability is no basis for inspiring anything other than anxiety, and trying to build a sense of moral purpose on the basis of fear is no substitute for politics.

Risk as pro- and anti-war politics

In terms of the political implications risk-consciousness, in a sense both Shaw and Heng are right: risk can be called on to serve both pro- and anti-war camps. What it cannot do is compensate for the lack of principled political arguments either for and against war. When risk is repeatedly mobilised as an argument for war, the cumulative effect is to reinforce cynicism. Inevitably, the dangers become exaggerated (whether deliberately, as part of a propaganda campaign, or out of genuine fear makes little difference in this respect), since war is precautionary. If the working assumption is 'better safe than sorry', going to war need not be based on any real threat: as Rumsfeld said of Iraqi WMD, 'Absence of evidence is not evidence of absence'. Notwithstanding Beck's (2002: 114) claim that it is 'the perceived globality of risk' which 'makes political action possible in the age of globalisation', elite attempts to connect with a political constituency on the basis of risk-perception are actually counterproductive, producing only distrust and suspicion when exaggerations are exposed. At the same time, since the need to avoid risk also extends to the way wars are conducted, Western governments virtually invite criticism. As Mick Hume remarked soon after the beginning of the Iraq invasion:

> The problems and casualties encountered to date are on a very small scale, judged by any historical perspective. But when you signal your intention to pull off some sort of 'safe', low-risk conflict, small setbacks can easily be perceived as big problems.

> By the same token, the coalition's defensive emphasis on avoiding civilian casualties means that, when some do occur, what would once have been seen as an inevitable consequence of war can now cause an international outcry.[17]

There was no shortage of criticism drawing attention to dangers and problems in Iraq, but this should not be mistaken for a political argument against war.

Deep down, Shaw knows this. His case study of Iraq accurately describes the emptiness of the debate about the war, whereby pros and antis traded risk assessments, each side trying to outdo the other in constructing the worst doomsday scenario (2005: 103–6). The trouble is that he has nothing better to offer and so joins in. Having thoroughly demolished the approach of body-counting as a strategy for encouraging opposition to war, for example, Shaw then signs a petition calling for more body counts (2005: 145, n8). He also seems to hope that electoral 'risk-rebound' due to 'the risks to which the USA ... exposed its *own* and other international troops in Iraq ... and the [war's] counterproductive effects for the risks of terrorism' will help his argument (2005: 123). Given that promoters of the cosmopolitan cause repeatedly urged Western governments to take greater risks, there is something repellent in seeing Shaw now hitching it to the bandwagon of risk-aversion. He even has the gall to claim that it was Bush who overturned the 'legitimate global order that was built after 1945', despite the fact that the advocates of human rights intervention spent years urging the West to dispense with the principles of sovereign equality and non-interference on which the post-war order was constructed (2005: 141). At least on this question Shaw is consistent, maintaining his support for 'the exercise of global authority'. The flip side of his opportunism in latching on to risk-aversion over Iraq is the ease with which his ostensibly anti-war argument slips into support for military intervention. Having disassociated capitalism and war through the 'mode of warfare' concept, Shaw's utopian vision of the historic de-legitimation of warfare entails no fundamental social transformation. Indeed, it does not even require the end of war, only its re-designation as 'armed policing' (2005: 142).

The idea of cosmopolitan military action is that it is simultaneously 'above' politics – a police action, rather than a Clausewitzean clash of wills – and a new political project, rallying people behind shared values. The combination is impossible to achieve in any convincing way: you cannot have a political project based on a rejection of politics. Similarly, looked at from the interests half of the values and interests equation, when 'interests' are understood in terms of 'preventing the worst', war becomes a merely pragmatic, non-political measure to avert potential threats, thereby making it more difficult to justify putting the lives of Western troops at risk. Cosmopolitanism is an anti-political outlook, a symptom of the difficulty of articulating interests or values rather than a solution to this problem.

Conclusion

This chapter has argued that risk cannot work as basis for new politics because it is a fundamentally anti-political outlook. The theorists of risk society argue that it is the spatio-temporal shifts of globalisation and the new sources and scope of 'manufactured risk' that have undermined established frameworks of political identification, but, it has been suggested here, the dynamics of politics in the risk society are better explained by the absence of the subject, the attenuation of political agency. As Joseph Camilleri and Jim Falk (1992: 59–61) argue, the problem of political agency at the level of the individual subject translates into a crisis of sovereignty at the level of the state. This is explored further in the next chapter, but for now it might be suggested on the basis of the foregoing discussion that the move away from justifying foreign policy in terms of national interests is a product of the failure of politics to engage people. Risk talk and cosmopolitanism are attempts to evade the consequences of this problem by instead presenting international intervention both as a technical matter of risk assessment and as a non-political police action carried out in the name of 'values'.

On the one hand, war is presented as something about which we have no choice – leaders are forced to action by the quasi-subjects of risk. On the other hand war is purely a matter of choice – it becomes a matter of 'doing the right thing' according to the dictates of the leader's conscience. In seeking to persuade people of the necessity of the 2003 Iraq war, Blair pursued both tacks. Unfortunately, so did the anti-war movement. Where the government emphasised the risks of inaction, its critics gave greater weight to the risks of action; where Blair's conscience told him he could not disappoint the suffering Iraqi people, the protestors called back: 'not in my name'. It is not, as the cosmopolitans would have it, that war-as-policing is above politics, but that there is no political content to contemporary debates about war: technical risk-assessment or personal conscience are the only basis for disagreement.

Chapter 6

Postmodern empire and the 'death of the subject'

As is widely recognised today, imperialism ain't what it used to be. It is 'empire lite' (Ignatieff 2003), 'incoherent empire' (Mann 2003), or 'empire in denial' (Chandler 2006). In one of the most celebrated recent contributions on the topic Michael Hardt and Antonio Negri (2000) draw a pointed contrast between the nationally-rooted imperialisms of old and the new phenomenon of global empire, understood as an amorphous network of power with no centre. Apart from Michael Mann, none of these analysts is suggesting that twenty-first century imperialism lacks power: in terms of wealth and military muscle the strength and reach of the imperial powers is greater than ever. Rather, what these commentators are all getting at, in different ways, is that contemporary imperialism appears to lack a sense of imperial mission. The terms in which international conflict is discussed today – US imperialism, Islamic terrorism – seem familiar, even a throwback to the past. Yet the content of these apparently recognisable categories has changed. Contemporary terrorism also seems to lack a grand narrative. Unlike in the case of past acts of terror, 9/11 was conspicuously not followed by a communiqué explaining the attack, setting out a political manifesto or listing demands (Gearson 2002: 11). Instead, bin Laden and al-Qaeda initially denied responsibility, while experts and media commentators were obliged to speculate about who had perpetrated the outrage and what their aims and objectives might be. In describing both imperialism and terrorism as 'postmodern' the intention here is to suggest that what is different about these phenomena today hinges on the postmodern crisis of political agency.

This problem of agency, the 'death of the subject' in postmodernist thought, presents itself in the international sphere as a problem of sovereignty. This is so in two senses, depending on whose sovereignty we are talking about. In regard to the Western state, as we saw in Chapter 1, the idea is that sovereignty is now voluntarily 'shared' or partially given up, as in multilateral institutions like the EU. An insistence on traditional forms of sovereign authority is seen as outdated and irrelevant in today's globalised and multilateral world: hence the European objection to Bush's US when it was seen to be aggressively asserting its own sovereignty rather than working in partnership with the 'international community'. The sovereignty of the non-Western state is seen as problematic partly in that it too may be understood as clinging to the outdated modern concept of sovereignty, but at the same time it is also seen as problematic for failing to achieve or maintain the status of modern sovereignty. These ideas correspond to Robert Cooper's (2004) categories of 'modern' and 'pre-modern' states or, in more familiar terms, to the categories of 'rogue' and 'failed' states. These are not so much separate classifications for different sets of states, however, but different ways of conceptualising the problems that non-Western states supposedly present. Saddam's Iraq, for instance, was simultaneously a 'rogue' state, allegedly threatening the West with its WMD, and also a 'failed' state in that the regime was not in full control of its territory and did not discharge its duty of care toward its own citizens, instead abusing their human rights (Elden 2007). This means that the West is engaged simultaneously in the apparently contrary tasks of knocking down non-Western states and building them up. As we shall see, these are not so contradictory as first appears, however, since the process of state-building, while it may often pay lip service to the ideas of sovereignty and self-government, means something very different in practice.

This chapter asks why sovereignty is seen as problematic in these various ways today, and explores the implications of the crisis of (sovereign) agency for our understanding of contemporary imperialism and terrorism. Established ideas about state sovereignty have been challenged theoretically as well as practically in the years since the end of the Cold War, and the chapter begins by considering some of these recent debates. It then goes on to examine what is distinctive about imperialism and terrorism today. As the preceding chapters have argued, the lack of purpose and mission simultaneously sets a more interventionist dynamic in motion and undercuts the coherence of attempts to project power internationally. As suggested in Chapters 2 and 3, both the 'ethical' interventions of the 1990s and the War on Terror were attempts to cobble together a sense of mission rather than being determined by the pursuit of definite strategic interests, yet precisely because the focus was on generating meaning, both frameworks resulted in actions which were more like media stunts. This chapter draws out the implications of this crisis of meaning for how the West relates to weaker states in the context of the War on Terror. Not only the new forms of intervention but also terrorism itself may be understood as an externalisation of the West's internal crisis of meaning – not in terms of a reaction against or resistance to Western power, but rather as a manifestation of the West's own weaknesses.

Sovereignty and the 'death of the subject'

The fall of the Berlin Wall brought many established ideas crashing to the ground, including in the academic discipline of International Relations (IR). Dramatic and unexpected international events were widely interpreted as having exposed the poverty of the narrow debates between neo-realism and neo-liberalism that had come to dominate the discipline, and as giving a great boost to a variety of newer approaches (Booth 1995). The discipline's mainstream orthodoxy of neo-realism, as exemplified by the work of Kenneth Waltz (1979), conceived the international sphere as an unregulated space of 'anarchy' in which states are egoistic actors pursuing their conflicting national interests. From the realist perspective, states are bound to act in this way precisely because of the logic of anarchy – that is, because there is no over-arching framework of world order. The liberal perspective could draw on a long tradition which emphasised its distinctiveness, repudiating the Hobbesean world of the realists in favour of a Kantian concept of perpetual peace. Yet neo-liberalism, associated most prominently with Robert Keohane and Joseph Nye (1977), while still highlighting the potential for cooperation rather than conflict, had converged with neo-realism to the point where both could be characterised as sharing a common rationalist, behaviourist outlook. As John Ruggie (1998: 3) puts it: 'they share a view of the world of international relations in utilitarian terms: an atomistic universe of self-regarding units whose identity is assumed given and fixed, and who are responsive largely if not solely to material interests that are stipulated by assumption'.

The main beneficiary of the shake-up in IR since the end of the Cold War has been the constructivist approach. A full account of the various strands of constructivist thought would be out of place here, but its interest for our discussion is two-fold. Firstly, constructivism has been offered as giving a new lease of life to the aspirations of liberalism, and it is important to examine it here because it has some clear points of connection with the sorts of 'ethical' policies which have been adopted by Western governments. Secondly, it is also worth examining some of the critiques which have been made of constructivism, particularly by postmodernist or post-structuralist IR theorists, since these shed some light on the question of agency both through the problems they highlight and the through limitations from which they suffer.

Constructivism and ethical foreign policy

The major innovation made by constructivism is to argue that the identities and interests of states are not given, but are socially constructed in the process of interaction. In Alexander Wendt's widely influential (1992) formulation, if the international sphere is anarchical, that is because states agree to make it so. State interests and identities are not determined exogenously, argues Wendt, but are 'endogenous to the state system', shaped by the interactions between states (and, some constructivists would emphasise, between states and other global actors). The relationships of power and competing interests which realism sees as an inevitable and eternal feature of international relations are, in this perspective, actually the product of the way states choose to understand their identities and interests. States' pursuit of self-interest, in other words, is no more than a particular way of constructing international relations rather than a pre-social state of nature in which individual actors are forced to compete for power. Just because states understood themselves in this way in the past, does not mean they should continue to do so. Thus, constructivism seems to offer a way to understand the increased importance of ethics, norms and altruistic behaviour on the part of states.

In part, the rise of constructivism reflects a feeling that 'static approaches to IR are particularly unsatisfying during the current era of global transformation' and that new developments demand new sorts of explanations (Finnemore and Sikkink 1998: 888). Yet there is more going on than simply a new scholarly research programme. Many contributions to the discussion are clearly concerned to promote, rather than simply to describe, processes of change, polemicising against other approaches in order to further an alternative agenda. Neo-realist orthodoxy is dismissed as 'Western ideology': a perspective, justified by 'white male Anglo-American professors of international relations', which favours the powerful and closes off the 'ideas about transcendence [and] emancipation' that constructivism wishes to open up (Booth 1995: 333). In this way, academic discussion seeks both to explain and also to justify the turn towards a system of 'other-help' rather than 'self-help' behaviour in international affairs. The sorts of claims made by Cooper (2004) about 'postmodern Europe' illustrate the connection between academic theorising and elite practice. The EU is held to exemplify exactly the sort of '"cooperative" security system, in which states identify positively with one another so that the security of each is perceived as the responsibility of all' which Wendt (1992: 400) takes as indicating the possibility of moving beyond egoistic behaviour.[1] Cooper's 'postmodern imperialism', driven by values rather than interests, also seems to confirm the constructivist hypothesis.

Although this approach is clearly intended to 'inject ... a dose of agency' (Mercer 1995) into theoretical understandings of international relations the better to explain real-world changes, Wendt has been criticised for not having an adequate theory of agency and change. In particular, his claim to be able to explain the end of the Cold War better than realist accounts has been contested (Bickerton et al. 2007b: 27–8; Chandler 2004: 29–31).[2] In so far as constructivism emphasises the process of interaction as decisive in the formation of identities and interests, this objection is a powerful one: constructivism does elevate process over agency. Yet it would not be true to say that Wendt offers no explanation of how change comes about, and it is instructive to examine what he does say on the matter.

According to Wendt, agency consists in the gap between the 'me' part of subjectivity defined by others, and the 'I' which actively assumes that role. This gap allows actors the possibility for 'self-reflection and practice specifically designed to transform their identities and interests and thus to "change the games" in which they are embedded' (1992: 419). His example is the 'New Thinking' initiated by Mikhail Gorbachev: this entailed a re-conceptualisation of the USSR's identity and interests whereby, through a process of 'altercasting' (treating the Other as if it already had a new identity), the Soviet Union was able to 'change the game' from one of mutual hostility and distrust to one of cooperation and amity. Hence, he argues that: 'if the United States and Soviet Union decide that they are no longer enemies, "the cold war is over"' (1992: 397). Accepting, for the sake of argument, that this 'altercasting' took place, the key question is why the USSR should have engaged in its New Thinking in the first place. Wendt's answer is that there was a domestic 'breakdown of consensus about identity commitments', leading to 'the government's decline of political legitimacy at home' (1992: 420). In other words, the change of identity and values internationally was caused at least in part by a domestic crisis of legitimacy, raising the possibility that perhaps the 'ethical' turn in Western foreign policy might have similar causes. This is a possibility that Wendt does not explore, however. He says he is 'suggesting for rhetorical purposes that the raw material out of which members of the state system are constituted is created by domestic society before states enter the constitutive process of international society' (1992: 402), but the implied importance of domestic politics cannot be pursued in his approach, since the whole thrust of his argument is that it is interactions between states which determine identities and interests. Constructivism advertises its status as a *social* theory,[3] but it is only 'social' in the narrow sociological understanding of the social as equivalent to interpersonal relationships, here extended to 'interpersonal' relations between states.

The postmodernist critique

Some postmodernist or post-structuralist IR theorists have paid particular attention to this issue of the relationship between the domestic and the international in the definition of states' identities and interests (Campbell 1992; Walker 1993); a concern which has led to an illuminating critique of constructivism. Maja Zehfuss, for example, offers a penetrating critique of Wendt and other leading constructivists by assessing their approach in relation to Germany's international military involvement in the post-Cold War era. As she observes, in this case the construction of a larger collective identity beyond the narrow self-interest of the nation-state did not lead, as Wendt supposes, to a more peaceful 'Kantian culture', but to greater military activity (2002: 83). In justifying involvement in Somalia and the Balkans in the early 1990s, German leaders disingenuously claimed that they were only responding to pressure from abroad, and that they had to act in order not to disappoint their 'friends and partners'. One 'Other-regarding' collective identity, centred around being a non-military power within an integrated Europe, was swapped for another 'Other-regarding' collective identity which involved being a military power for humanitarian and human rights causes. As we saw in Chapter 2, conflict in the Balkans was presented as a defining moment for Europe's collective identity, but hardly in a peaceful fashion: as Zehfuss notes, German leaders came to see military deployment and the creation of a standing European security force as a means to achieve integration, instead of European integration meaning that Germany could be a non-military power. The claim to be acting in accordance with the needs and demands of others, rather than from self interest, was a way of neutralising objections to a highly controversial change in policy which was actually designed to boost Germany's international standing; while the turn toward 'ethical' military action offered a way to give purpose and direction to German politics. The domestic meaning of military involvement in relation to the country's Nazi past underwent a shift, summed up in the re-interpretation of the 'Never Again' slogan, from being a repudiation of war to being an argument in favour of war to halt alleged Nazi-style atrocities in the former Yugoslavia. As Foreign Minister and former peace activist Joschka Fischer said at the time of the Kosovo conflict, he had: 'not only learned the lesson "never again war", but also "never again Auschwitz"' (quoted in Deichmann 2000).

The strength of the post-structuralist critique – the thing that makes it suspicious of constructivist claims about identity – is also the source of its weakness, however. This is its hostility to the concept of the subject. As Jenny Edkins and Véronique Pin-Fat (1999: 1) explain, although constructivism offers a view of the subject/sovereign state as constructing its identity inter-subjectively, through processes of social interaction, or see it as shifting across different subject positions, this perspective still leaves the subject intact as, in Wendt's (1992: 404) telling, an 'ego' which confronts its 'alter'. Instead, they argue, the category of the subject is itself 'impossible': the subject 'does not exist', except as a never-completed performance. Where Wendt (1992: 404) invokes the symbolic-interactionist concept of the 'looking-glass self' – the idea that our self-identity is shaped by how we are perceived by others – Edkins and Pin-Fat counter with psychoanalyst Jacques Lacan's notion of the 'mirror stage': the moment of mis-recognition when, according to Lacan, the fiction of the self is created. Extending the idea to state sovereignty, they argue that both subject and sovereign are 'master signifiers' – equivalent, in Lacanian terminology, to the Phallus, or to what Derrida calls the *logos* – which function to stabilise the phallogocentric symbolic systems of both language and society.

In the post-structuralist view of language, meaning is never finally fixed or, to put it another way, is never present in the sign: instead, since meaning is only produced by difference, it is always endlessly deferred along the chain of signifiers. In order for language to work as an orderly system, however, that absence of meaning has to be managed or covered up in some way. In language, this happens through what Derrida calls phonocentrism, the privileging of speech over writing, whereby the speaking subject appears to be the origin and source of meaning, rather than meaning being produced by the differences between signs. Such a subject is really no more than a convenient fiction, from this anti-humanist perspective which maintains that language 'speaks us'.

Similarly, for Lacan the unconscious is structured like a language, but in the same way that Derrida views language – as an endless play of signifiers. In a post-Saussurean re-working of Freud's account of the subordination of unconscious drives and desires to a rational ego – the Oedipal passage from the pleasure principle to the reality principle through conformity to the incest prohibition – Lacan understands the formation of a stable sense of self as dependent on subordination to the Law of the Father, or the Phallus. This assertion of order stands in for or covers up the lack at the centre of the system, in this case our desire for wholeness, our desire to merge with the (m)Other.[4] It is worth emphasising the anti-humanism implicit in this outlook: whereas Freud's slogan was 'where Id was there shall Ego be', the Lacanian subject is always 'decentred', marked by a 'lack', an absence of meaning which s/he strives to fill.

Edkins and Pin-Fat (1999: 6) extend this perspective, by analogy, to the analysis of state sovereignty. The absence of meaning is construed here as an 'antagonism at the heart of the social order', though they unfortunately neglect to mention what that antagonism is or to tell us anything whatever about it: at least in their account, it really is a 'lack'. Still, let us take it as read that we do live in an antagonistic, divided society. What the 'master signifier' of sovereignty does is to fix that play of meaning or social antagonism, by providing a 'nodal point around which meaning is articulated'. Sovereignty is thereby understood as equivalent to the Derridean *logos* or the Lacanian Phallus: an imposition of absolute authority, to which we subordinate ourselves as subjects. As their co-editor, Nalini Persram (1999: 172), puts it: 'Subjectivity … came into being by virtue of the myth and promise of sovereignty for the subject within the social order, which also claimed sovereignty for itself'. From this point of view, constructivism fails to get to the heart of the matter – or worse, it appears to question subjectivity and sovereignty but actually leaves them undisturbed. In a spirited attack, Persram rejects attempts to incorporate postmodern approaches into the constructivist camp, denouncing the 'pseudo-progressive vocabulary of intersubjectivity and all the rest' (1999: 171). The insistence on maintaining a critical posture seems attractive, but what she really means is that post-structuralists like her are better at demolishing the subject than are the constructivists.

Since subjectivity and sovereignty really are degraded today, poststructuralists' relentless hostility to these concepts affords greater insight, at least some of the time, than seems to be available to writers who put themselves at the service of attempted new grand narratives. Yet ultimately the attack goes nowhere, offering only a tiresome repetition of the sorts of criticisms made by Althusser and Foucault in the 1970s. By way of illustration, we can examine the first two case studies in the collection edited by Edkins *et al.*

In the first of these, David Campbell reprises the argument about the Bosnian war made at greater length in his 1998 book *National Deconstruction*. Unlike many commentators, he is sensitive to the fact that the attention paid to Bosnia by the 'international community' was more about shoring up the West's self-image than it was about saving the victims who were the ostensible focus of concern. Drawing on Baudrillard and others, he makes a similar point about the West's 'self-serving morality of pity and victimhood' (Campbell 1999: 23) to that discussed in Chapter 2 in terms of a narcissistic search for meaning. Having gained this insight, however, he then throws it away, joining the chorus of those urging tougher Western intervention while welcoming the elevation of humanitarianism as a limit on state sovereignty. The only difference is that he gets the latter argument from Derrida instead of from *The New York Times* or *The Guardian*. Campbell's critical orientation leads him to question humanitarianism as a new way of endowing Western authority with meaning, but his assumption that it is the *strength* of sovereignty which is the problem leads in the opposite direction, preventing him from understanding why the exercise of Western power should have taken this peculiar form. Hence, he identifies the underlying problem as 'realism', suggesting that Western leaders were as committed as nationalist Serbs and Croats to the worship of sovereignty, and that they shared similar assumptions about 'autonomous and settled identities' and about the 'alignment between state and nation' (1999: 28). In this reading, it is an 'unwillingness to make multiculturalism [the political] goal' of intervention (1999: 33) which hampers effective international action – a conclusion belied by the fact that just a few months after Campbell had reached it, NATO was bombing Yugoslavia in the name of … multiculturalism, teaching 'fascistic' Serbs the value of tolerance.

The strengths and limitations of the post-structuralist approach are illustrated even more vividly in Cynthia Weber's analysis of the 1994 US-led UN intervention in Haiti. Her conceit is that, in intervening in Haiti to remove the military junta and restore President Jean-Bertrand Aristide to office, the US engaged in a transvestite masquerade, disavowing its own phallic power as a way of exercising it all the more effectively. Clinton, she suggests, laid claim: 'a different kind of US sovereign subjectivity by subtly rewriting US foreign policy toward the Caribbean as a male transvestite' (1999: 51). That is to say, the US did not act in its own name, but only took action 'reluctantly', to enforce the will of the UN; not invading but staging an 'intervasion' which took the form of a 'soft landing' rather than a 'forced entry'. The effect of this masquerade of not possessing phallic power was to reinforce the fact of US dominance – much as the male transvestite draws attention to that which he pretends not to have – so that: 'the United States in male masquerade appears to be a more sovereign state than all sovereign states'. The trope of transvestism makes the analysis an entertaining read, but more importantly it demonstrates Weber's sensitivity to the distinctive way that US power was exercised in the Haiti intervention, not as a direct assertion of authority but indirectly, in a way that seemed calculated to disguise and disclaim US power and interests. The question, however, is why the US was 'wearing a dress' in Haiti. Weber's implausible answer is that America did not want to look like a bully in its own back yard – why not, we may wonder – and that it was attempting to escape from castration anxiety, fearing the loss of the phallic power to make meaning that it had gained in the 1991 Gulf War (1999: 43). Yet this argument is circular: the US disavows its power because of fear of exercising it directly. We are still none the wiser as to why this might be the case. The approach which enables Weber to pose the interesting question of why it now seems difficult for the West to project power directly also closes off an exploration of possible answers. She too discards her insight, concluding that both sovereignty and subjectivity should be understood as performance rather than stable facts: a conclusion that diverts us away from addressing the specificity of the way Western power is exercised in the post-Cold War era, and points instead toward some timeless platitude about the 'performative' nature of subjectivity and sovereignty *per se*.

Paradoxically, the postmodernist approach depends on taking the modern conceptions of subjectivity and sovereignty as fixed objects of critique, in order that its deconstruction of them can have some force. The problem derives from the anti-essentialist assumptions of post-structuralism: there is only appearance, never essence, in this approach. Sovereignty can only be treated as a 'master signifier' – an arbitrary form which occupies a particular place in the system – never as having a social essence. As discussed in Chapter 4, this approach derived from post-war thinking about the 'relative autonomy' of ideology, where the impulse was to explain the absence of revolutionary class consciousness. The effect has been to justify the absence of political agency by demolishing the category of the subject in theory. The final strand of IR thought to be considered here, however, does hold out the possibility of uncovering the 'essence' of state sovereignty.

Sovereignty and civil society

Justin Rosenberg offers a quite different critique of realism from that of the constructivists. The realist orthodoxy of IR theory, he suggests, was the apologetic, ideological form of post-war imperialism. What the realists theorised as 'anarchy' is the sphere of market exchange, in which sovereign individuals/states pursue their interests, while the real power relations of production disappear from view. Thus, the realist theory of IR was the most 'appropriate' perspective for the particular form that imperialism assumed under Pax Americana during the second half of the twentieth century. Arguing that 'Every historical episode of imperial expansion elaborates its own distinctive ideological legitimation', Rosenberg says that:

> For the twentieth-century United States [this] means the liberal idea of freedom, and a discipline of IR which concentrates on the purely political world of sovereign equality and anarchical competition in which the imperial character of American world power is least visible.
>
> (1994: 172)

Despite the withdrawal of the imperial powers from their overseas territories during the era of decolonisation, indirect domination continued through the subordination of newly-independent states in the world market. The supposed end of empire was really a shift from direct political control to an 'empire of civil society', argues Rosenberg, in which power was exercised through the non-political, private realm of economic exploitation.

Hence, the extension of sovereignty after the Second World War, even though it entailed the formal recognition of sovereign equality, did not fundamentally alter the relationships of *inequality* founded on the social power of capital. Rosenberg points out that this change in the form of imperialism suited the needs of the hegemonic power, the US, which presented itself as 'anti-imperialist', in contrast to the old colonial powers of Europe:

> When do the interests of a rising imperial power promote not political subjection but political independence? They do so when the political independence in question is not substantive political possession of resources by an autarchic state (in either communist or radical nationalist forms) but rather the consolidation of sovereignty. This breaks the political link with the former imperial power, while opening the newly demarcated sphere of 'the economy' to the private power of foreign capital, that is, to the social form of dependence mediated by things. Historically, the US fought communism and anti-Western radical nationalism and supported the emergence of sovereign independence, irrespective of whether it took a democratic political form.
>
> (1994: 169)

This is certainly a better account of decolonisation than that offered by the constructivists. As David Chandler (2004: 64) points out, the constructivists tend to read back into history the elevation of normative values they discover in the present, understanding decolonisation as resulting from the international adoption of a more morally-enlightened perspective. Martha Finnemore and Kathryn Sikkink (1998: 887), for example, maintain that: 'decolonization was driven by a profoundly normative agenda and … explicitly sought to reconstitute the identities of both the new states and their former colonizers'. Whereas this type of explanation is 'social' only in the sense that it is interested in the inter-personal interactions between different actors, Rosenberg's Marxist account derives the change in the form of imperial rule from the core, defining relationship of capitalist society.

Elegant though Rosenberg's critique of realism is, however, it is not without its problems. Firstly, in challenging the false separation between the private sphere of economic exploitation and the public political world of free individuals/states Rosenberg tends drastically to underestimate the importance of the political. Secondly, even as he assembled his critique of realism, this 'orthodoxy' was already in decline, increasingly challenged by the newer constructivist approaches. If realism was the ideological form of an imperialism which promoted the freedom of sovereign states, the question logically arises of what new developments today's IR might be theorising.

Rosenberg's approach is evidently inspired by the contrast Marx draws between the exploitative relationships of the 'hidden abode of production' and the sphere of market exchange, which he describes sardonically as 'a very Eden of the innate rights of man' (Marx 1976: 279–80). Just as, within the modern nation-state, capitalism freed people from relationships of direct dependence and coercion, subordinating them instead to new hierarchical class relations but mediated by the exchange of commodities; so in the international sphere the direct and visible coercion of empire is replaced by the invisible coercion of private economic relationships. The public sphere of politics is indeed an imperfect realm of freedom since that freedom is undercut by the inequalities spontaneously reproduced through the relationships of production. Yet Marx's intention was not simply to rubbish the claims of freedom and equality made on the basis of the separation of the political realm but to show how the possibility of freedom was limited by the hidden relationships of production. After all, it is the fact that capitalism creates this apparently 'separate' sphere of political freedom which helps to create the possibility for social transformation through the exercise of conscious collective agency.

The development of the system of equal sovereign states – analogous, in Rosenberg's account, to the free and equal relationships among sovereign individuals within capitalist society – appears as a more perfect form of capitalist empire, in which the 'dull compulsion' of the wage-labour/capital relationship makes direct coercion unnecessary most of the time. The formal equality among sovereign states that was institutionalised in the post-war UN system appears as a sign of imperialism's strength: direct forms of domination could be dispensed with in favour of a principle of political non-interference and sovereign equality because the hidden inequalities of exploitation ensured the subordination of weaker states. Yet the unfortunate effect of Rosenberg's critique is to downgrade the importance of the sphere of politics. If we follow through the logic of his argument we would conclude that the winning or losing of sovereign independence for Third World states was really neither here nor there – it did not alter the basic relationship of power, exercised through surplus-extraction in the 'non-political' abode of production, which could carry on quite well without the need for direct political domination and coercion.

Yet this is not really what happened. The extension of sovereignty in the process of decolonisation was something that in many cases was fought over tooth and nail. Britain, for example, went to war in Malaya and Kenya against independence movements; France did the same in Algeria and Vietnam. Where former colonies became sovereign states, this often involved an active assertion of sovereignty and self-government, rather than simply the peaceful withdrawal of the former colonial powers. As discussed in Chapter 4, the process also entailed an ideological retreat on the part of the colonial powers, who found that the vocabulary of race and empire through which they had understood and justified their domination was now tainted by the barbarism of two world wars and challenged by anti-imperialists. A balanced account has to acknowledge that the retreat from empire and the establishment of the principle of sovereign equality was a huge reversal for the West, even though it is true that, as Rosenberg points out, informal mechanisms of domination ensured continuing global inequality.

Moreover, Pax Americana did not mean the promotion of sovereignty in any straightforward sense: rather, new forms of regulation were adopted under the aegis of the Cold War. The period of post-war 'peace' in fact entailed the US engaging in continual military activity, bombing somewhere virtually every year after 1945 (Blum 2000: 93–4). The 'peace' of the Cold War security regime entailed almost constant conflict in the Third World and new forms of imperial discipline as regimes were brought down or propped up in accordance with Western interests. Rosenberg is careful to point out, in the passage quoted above, that the US attacked states which asserted their independence in ways that thwarted imperialism through 'substantive political possession of resources' within a nationalist or communist framework, and one could add that Third World nationalism and Soviet communism offered only limited and flawed alternatives to imperial rule. But this only underlines the importance of the political sphere – as well as highlighting the importance to former colonial possessions of winning the right to self-government, even if their exercise of that freedom was undermined by indirect economic domination and the Cold War security framework.

Rosenberg is right to suggest that the essence of sovereignty is to be found in the private relationships of production, in the sense that this is what creates the political as a distinct and separate sphere. This does not diminish the importance of the political as the arena in which conceptions of the 'national interest' or 'popular will' are formed, however. Today, as discussed further below, it is exactly the right to self-government, embodied in the modern concept of sovereignty, that is under threat, both in direct assaults on weaker states and in so-called 'state-building' measures. As Christopher Bickerton et al. (2007a: 9) point out, an oddity of the contemporary assault on the concept is that it is often pitched against 'Westphalian' sovereignty, as if the problem today was seventeenth-century absolutism. In fact what is under attack, as they go on to observe, is the modern conception of sovereignty that emerged with the Enlightenment: the idea of sovereignty as the expression of the popular will. This is not to say, of course, that the 'popular will' or 'national interest' is uncontested or consensual. Indeed, the opposite is true – as becomes obvious when claims to be acting in the 'national interest' are invoked against domestic dissenters. Yet it is only through the engagement and contest of clashing interests in the political sphere that the idea of a national will or interest is formed. As Alexander Gourevitch argues, 'the idea of the national interest is dependent upon domestic conflict'. In a situation like that in Western societies today, when such conflict is negligible and political contestation fails to take place, the 'national interest' becomes much harder to define, since it is 'only when the fundamental organising institutions of society are challenged that the question of the national interest poses itself in a consistent way' (Gourevitch 2007: 64). Instead, the elite becomes incoherent and directionless, unable clearly to define the direction and purpose of their state policies.

What happens when society fails to engage its members in the political clash of interests? This is the moment in which we find ourselves, and the rest of this chapter will outline some of its consequences.

Postmodern empire

'This is where our epistemology starts, with rejecting the hubris of perfect rationality', says postmodernist theorist of postmodern war Chris Hables Gray: 'perfect knowledge is a chimera'. The surprise conclusion he draws from this humble beginning is that it was, therefore, legitimate to invade Afghanistan:

> Can you say that the sovereignty of Afghanistan is being assaulted when that sovereignty means the enslavement of woman, the persecution of religious and ethnic minorities, and the direct support of aggressive international terrorism?
>
> [...]
>
> The whole system has to change, and that means establishing new rules that put human rights above national sovereignty ...
>
> (Gray 2002)

Gray's emphasis on postmodern indeterminacy and uncertainty somehow leads him to endorse the practical deconstruction of other people's sovereignty – on the bizarre but convenient grounds that because of our own epistemological modesty we cannot know for sure that Afghanistan is a sovereign state. At one level, this is simply an apology for the bombing (which was in full swing when Gray penned these lines), invoking the cosmopolitan argument that human rights should 'trump' national sovereignty. Perhaps, however, it is more than that: we might interpret Gray's apologia as a theoretical rationalisation of the real process whereby the West's own sense of uncertainty and indeterminacy means that legitimacy is sought in foreign intervention and regulation. This, in microcosm, captures the dynamic of postmodern imperialism.

The assault on sovereignty

The consequences of the West's own internal crisis of meaning have been most sharply posed in the redefinition of sovereignty abroad. As noted above, the non-Western state is seen to present problems both because it is too strong and because it is too weak. On the one hand, it is the unrestrained sovereignty of states that is seen as problematic – what is sometimes referred to as 'sovereign impunity'. Here the problem is that the sovereign state is a law unto itself – in other words, it is sovereign. This view implies that the non-Western state has to be cut down to size, restrained through force if necessary by the 'international community', in order that sovereignty does not become a 'tyrant's charter', allowing states to assert their strength, menace their neighbours and abuse their own citizens. This is the state as victimiser who needs to be policed and regulated. If, in this view, the state appears to be too strong, on the other hand it is also seen as too weak: the West also has the task of building-up the non-Western state, preventing or repairing state 'failure'. Here the danger comes not from strong, aggressive states but from the weakness and lack of cohesion of the state, understood as a breeding-ground for chaos – in the form of humanitarian crisis or civil conflict, for example. This is the state as victim, as incapable of regulating itself and in need of what Vanessa Pupavac (2001) calls 'therapeutic governance'.

As discussed in Chapter 2, in the humanitarian and human rights interventions of the 1990s, the idea developed that the principle of non-interference in a state's internal affairs had to be abandoned or at least modified in cases of humanitarian crisis or human rights abuse. From the imposition of 'safe areas' and no-fly zones in Iraq in 1991, through to the establishment of international protectorates in Bosnia and Kosovo, the territorial integrity and right to self-government of weaker states has been repeatedly called into question. From time to time, the option of re-colonisation has been floated, as in the British media's early enthusiasm for a complete takeover of Somalia, or David Rieff's (1999: 10) call for a 'recolonization of part of the world' under a system of 'liberal imperialism'. Over time, however, as Chandler (2006: 31) observes, the emphasis has shifted away from a confrontational 'right to intervene' towards the less provocative idea of a 'responsibility to protect', as developed by the International Commission on Intervention and State Sovereignty (ICISS 2001). The idea is that states have responsibilities to the international community as well as to their own citizens, and that the international community has a duty to intervene if states will not or can not meet these responsibilities. Yet the redefinition of sovereignty as 'responsibility' effectively means the end of sovereignty. The non-Western state is no longer understood as sovereign – as accountable to no higher power than its own citizens – but as necessarily held to account from above by international actors.

It is not a question of Western states directly imposing their own sovereignty as in the days of colonialism, when dependent territories and possessions were the property of the imperial powers and subject to their sovereign rule. But neither is it simply a case of the formal equality of sovereignty being extended to non-Western states while power is exercised informally through economic relationships, as in Rosenberg's 'empire of civil society'. Instead, the West takes on a highly interventionist role in overseeing and regulating the behaviour of weaker states, presenting this simultaneously as confirmation of its own legitimacy in acting in the name of internationally-agreed norms of governance, and as a purely technical and administrative process. It recalls the dynamics of official multiculturalism discussed in Chapter 4, characterised by Žižek (2000: 216) in terms of an 'intricate police apparatus' which allocates each group its 'proper place within the social structure'. This stands equally well as a description of the processes of therapeutic governance, at once supposed to be evidence of 'values' – pre-eminently the value of tolerance – and a technical matter of regulation, decided on by 'various ethico-legal "committees"'. Chandler describes this as 'empire in denial': a form of imperial domination which disavows its own power.

As Chandler (2006: 57–61) observes, the view of the non-Western state as in need of therapy reflects contemporary understandings of war – as in Kaldor's concept of 'new wars' – not as a clash of interests, a pursuit of politics by other means, but as a pathological condition from which the non-Western state suffers, or as a criminal act which its leaders perpetrate. This view of other people's wars as essentially non-political, as a form of psycho-social breakdown and/or criminality, also casts the international community in the non-political role of therapist-cum-policeman. Hence there has been a transition in the post-Cold War era, from peacekeeping, in which the UN acted as referee – monitoring ceasefires, keeping warring sides apart – toward peace-building, in which the role of the international community is to regulate the internal conduct of states traumatised by war or other forms of breakdown. Just as the conflicts themselves are understood not as a political clash of interests but as pathological and/or criminal behaviour, so too the West's role is seen to be 'above' politics. Hence, although international intervention is often justified in highly-charged, moralistic terms as a battle of good and evil, it is simultaneously a de-politicised and technical process, not dissimilar from the requirements placed on candidate members of the EU to adopt the correct legal frameworks. The un-elected international administrators who rule in Bosnia and Kosovo, for example, see themselves as simply 'doing the right thing'. As the UN's High Representative in Bosnia, Lord Paddy Ashdown explained his approach to governing the country in terms of 'doing what I think is right', apparently assuming that his personal moral sense would coincide with the interests of the Bosnian people (Chandler 2006: 53). International rule is thereby cast as a matter, not of politics, but of ethics and norms which are embodied in the personal conscience of figures such as Ashdown. The sorts of patterns discussed at the national level in Chapter 5, whereby politicians justify decisions in terms of their personal conscience, and advisors such as Giddens recommend a therapeutic model of governance, are thereby repeated at the international level.

The rule of international administrators in Bosnia and Kosovo is as high-handed as that of any colonial governor (Knaus and Martin 2003).

Although Bosnia is a formally sovereign state, its government is entirely subordinate to the international community. After more than a decade of post-war 'independence', as Chandler (2006: 65) notes, 'not one piece of substantial legislation has been devised, written and enacted by Bosnian politicians and civil servants without external guidance'. It should be emphasised that the effect of this style of rule is entirely counter-productive, in that it leaves underlying conflicts unresolved and only succeeds in creating what Chandler describes as 'phantom states': entities which may meet externally-imposed standards of governance but which lack the domestic legitimacy that can only come from self-government. Whether understood as victim or victimiser, the non-Western state is assumed to be incapable of genuine self-government: its elections must be monitored, its legislation guided by international 'experts'. Such states are not really sovereign, and their governments are not held to account by their own populations through a process of political contestation, but are rather regulated by the 'international community'.

War for values

We should take seriously the claim that international intervention by Western states is 'other-directed'. This is not to say that it actually benefits those on the receiving end. Quite the reverse: the results are at least as destructive as traditional imperialism, if not more so. But it is to suggest that the dynamic driving post-Cold War intervention is about seeking legitimacy in what the West claims to do for others. In that sense, since the ultimate goal is to solve a problem at home, the other-directed ethics are actually self-directed. Yet the problem is not, as some radical critics have suggested, that the ethical claims are simply a sham, designed to hide selfish interests (Heuer and Schirmer 1998). Rather, it is an inability to formulate a clear sense of national interest or strategy that leads Western states to seek legitimacy in other-directed international intervention.

The other-directed actions that are undertaken in order to fill the emptiness at the heart of the Western state sometimes involve those others having to fight and die in order that 'our values' might live. Blair made this clear in a series of three major foreign policy speeches in 2006, in which he emphasised the key values of tolerance and democracy, and presented post-war Afghanistan and Iraq as struggling to realise them. Their struggle was understood as helping the West to overcome its own lack of confidence and cohesion. In the first speech he said it would be wrong to 'walk away from those engaged in a life or death battle for freedom':

> The fact of their courage … should give us courage; their determination should lend us strength; their embrace of democratic values, which do not belong to any race, religion or nation, but are universal, should reinforce our own confidence in those values.[5]

Similarly, in the second speech he interpreted ongoing conflict in Afghanistan and Iraq as 'a battle utterly decisive in whether the values we believe in triumph or fail', and pointed to elections there as a 'symbol of hope, and of belief in the values we too hold dear'.[6] In the third speech, the Iraqis' struggle in their own bitterly divided country became a means to mend divisions in Britain and the wider international community. 'The war split the world', he noted, but: 'The struggle of Iraqis for democracy should unite it'. Their struggle, 'so critical to our own values', was also going to give 'renewed vigour and confidence' to the West.[7] The clear intention was to bolster confidence in 'our values' by discovering people fighting for them somewhere else.

In the same series of speeches, Blair also re-presented the weakness of 'our values' as an external threat. He identified the enemy as 'the ideology represented by Saddam and Mullah Omar', no doubt fully aware that the secular Baathist and the ultra-religious Taliban leader had almost nothing in common ideologically. They were yoked together, however, as examples of 'extremists' who were hostile to the values which, though 'universal', also made London 'special':

> the same ideology killed people on the streets of London, and for the same reason. To stop cultures, faiths and races living in harmony; to deter those who see greater openness to others as a mark of humanity's progress; to disrupt the very thing that makes London special [and the thing that] would in time, if allowed to, set Iraq on a course of progress too.[8]

The terms of Blair's presentation of the War on Terrorism recall Kaldor's (1999: 58) notion that nationalists in the former Yugoslavia were waging war against 'a secular multicultural pluralistic society' and were dedicated to 'eliminating an internationalist humanitarian outlook ... globally'. The values to be celebrated at home – 'diversity' and 'tolerance of difference' – are understood as threatened by extremists who 'disagree with our way of life, our values and in particular in our tolerance'.[9] In this way 'democratic values', equated with tolerance, can be furthered by invading other countries to defeat extremists who hate tolerance. War and intervention are ways to prove our commitment to 'our values'.

At the same time, understanding war and terrorism as an attack on 'our values' could be seen, as Baudrillard (1994) suggests, as the West 'longing for an impossible violence against itself'. From the cosmopolitans who wished that Western troops could be killed in Kosovo, through the neoconservatives at the Project for the New American Century fantasising about a 'new Pearl Harbour', to Blair's idea of Afghans and Iraqis dying in order to 'reinforce our own confidence', the tendency is to externalise the West's problems. The doubts and divisions at home are played out abroad, so that the internal weakness of 'our values' is instead understood as an external threat which can be confronted.

In contrast to the claim that contemporary terrorism is an attempt by an external force to wipe out the West's values, Baudrillard (2002: 7) argues that: 'The West ... has become suicidal, and declared war on itself'. Somewhat similarly, Zehfuss (2007) interrogates the way that in the War on Terror 'our profound vulnerability comes to be represented as inflicted by others', arguing that 'this "we" only comes about through the violent gesture of ... acting as a "we"'. That is to say, the 'violent gestures' against others are actually about constructing the Western self. This argument is persuasive in so far as it identifies the War on Terror as an external projection of the West's inner problems. However, this is not evidence of the impossibility of the subject, as the postmodernists would have it, but is rather a consequence of the death of politics.

Postmodern terror: the West at war with itself

As Jason Burke observes, in the initial reactions to 9/11 al-Qaeda was mis-leadingly characterised as an immensely powerful global 'super-organisation'. Western officials and journalists suggested, for example, that its base in the Tora Bora caves in Afghanistan was some sort of high-tech complex kitted-out like the lair of a Bond movie master-villain, 'replete with subterranean computer rooms, secret passageways, laboratories and such-like', whereas the prosaic reality was a 'paltry, rubble and excrement-filled' mess (Burke 2006: 7). To the extent that the al-Qaeda of the West's imagination existed as a coher-ent organisation, it was defeated in Afghanistan. Yet it is better understood, Burke suggests, as an idea – and in that respect al-Qaeda has proved much harder to defeat (see further Burke 2004). Even as an idea, Islamist terror-ism has tended to be seen as an entirely external problem – an ideology which might attract some domestic sympathisers who are then radicalised and indoctri-nated, most likely abroad, but definitely a foreign phenomenon. It has become increasingly apparent, however, that the 'idea' of al-Qaeda feeds off trends in Western societies as much as it does off radical interpretations of Islam in the Middle East.

This is particularly clear in the case of the British-born suicide bombers who carried out the 7/7 attacks on the London transport system in 2005. As Munira Mirza et al. (2007: 5) point out in their investigation of attitudes among British Muslims, 'the growth of Islamism in the UK is not solely a foreign problem, but something that must be understood in relation to polit-ical and social trends that have emerged in *British* society over the past two decades'. They suggest that the 'weakening of older, collective forms of iden-tity, such as nationalism, political parties, or trades unions' in the recent past has led to a more general disengagement and alienation in Western societies, of which home-grown radical Islamism is only the most extreme manifes-tation (2007: 17). Hence, as they observe, the antipathy to Western values voiced by radical Islamists is 'not exclusive to Muslims and can also be found in wider society':

> although Islamism appears otherworldly to our modern sensibilities, we should consider the way in which its animosity towards the West chimes with certain ideological trends that have long been fashionable amongst the Western intelligentsia. For instance, prominent members of the anti-globalization movement attack the 'greedy' consumerism and materialism of capitalist society; culturally relativist social theory bemoans the dominance of 'euro-centric' scientific and cultural knowledge; environmentalist groups celebrate the spiritual richness of pre-industrial, rural life; and certain strands of radical feminism condemn the sexualisation of women in the West, leading to the bizarre claim by one Muslim feminist that: 'just about everything that Western feminists fought for in the 1970s was available to Muslim women 1,400 years ago'.
>
> (Mirza *et al.* 2007: 16)

The Islamists' condemnation of Western decadence is not so much a foreign ideology confronting the West from without, as Blair maintains, but rather a violent manifestation of the West's own self-loathing.

The decline of traditional forms of collective identification and social engagement mentioned by Mirza *et al.* has been compounded by the growth of identity politics, initially promoted, as we saw in Chapter 4, by the Left in response to its own weakness but now enshrined in the official policies of multiculturalism and diversity. Ironically, it was the multiculturalist approach to 'community relations' that, in Kenan Malik's (2006) words, 'helped create a space for the growth of Islamic militancy' by relating to people on the basis of their differences and identities. A complementary relationship developed between the Left's promotion of difference as an alternative to the universal subject, and the official use of multiculturalism as a response to the urban unrest of the 1980s, promoting religious and cultural leaders. Multiculturalism did not create radical Islamism but, as Malik argues, it 'fostered a more tribal nation, created a grievance culture, strengthened the hand of conservative religious leaders, undermined progressive trends within the Muslim communities and created a vacuum into which radical Islam stepped'. The contemporay understanding of grievances among British Muslims, centred around the idea of 'Islamophobia', simply repeats the pattern, continuing to promote the sense of separation, difference and victimhood that Malik identifies.

Of course, it might be objected that attacks by home-grown British terrorists are one thing but that 9/11 or al-Qaeda's involvement in the ongoing terror in Iraq are a different matter. Yet the underlying dynamic of al-Qaeda's development as a self-consciously 'global' phenomenon is not dissimilar from that which has led a small number of British Muslims to become suicide bombers. As Marc Sageman's (2004: 74–5) study of al-Qaeda members shows, they are not drawn from the ranks of the marginal and dispossessed. Around three-quarters of members in his sample were upper or middle class. About the same proportion had a secular education, and over 60 per cent had some college education. Al-Qaeda members are, as he remarks, 'truly global citizens', familiar with the West, fluent in several languages, better educated than average and trained as professional or semi-skilled workers (2004: 76–8). These 'global citizens' are not engaged in a purposeful political struggle with practical aims and concrete objectives: they practice a form of terrorism which has more the character of an individual, ethical gesture than a collective political act.

The global jihadis are not the representatives of national liberation struggles in the Third World, but are the product of the failure of such struggles. As Olivier Roy (1994: 51–2) argues, the rise of political Islamism in the 1980s resulted from the 'general loss of prestige of progressive ideologies and the failure of the "Arab socialist" model'. Just as the decline of left-wing politics in Western societies created space for the growing influence of radical Islamism as an expression of alienation, so too in the Middle East and North Africa, Roy (1994: 194) suggests, Islamism grew as a 'movement embodying the protest and frustration of a generation of youth that has not been integrated socially or politically'. If radical Islamism was premised on the decline of socialist and nationalist politics, al-Qaeda represents a further degeneration.

The imagined constituency in whose name al-Qaeda acts is the *ummah* – the worldwide community of Muslims, abstracted from local contexts. As Faisal Devji (2005: 16) notes, al-Qaeda shows scant regard for conventions of 'correct' Islamic practice or for 'inherited forms of Islamic authority'. It is in fact premised on cutting free from rooted local struggles, taking flight instead for the fantasy of a global jihad. The locations in which this jihad develops – Afghanistan, Bosnia, Chechnya, Iraq – are viewed as places in which to act out the fantasy, rather than territories in which tangible problems are to be addressed (Devji 2005: 27–8; Roy 2004: 68). Similarly, al-Qaeda's references, in statements by bin Laden and others, to real injustices such as the dispossession of the Palestinians, are used opportunistically for their symbolic value rather than actually being the focus of struggle (Devji 2005: 68–71). Indeed, as Brendan O'Neill observes, bin Laden's statements are more like a recycling of opinions from the Western media and the 'blogosphere' than a distinctive set of ideological or religious beliefs. Thus, bin Laden criticises the Bush administration for not allowing enough time for weapons inspections in Iraq, for rushing in to a war for oil, and for handing out contracts to corporations, such as Halliburton, with links to administration officials. After the 2004 Madrid train bombings, bin Laden echoed the Spanish protestors' complaint that their leaders had: 'compromised their security'. Like many a blogger, he repeats familiar radical complaints about 'big media' and even recommends the work of *The Independent* journalist Robert Fisk.[10] Similarly, Devji (2005: 6) notes that in his initial response to 9/11 bin Laden seemed to echo the sorts of conspiracy theories popularised in television shows such as *The X-Files* and films by Oliver Stone. Whether among British-born radical Muslims or the leaders of al-Qaeda, the outlook appears to be closer to the sort of disillusioned self-critique found in Western culture than a foreign ideology confronting the West from without.

A number of analysts have compared al-Qaeda terrorism with the 'propaganda of the deed' of anarchists and revolutionaries in Russia at the turn of the twentieth century (for example, Roy 2004: 57). The comparison makes sense in so far as spectacular acts of terror are understood by their perpetrators as inspiring the Muslim *ummah* to rise up. Yet even this judgement seems too generous: the *ummah* figures more as an imaginary, admiring audience than as a real constituency who are called to action. Since it has no positive proposal, only negation, contemporary terrorism may reasonably be described as nihilistic, as exemplified in al-Qaeda's typical modus operandi, the suicide or martyrdom operation (Gupta 2004). The suicide of the 'martyr' is not the unfortunate but necessary by-product of such operations, but their central goal. This cannot be understood solely in religious terms, as devaluing life in favour of the paradise beyond, however. As Roy (2004: 178) asks, why should it be that this sure-fire route to paradise has only recently been discovered? Although it entails a literal dissolution of the self, the al-Qaeda suicide operation paradoxically also indicates an inflated, narcissistic sense of self-importance. Roy comments, for example, on the will that the leading 9/11 hijacker, Muhammad Atta, apparently carried around for years prior to his death, which specified the details of his funeral in a way that showed 'a sort of exaggerated self-indulgence' (2004: 178–9, n51). Similarly, as Devji has remarked, the videotaped statements by British 7/7 bombers Shehzad Tanweer and Mohammad Sidique Khan are not only full of media-derived references to images of jihad, copying the dress, body language and sound-bites of bin Laden and other figures, but are also designed to secure their immortality, not in a religious sense, but via the media.[11]

Perhaps a more illuminating comparison than those drawn between al-Qaeda and previous forms of terrorism is the parallel that Devji (2005: 12–13) suggests between the jihadis and other contemporary global movements, such as the anti-globalisation, environmentalist or anti-war protests. These too bring together heterogeneous groups of people who have little in common in terms of either interests or even ideas, and are more about individuals making an 'ethical' statement. In this context, the political reference points invoked in al-Qaeda statements – Palestine, Afghanistan, Iraq – feature only as the pitiable victims who justify the other-directed ethical action of the 'martyr'. In devising their spectacular, made-for-TV acts of terrorism, complete with secondary texts in the form of websites, videos and audiotapes, today's jihadis are the mirror image of the violent gestures of 'other-directed' Western foreign policy, in which the importance of media spectacle is elevated in the absence of any more concrete strategic objectives.

Conclusion

For the moment at least, the West has no answer to the nihilistic terrorism of al-Qaeda. The by now often repeated slogan that 'we love death more than you love life' signals the ability of a handful of individuals to bring Western cities to a standstill or to tie down the world's most powerful military machines in Iraq. Any power they have derives solely from the incoherence and risk-aversion of the Western elite themselves. The suicide-terrorist's staging of his own death is similar to the West's use of violent gestures as a way to assert its 'values', and both involve narcissistic media performances. In both cases, the victimhood of others is held to justify the violent act; both sets of gestures are 'ethical' rather than political.

These symmetrical phenomena – of Other-regarding imperialism and nihilistic terrorism – are both products of the crisis of political agency that has followed the end of the Cold War, signalling the end of previously-established forms of political identification and action. Where the West has sought a new sense of purpose and mission in ethical foreign policy actions, these have entailed the deliberate abrogation of the post-1945 principles of sovereign equality and non-interference, creating a new global space of regulatory governance rather than self-government. This was never a confident and assertive imperialism but always an empire 'in denial', in Chandler's phrase, an imperialism which could not speak in its own name because it had no coherent view of its own strategic interests. In staging the spectacle of war for values, the West created a new form of ethical anti-politics that has found its echo in al-Qaeda. Cosmopolitan law-enforcement meets cosmopolitan terrorism: not so much a clash of interests as a violent working-out of the emptiness of postmodern politics.

Conclusion
Beyond postmodernity

This book has argued that postmodernist thought – or at least some of it – can offer an insight into the nature of politics today. As suggested in Chapter 6, however, the hostility to the subject which allows postmodernism its insight also limits its potential as a critique. The title of this concluding chapter might seem like a contradiction in terms, since for postmodernism there can be no 'beyond': we are stuck in the perpetual present. Yet unless we are content with the bleak pessimism of postmodernism, we had better try to think beyond it, since there is no going back.

The 'death of the subject' theorised by postmodernism has been treated here, following James Heartfield (2002), as a real historical event: the political defeat of the working class. The end of meaningful political contestation and engagement is what has given rise to the problems considered here, all of which are, at root, products of a crisis of political agency; of an inability to imagine history being made by humanity. As Zaki Laïdi (1998) argues, this has left us in a 'world without meaning' in which, in the absence of any vision of the future, international affairs are dominated by reactive crisis-management and risk-avoidance.

This is the world as the postmodernists said it was – a world where political subjectivity has become 'impossible' and grand narratives have lost their meaning as a guide to future action. For this reason alone, postmodernism offers a greater insight than approaches which view the present as simply a continuation of the past, or those which endorse attempts to recapture a sense of purpose and meaning through war and intervention. Doubting the 'reality' of war points up the fact that it is staged as a media spectacle, in a way that more conventional accounts of propaganda tend to miss. Where radical critics assume we are still living in the old world of straightforward power and interest, commentators such as Baudrillard grasp that international action is not the pursuit of definite interests but the pursuit of 'the absence of politics by other means'. Attuned to the discursive construction of subjectivity and sovereignty, the postmodernists see more clearly than most how humanitarian intervention and the War on Terror have been a narcissistic search for meaning and purpose.

As far as the 'death of the subject' goes, the theory preceded the event, of course, and was in fact a contributory factor in bringing it about. Pitching their own disillusionment with the universal subject as a hostility to universalism and humanism as such, the latter were understood as the oppressive ideological impositions of discourse and power. Yet all along, the problem was not that such ideas were too strong but that they were too weak. Today, claims are still made about universal values and humanism. The problem with such claims is not that they show the undue strength of these ideas in contemporary society, but that they are invoked in a degraded and debased form, used in such a way that they imply their opposite.

Today we are told that Western societies are in the process of 'humanising modernity' and waging 'humane wars'; that human rights have been elevated into the operating principle of state policy, valuing the individual as never before. In reality, the reverse is true. The humanitarian militarism of the 1990s tended to produce a pornography of 'Evil' than rather than to elaborate any more positive vision. As Michael Ignatieff (1998: 18) puts it:

> In the twentieth century, the idea of human universality rests less on hope than on fear, less on optimism about the human capacity for good than on dread of human capacity for evil, less on a vision of man as maker of his history than of man the wolf toward his own kind.

The journalists and intellectuals who advocated 'ethical' military intervention in the wars and crises of the 1990s did so on the basis of a sometimes exaggerated fear of this 'human capacity for evil'. Their tendency to emphasise what one writer on Bosnia calls 'the dark and ugly side of human nature' (Ahmed 1995: 22) chimed with official efforts to work up a grand set of 'values' out of their interventions in other people's local wars.

These efforts invariably meant invoking the barbarism of the Holocaust – Saddam was Hitler, the Serbs were the new Nazis, al-Qaeda were 'Islamo-fascists'. The inflation served a conventional propagandistic purpose, of course, but as we have seen it also helped to bolster the sense that by combating these supposedly titanic figures of evil the West must be engaged in a meaningful and important mission. The claim to be fighting wars for some humanist purpose, in other words, was made by pointing to how terrible humanity could be. Leaders have returned to the theme repeatedly, and have built the moral lesson of the Holocaust into the fabric of Anglo-American culture, from President Clinton's dedication of the Holocaust museum in Washington in 1993 to the Blair government's inauguration of an annual Holocaust Memorial Day in Britain since 2001. An opinion poll commissioned by the Holocaust Memorial Day Trust just before the 2007 commemoration indicated the lesson being taught: 41 per cent of those polled thought 'a Holocaust could happen in Britain', and 36 per cent thought that 'most people would stand by and do nothing in the event of genocide' in the UK. 'We need to be constantly on our guard', said the Trust's chairperson:

> With increasing levels of hate-crime, prejudice and ignorance towards those that are in some way different to ourselves, we really need to be vigilant in tackling prejudice and intolerance. As genocides in Europe, Rwanda and Bosnia have shown, it doesn't take much to turn these negative conditions into something far more calamitous.[1]

This constant 'need for vigilance' to police intolerance is the lesson continually drawn from the Holocaust and more recent events which are interpreted as analogous to it. We are seen by our leaders – and, if the poll evidence is anything to go by, to some degree see each other – as a Holocaust waiting to happen. This is the anti-human moral lesson drawn time and again, not just in relation to the past but also in the present: the West's 'wars for humanity' presume a degraded view of the human condition in which people exist only as victims or victimisers.

The values which are claimed to be the basis of a universalist outlook on the part of Western governments today – pre-eminently democracy and human rights – on closer inspection reveal an anti-universalist perspective. Democracy is now understood as something the West does to weaker countries, often by force. Even when it does not entail military invasion, 'democratisation' means integration into international networks of normative regulation, rather than genuine self-determination. Similarly, support for human rights does not presume an autonomous, self-governing subject who is the bearer of those rights. Rather, it entails external enforcement in support of victims who cannot exercise those 'rights' on their own behalf (see further Chandler 2002). This is a recipe for perpetual interference in the affairs of weaker states and implies an elitist, rather than a universalist outlook.

As we saw with Toulmin's (1990) account of 'humanising modernity', what is presented today as 'humanism' in fact means adopting an attitude of humility about human frailty and fallibility. Self-limitation, as the risk society theorists tell us, is the 'goal' that emerges; we are united in our common humanity, but only insofar as this is understood in terms of shared vulnerability and fear. None of these trends indicate the strength of Enlightenment ideas of humanism and universalism, as the postmodernists seem to believe.

For all that it is attuned to contemporary sensibilities, politically it is as if postmodernism has got stuck in a time warp somewhere in the early 1980s, still trying to kill off the subject. In one sense, this is perverse: it is the attenuation of political agency that, as we have seen, gives rise to a host of contemporary problems. On the other hand, it is worth considering why the critique of the subject carries on. The 'death of the subject' has appeared in scare quotes throughout this book because the subject as such is not really dead. The phrase is perhaps best translated as the 'death of politics' – or at least the death of the politics of the past. But actual human subjects are still very much alive, even if today we live in a society that encourages us to be afraid of our power and potential.

Notes

Introduction: postmodernism and 9/11

1 Edward Rothstein, 'Attacks on US Challenge the Perspectives of Postmodern True Believers', *New York Times*, 22 September 2001, http://www.criminology.fsu. edu/transcrime/articles/Attacks%20on%20U_S_%20Challenge%20Postmodern %20True%20Believers.htm.

2 Roger Rosenblatt, 'The Age of Irony Comes to an End', *Time*, 24 September 2001, http://www.time.com/time/covers/1101010924/esroger.html.

3 Andrew E. Busch, 'September 11 and the Return to Reality', Editorial, John M. Ashbrook Center for Public Affairs, Ashland University, October 2001 (http://www.ashbrook.org/publicat/oped/busch/01/reality.html); Kenneth Westhues, 'Postmodernism, Political Correctness, and the Attacks of September 11', Panel presentation at the Tenth Anniversary Meeting of the Society for Academic Freedom and Scholarship, University of Western Ontario, 4 May 2002 (http:// arts.uwaterloo.ca/~kwesthue/postmodernism.htm).

4 John Leo, 'Campus hand-wringing is not a pretty sight', *uexpress.com*, 30 September 2001, http://www.uexpress.com/johnleo/?uc_full_date=20010930.

5 Charles R. Kesler, 'Our Fighting Faith: Why We Roll', *National Review*, 10 September 2002, http://www.nationalreview.com/script/printpage.asp?ref=/ comment/comment-kesler091002.asp.

6 For details of The Coup's *Party Music* and other controversial album covers see http://www.tabootunes.com/gallery.html. On the censorship of films and television programmes see David Lister, 'How do you entertain when fantasy becomes horrible reality?', *The Independent*, 12 November 2001.

7 Apparently with some success – see, for example: Mark Goldblatt, 'French Toast', *National Review Online*, 13 December 2001, http://www.nationalreview. com/comment/comment-goldblatt121301.shtml.

8 Stanley Fish, 'Postmodern warfare: the ignorance of our warrior intellectuals', *Harper's Magazine*, July 2002, http://web.pdx.edu/~tothm/religion/ postmodern%20warfare.htm.

9 Douglas Kellner, 'The Politics and Costs of Postmodern War in the Age of Bush II', undated but c. February 2002 (http://www.gseis.ucla.edu/ faculty/kellner/papers/POMOwar.htm); Victor Davis Hanson, 'Postmodern War', *National Review Online*, 7 March 2003 (http://www.nationalreview.com/hanson/ hanson030703.asp); Anis Shivani, 'America's hyperreal war on terrorism', *Dawn*, 5 November 2001 (http://www.dawn.com/2001/11/05/op.htm).

10 This is why, as Krishan Kumar's (1995: 116–18) account suggests, when critics seek to characterise postmodernity in terms of 'objective' economic changes,

as opposed to subjective perceptions of the world – as in Fredric Jameson's idea of 'late capitalism', Scott Lash's concept of 'disorganised capitalism' or David Harvey's notion of 'flexible accumulation' – the line between the two becomes blurred as these 'objective' changes are understood in terms of subjectivity and the centrality of culture.

11 Available at http://www.wesjones.com/eoh_response.htm.

12 Stanley Fish, 'Condemnation Without Absolutes', New York Times, 15 October 2001, http://humanities.psydeshow.org/political/fish-column.htm.

1 Postmodern war in a world without meaning

1 In explaining his use of the term 'postmodern state', Cooper (2004: 188, n6) cites Toulmin and Coker. Coker (2001: 15) in turn describes Toulmin's Cosmopolis as 'seminal'.

2 Toulmin's discussion of Renaissance attitudes to truth and knowledge bears some similarity to Alan Sokal's (1996) hoax article calling for a postmodern science.

2 The humanitarian spectacle

1 Ronald Reagan, 'Better tomorrows as a noble vision approaches fruition', The Sunday Times, 6 December 1992.

2 George H. W. Bush, 'Address to the Nation on the Situation in Somalia', 4 December 1992, http://bushlibrary.tamu.edu/research/papers/1992/92120400.html.

3 Similarly, Greg Philo et al. (1999: 224–5) note that US air drops of aid to the massive refugee camps which developed on Rwanda's borders in the wake of the mass killings of 1994 were 'a classic example of a publicity stunt which contributed nothing to resolving a crisis'. With aid coming in by road, the air drop was not necessary and much of the 'aid' was in any case useless: the parcels contained 'dirty clothes, gruyere cheese (labelled "perishable needs refrigeration"), ski-mittens, biscuits (labelled "do not drop"), chocolate and flour from Sainsbury's'. On the ground, meanwhile, NGOs were keen 'to help orphaned and abandoned children, [but] few were interested in digging latrines', an activity which would have been more useful in the midst of a cholera epidemic, but less photogenic.

4 Robinson also highlights the importance of 'policy uncertainty' as a key factor in determining the degree of media influence (2002: 30–2).

5 Keeble mentions Germany and Japan as the main rivals. He also adds two further reasons for the Gulf War: that it served as a warning to other potentially hostile Middle Eastern states; and that it showcased British and American arms technology (1997: 11–12).

6 As Susan Woodward (1995: 325) suggests, the money could have been spent much more effectively if the objective was humanitarian relief: 'European governments spent fabulous sums on the spectacular evacuations of children for medial care in their capitals when the medical skills were available locally and the repair of damaged equipment would be far less costly'.

7 Gearóid Ó Tuathail (1999) coins the term 'videocameralists' to capture a similar idea, describing journalists as 'information age agitators for "something to be done" about the collapse of governance and the transparent violation of human rights in Bosnia'.

8 Omaar, herself a Somali, was later sacked from Africa Watch for publicly criticising Operation Restore Hope. Yet the logic of her own argument was for extensive international involvement in her country, and she continued to stress that she was 'not opposed to the use of force as such' (The Times, 5 December 1992).

9 This was not the first instance of intense competition between NGOs, but other writers also highlight the intervention in Somalia as particularly marked by such rivalry (de Waal 1997, Maren 1997).

10 Those in the media sometimes also view themselves in these terms, imagining that their own opinions represent those of the majority. One veteran BBC journalist told me that during the 1991 Gulf War a senior BBC manager described himself as a 'barometer of public opinion' in justifying to staff his decision to delay transmission of a programme about British weapons exports to Iraq.

11 See, for example: 'Clinton: Serbs must be stopped now', CNN, 23 March 1999 (http://www.cnn.com/US/9903/23/u.s.kosovo.04/); 'Transcript: Clinton justifies US involvement in Kosovo', CNN, 13 May 1999 (http://www.cnn.com/ALLPOLITICS/stories/1999/05/13/clinton.kosovo/transcript.html); 'Transcript: Clinton speaks at Memorial Day Event', CNN, 31 May 1999 (http://www.cnn.com/ALLPOLITICS/stories/1999/05/31/clinton.transcript/transcript.html).

3 The media war on terrorism

1 Baudrillard's (2006: 87) response to the pictures of torture and abuse from Iraq is much closer to the mark: 'those who live by the spectacle will die by the spectacle'.

2 The allegedly manipulated image is available at http://www.thememoryhole.org/media/evening-standard-crowd.htm.

3 The pictures, and the newspaper's note about the incident, are reproduced at http://www.sree.net/teaching/lateditors.html.

4 'A Tale of Two Photos', *Information Clearing House*, 15 April 2003, http://www.informationclearinghouse.info/article2838.htm.

5 'CNN statement about false claim it used old video', *CNN Online*, 20 September 2001, http://www.cnn.com/2001/US/09/20/cnn.statement/.

6 Rafat Ali, 'In Frantic Hunt for News, Readers Peruse Foreign Papers', *Globalvision News Network*, 11 October 2001, http://www.gvnews.net/html/Corp/press4.html.

7 'Dyke Slates "gung ho" war reports', *BBC Online*, 24 April 2003, http://news.bbc.co.uk/1/hi/entertainment/tv_and_radio/2973163.stm.

8 *Al-Jazeera Exclusive*, BBC2, 1 June 2003.

9 See http://www.welovetheiraqiinformationminister.com for a collection of his statements. The al-Sahaf action figure is available from http://herobuilders.com.

10 *The Washington Post* reported that of the 253 US troops killed by enemy fire in Iraq by the beginning of November 2003, 139 had died since 1 May (http://www.washingtonpost.com/wp-dyn/articles/A54882-2003Nov2.html). November 2003 then turned out to be the worst month so far, with a further 79 American deaths (Channel Four News, 1 December 2003).

11 'Vindication: A Statue Falls', *MediaLens*, 11 April 2003, http://www.medialens.org/alerts/2003/030411_Vindication.html.

12 Joanna Glasner, 'Military Cameramen Head to Gulf', *Wired News*, 13 March 2003, http://www.wired.com/news/business/0,1367,58021,00.html.

13 *Correspondent*, BBC2, 18 May 2003, http://news.bbc.co.uk/nol/shared/spl/hi/programmes/correspondent/transcripts/18.5.03.txt.

14 'The Battle for Ideas in the US War on Terrorism', American Enterprise Institute, 29 October 2001, http://www.aei.org/events/filter.,eventID.364/transcript.asp. Ledeen wrote up his speech as 'We'll Win This War', *The American Enterprise*, December 2001, http://www.taemag.com/issues/articleID.15447/article_detail.asp.

15 'Deputy Secretary Wolfowitz interview with Sam Tannenhaus', *Vanity Fair*, 9 May 2003, http://www.defenselink.mil/transcripts/2003/tr20030509-depsecdef0223.html.

16 Full Text of Tony Blair's Speech, *Guardian Unlimited*, 5 March 2004, http://politics.guardian.co.uk/speeches/story/0,11126,1162992,00.html.
17 The speech is available at http://politics.guardian.co.uk/labourconference2001/story/0,1220,561985,00.html.
18 'Blair fears terror "nightmare"', *BBC Online*, 28 February 2003, http://news.bbc.co.uk/1/low/uk_politics/2808689.stm.
19 'Afghanistan hailed "a triumph for human rights in 2001"', US Department of State, 5 March 2002, http://usinfo.state.gov/cgi-bin/washfile/display.pl?p=/products/washfile/topic/rights&f=02030406.ndh&t=/products/washfile/newsitem.shtml.
20 *Correspondent*, BBC2, 18 May 2003, http://news.bbc.co.uk/nol/shared/spl/hi/programmes/correspondent/transcripts/18.5.03.txt.
21 Media reactions were similar. The *Sun* urged its readers to 'smile at a Muslim' (editorial, 24 September 2001), while the BBC issued guidelines instructing journalists that they 'must avoid giving any impression that this is a war against Islam' (BBC, *War in Afghanistan: Editorial Policy Guidelines*, 25 September 2001).
22 'Berlusconi hails "great" Islam', *BBC Online*, 2 October 2001, http://news.bbc.co.uk/1/hi/world/europe/1575619.stm.
23 Frank Furedi, Epidemic of fear, *spiked*, 15 March 2002 (http://www.spiked-online.com/Articles/00000002D46C.htm); 'Hollywood on terror', Australian Broadcasting Corporation, 21 October 2001 (http://www.abc.net.au/correspondents/s397008.htm). For details of the ICT see Der Derian 2001: Chapter 7.
24 Brendan O'Neill, 'Gulf War meets Culture War', *spiked*, 27 February 2003, http://www.spiked-online.com/Articles/00000006DC92.htm. As Faisal Devji (2005: 25–6) notes, this sensitisation to cultural difference was put to use in devising deliberately culturally-degrading forms of treatment for Iraqi prisoners in Abu Ghraib prison.
25 See Schivelbusch 2003: 229–30. He also notes that the Nazis admired and emulated Anglo-American propaganda techniques, and were seen by others as 'American' in their methods of mass manipulation (227, 284–6).

4 Culture wars and the post-Vietnam condition

1 Patrick J. Buchanan, '1992 Republican National Convention Speech', Houston, 17 August 1992, http://www.buchanan.org/pa-92-0817-rnc.html. See also 'The Cultural War for the Soul of America', Buchanan's 14 September 1992 response to the debate over his speech, http://www.buchanan.org/pa-92-0914.html.
2 Somewhat similarly, in his survey of 'postmodern politics' Hans Bertens (1995: 192) argues that: 'the politics of difference always turn out to be a new version of what might somewhat paradoxically be called the politics of (western) uniformity'.
3 Žižek (2000: 393, n45) says the change is usually understood as a shift from redistribution to recognition. Yet demands for recognition may well involve a demand that resources be allocated to a particular minority and, as he observes, the redistributionist politics of the reformist Left posited the state as the universal in much the same way as demands for identity-recognition.
4 Theoretically this probably results from Žižek's Lacanianism, which in its deconstruction of the subject is not really compatible with the Marxist outlook with which Žižek seeks to combine it.
5 Jack Straw, 'The Future For Democracy – Politics in a Spectator Society', LSE and Fabian Society Public Lecture, 28 June 2006.

5 Security and vulnerability in the 'risk society'

1 Giddens – Lord Giddens since 2004 – has been an advisor to Tony Blair and is credited with providing the intellectual underpinnings of New Labour's 'Third Way' politics. It is difficult to assess the extent to which Giddens or Beck have had a direct influence on official policy, but at the least they have theorised developments which were happening spontaneously, lending a vocabulary and theoretical framework to the discussion.

2 Mulgan was speaking at the 'Panic Attack: Interrogating our obsession with risk' conference, The Royal Institution, London, 9 May 2003.

3 See, for example, Ulrich Beck, 'Living in a World Risk Society', Hobhouse Memorial Public Lecture, London School of Economics, 15 February 2006, http://www.lse.ac.uk/collections/sociology/pdf/Beck-LivingintheWorldRiskSociety-Feb2006.pdf.

4 Giddens's 'critical theory without guarantees' is identical to Stuart Hall's (1983) 'Marxism without guarantees' in this respect.

5 Ulrich Beck, 'Living in a World Risk Society', Hobhouse Memorial Public Lecture, London School of Economics, 15 February 2006, http://www.lse.ac.uk/collections/sociology/pdf/Beck-LivingintheWorldRiskSociety-Feb2006.pdf.

6 Hence, for example, not just particular 'risky' behaviours but whole categories of people may be condemned, designated as being 'at risk' just by virtue of who they are – a label which, as Lupton (1999: 113) remarks, 'often serves to reinforce the marginalised and powerless status of individuals'.

7 In July 2005 British police shot dead a Brazilian electrician, Jean Charles de Menezes, who they thought was a suicide bomber, and in June 2006 they arrested two brothers wrongly suspected of involvement in a bomb plot, shooting and wounding one of them in the process.

8 For an overview of media commentaries at the time which questioned the seriousness of the threat and/or used the alleged plot as an occasion to criticise US and UK political leaders, see the Center for Media and Democracy's 'Source Watch' site at: http://www.sourcewatch.org/index.php?title=Liquid_bomb_plot_August_2006. A leading doubter was Craig Murray, the former British ambassador to Uzbekistan, who wrote an article for *The Guardian* (18 August 2006) urging readers to 'Be very wary of politicians who seek to benefit from terror'.

9 *Smallpox 2002: Silent Weapon*, BBC 2, 5 February 2002 (http://www.bbc.co.uk/drama/smallpox2002/); *Panorama*: 'London under attack', BBC 1, 16 May 2004 (http://news.bbc.co.uk/1/hi/programmes/panorama/3686201.stm); *Dirty War*, BBC 1, 26 September 2004 (http://news.bbc.co.uk/1/hi/programmes/dirty_war/3654566.stm).

10 Ulrich Beck, 'Living in a World Risk Society', Hobhouse Memorial Public Lecture, London School of Economics, 15 February 2006, http://www.lse.ac.uk/collections/sociology/pdf/Beck-LivingintheWorldRiskSociety-Feb2006.pdf).

11 Jack Straw, 'The Future For Democracy – Politics in a Spectator Society', LSE and Fabian Society Public Lecture, 28 June 2006. Straw's exposition of the problems, and his proposed remedies seem heavily coloured by Giddensian sociology. He recommends, for example, re-establishing more local, face-to-face points of contact between politicians and the public: a suggestion that recalls Giddens's (1990: 80) idea of 'facework'.

12 Jack Straw, 'The Future For Democracy – Politics in a Spectator Society', LSE and Fabian Society Public Lecture, 28 June 2006.

13 Joe Kaplinsky, 'Precaution goes to war', *spiked*, 17 July 2002, http://www.spiked-online.com/Articles/00000006D986.htm. In reply to a reporter who asked 'is there any evidence to indicate that Iraq has attempted to or is willing to supply

terrorists with weapons of mass destruction?', Rumsfeld replied: 'as we know, there are known knowns; there are things we know we know. We also know there are known unknowns; that is to say we know there are some things we do not know. But there are also unknown unknowns – the ones we don't know we don't know'. (Department of Defense News Briefing, 12 February 2002, http://www.defenselink.mil/transcripts/2002/t02122002_t212sdv2.html.)

14 Tony Blair, 'Foreign Policy Speech III', Washington, DC, 26 May 2006, http://www.number10.gov.uk/output/Page9549.asp.

15 Ulrich Beck, 'Living in a World Risk Society', Hobhouse Memorial Public Lecture, London School of Economics, 15 February 2006, http://www.lse.ac.uk/collections/sociology/pdf/Beck-LivingintheWorldRiskSociety-Feb2006.pdf.

16 Tony Blair, 'Doctrine of the International Community', 23 April 1999, http://www.number10.gov.uk/news.asp?NewsId=363.

17 Mick Hume, 'The dangers of a risk-averse war', *spiked*, 26 March 2003, http://www.spiked-online.com/Articles/00000006DD03.htm.

6 Postmodern empire and the 'death of the subject'

1 See also Ruggie (1998: 173) who describes the EU as 'the first truly postmodern international political form'.

2 Wendt has also been criticised for his decision to stay within a state-centric framework. Other constructivists have instead emphasised the role of non-state actors: Finnemore and Sikkink (1998), for example, emphasise the importance of 'norm entrepreneurs' working through 'transnational advocacy networks'. For an excellent critique of those constructivist approaches which foreground the importance of 'global civil society' organisations see Chandler 2004.

3 The title of Wendt's 1999 book, *Social Theory of International Politics*, highlights this claim in contrast to Waltz's (1979) *Theory of International Politics*.

4 In Lacanian terms, this would be the 'return to the Real' that, in Žižek's (2002) argument, 9/11 failed to achieve.

5 Tony Blair, 'Foreign Policy Speech I' ('Clash about civilisations'), London, 21 March 2006, http://www.number10.gov.uk/output/Page9224.asp.

6 Tony Blair, 'Foreign Policy Speech II' ('Global alliance for global values'), Australian Parliament, 27 March 2006, http://www.number10.gov.uk/output/Page9245.asp.

7 Tony Blair, 'Foreign Policy Speech III', Washington, DC, 26 May 2006, http://www.number10.gov.uk/output/Page9549.asp.

8 Tony Blair, 'Foreign Policy Speech I' ('Clash about civilisations'), London, 21 March 2006, http://www.number10.gov.uk/output/Page9224.asp.

9 Tony Blair, 'Foreign Policy Speech III', Washington, DC, 26 May 2006, http://www.number10.gov.uk/output/Page9549.asp.

10 Brendan O'Neill, 'Bin Laden's script: ghost-written in the West', *spiked*, 13 December 2005, http://www.spiked-online.com/index.php?/site/article/512/.

11 See Devji's interviews with Brendan O'Neill in 'An Explosion of Pity', *spiked*, 21 July 2006, http://www.spiked-online.com/index.php?/site/article/1284/; and from the Institute of Contemporary Arts, 24 July 2006, at http://www.brendanoneill.net/DevjiICA.htm.

Conclusion: beyond postmodernity

1 '41% Believe a Holocaust Could Happen in Britain', Holocaust Memorial Day website, http://www.hmd.org.uk/press/2007_hmd_survey_results_2007/.

References

African Rights (1993) *Human Rights Abuses by the United Nations Forces*. London: African Rights.

Ahmed, Akbar S. (1995) '"Ethnic Cleansing": A Metaphor for our Time?', *Ethnic and Racial Studies*, Vol. 18, No. 1, January, pp. 1–25.

Altheide, David L. (2002) *Creating Fear: News and the Construction of Crisis*. Hawthorne, NY: Aldine de Gruyter.

Althusser, Louis (1984) *Essays on Ideology*. London: Verso.

Anderson, Perry (1980) *Arguments Within English Marxism*. London: New Left Books.

Anderson, Perry (1998) *The Origins of Postmodernity*. London: Verso.

Aron, Raymond (1968) *Democracy and Totalitarianism*. London: Weidenfeld and Nicholson.

Baudrillard, Jean (1988) *Selected Writings*. Stanford, CA: Stanford University Press.

Baudrillard, Jean (1994) 'No Reprieve for Sarajevo', *Libération*, 8 January, http://www.uta.edu/english/apt/collab/texts/reprieve.html.

Baudrillard, Jean (1995) *The Gulf War Did Not Take Place*. Bloomington, IN: Indiana University Press.

Baudrillard, Jean (1996) 'When the West Stands in for the Dead', in Thomas Cushman and Stjepan G. Meštrović (eds.) *This Time We Knew: Western Responses to Genocide in Bosnia*. New York, NY: New York University Press.

Baudrillard, Jean (2002) *The Spirit of Terrorism*. London: Verso.

Baudrillard, Jean (2006) 'War Porn', *Journal of Visual Culture*, Vol. 5, No. 1, pp. 86–8.

Beck, Ulrich (1992) *Risk Society: Towards a New Modernity*. London: Sage.

Beck, Ulrich (1998) 'Politics of Risk Society', in Jane Franklin (ed.) *The Politics of Risk Society*. Cambridge: Polity.

Beck, Ulrich (1999) *World Risk Society*. Cambridge: Polity.

Beck, Ulrich (2000a) *What is Globalisation?* Cambridge: Polity.

Beck, Ulrich (2000b) 'The cosmopolitan perspective: sociology of the second age of modernity', *British Journal of Sociology*, Vol. 51, No. 1, January/March, pp. 79–105.

Beck, Ulrich (2002) 'Terror and Solidarity', in Mark Leonard (ed.) *Re-Ordering the World: The Long-term Implications of 11 September*. London: The Foreign Policy Centre.

Beier, J. Marshall (2006) 'Outsmarting Technologies: Rhetoric, Revolutions in Military Affairs, and the Social Depth of Warfare', *International Politics*, No. 43, pp. 266–80.

Bell, Daniel (1976) *The Coming of Post-Industrial Society*. New York, NY: Basic Books.

Bell, Daniel (2000) *The End of Ideology*. Cambridge, MA: Harvard University Press.

Bell, Martin (1996) *In Harm's Way* (Revised Edition). Harmondsworth: Penguin.

Bell, Martin (1998) 'The Journalism of Attachment', in Matthew Kieran (ed.) *Media Ethics*. London: Routledge.

Ben-Ami, Daniel (2001) *Cowardly Capitalism: The Myth of the Global Financial Casino*. London: John Wiley.

Bertens, Hans (1995) *The Idea of the Postmodern*. London: Routledge.

Best, Steven and Douglas Kellner (2001) *The Postmodern Adventure*. London: Routledge.

Bibby, Michael (1999) 'The Post-Vietnam Condition', in Michael Bibby (ed.) *The Vietnam War and Postmodernity*. Amherst, MA: University of Massachusetts Press.

Bickerton, Christopher J., Philip Cunliffe and Alexander Gourevitch (2007a) 'Introduction: The Unholy Alliance against Sovereignty', in Christopher J. Bickerton, Philip Cunliffe and Alexander Gourevitch (eds.) *Politics without Sovereignty: A Critique of Contemporary International Relations*. Abingdon: University College London Press.

Bickerton, Christopher J., Philip Cunliffe and Alexander Gourevitch (2007b) 'Politics without Sovereignty?', in Christopher J. Bickerton, Philip Cunliffe and Alexander Gourevitch (eds.) *Politics without Sovereignty: A Critique of Contemporary International Relations*. Abingdon: University College London Press.

Blum, William (2000) *Rogue State: A Guide to the World's Only Superpower*. Monroe, ME: Common Courage Press.

Boltanski, Luc (1999) *Distant Suffering: Morality, Media and Politics*. Cambridge: Cambridge University Press.

Booth, Ken (1995) 'Dare not to Know: International Relations Theory versus the Future', in Ken Booth and Steve Smith (eds.) *International Relations Theory Today*. Cambridge: Polity.

Boutros-Ghali, Boutros (1992) *An Agenda for Peace* (UN document A/47/277-S/24111: Report of the Secretary-General pursuant to the statement adopted by the Summit Meeting of the Security Council on 31 January 1992), 17 June, http://www.un.org/Docs/SG/agpeace.html.

Brown, Sheila (2003) 'From the "Death of the Real" to the Reality of Death: How Did the Gulf War Take Place?', *Journal for Crime, Conflict and the Media*, Vol. 1, No. 1, http://www.jc2m.co.uk/Issue1/Brown.pdf.

Burke, Jason (2004) *Al-Qaeda: The True Story of Radical Islam* (Revised Edition). London: Penguin.

Burke, Jason (2006) 'Preface', in Martin Bright, *When Progressives Treat with Reactionaries: The British State's Flirtation with Radical Islam*. London: Policy Exchange.

Camilleri, Joseph A. and Jim Falk (1992) *The End of Sovereignty? The Politics of a Shrinking and Fragmenting World*. Aldershot: Edward Elgar.

Campbell, David (1992) *Writing Security: United States Foreign Policy and the Politics of Identity*. Minneapolis, MN: University of Minnesota Press.

Campbell, David (1998) *National Deconstruction: Violence, Identity, and Justice in Bosnia*. Minneapolis, MN: University of Minnesota Press.

Campbell, David (1999) 'Violence, Justice, and Identity in the Bosnian Conflict', in Jenny Edkins, Nalini Persram and Véronique Pin-Fat (eds.) *Sovereignty and Subjectivity*. Boulder, CO: Lynne Rienner.

Carruthers, Susan (2000) *The Media at War: Communication and Conflict in the Twentieth Century*. Basingstoke: Macmillan.

Carruthers, Susan (2001) 'New Media, New War', *International Affairs*, Vol. 77, No. 3, pp. 673–81.

Chandler, David (2003) 'Culture Wars and International Intervention: An "Inside/Out" View of the Decline of the National Interest', unpublished paper.

Chandler, David (2004) *Constructing Global Civil Society: Morality and Power in International Relations*. Basingstoke: Palgrave Macmillan.

Chandler, David (2006) *Empire in Denial: The Politics of State-building*. London: Pluto Press.

Chesterman, Simon (1998) 'Ordering the New World: Violence and its Re/Presentation in the Gulf War and Beyond', *Postmodern Culture*, Vol. 8, No. 3, May, http://www.iath.virginia.edu/pmc/text-only/issue.598/8.3chesterman.txt.

Chomsky, Noam (1992) 'The Media and the War: What War?', in Hamid Mowlana, George Gerbner and Herbert I. Schiller (eds.) *Triumph of the Image*. Boulder, CO: Westview Press.

Cica, Natasha (2001) *Truth, Myth or Genocide?* (research paper). London: Holocaust Educational Trust.

Clarke, Walter (1997) 'Failed Visions and Uncertain Mandates in Somalia', in Walter Clarke and Jeffrey Herbst (eds.) *Learning from Somalia: The Lessons of Armed Humanitarian Intervention*. Boulder, CO: Westview Press.

Coker, Christopher (2001) *Humane Warfare*. London: Routledge.

Combs, James (1993) 'From the Great War to the Gulf War: Popular Entertainment and the Legitimation of Warfare', in Robert E. Denton (ed.) *The Media and the Persian Gulf War*. Westport, CT: Praeger.

Cooper, Robert (2004) *The Breaking of Nations: Order and Chaos in the Twenty-first Century* (Revised Edition). London: Atlantic Books.

de Waal, Alex (1997) *Famine Crimes: Politics and the Disaster Relief Industry in Africa*. London: African Rights.

de Waal, Alex (1998) 'US War Crimes in Somalia', *New Left Review*, No. 230, pp. 131–44.

Dean, Mitchell (1999) *Governmentality: Power and Rule in Modern Society*. London: Sage.

Debord, Guy (1967) *The Society of the Spectacle*, http://www.bopsecrets.org/SI/debord/index.htm.

Deichmann, Thomas (2000) 'From "Never Again War" to "Never Again Auschwitz": Dilemmas Of German Media Policy In The War Against Yugoslavia', in Philip Hammond and Edward S. Herman (eds.) *Degraded Capability: The Media and the Kosovo Crisis*. London: Pluto Press.

Der Derian, James (1992) *Antidiplomacy: Spies, Terror, Speed and War*. Cambridge, MA and Oxford: Blackwell.

Der Derian, James (2001) *Virtuous War: Mapping the Military-Industrial-Media-Entertainment Network*. Boulder, CO: Westview Press.

Der Derian, James (2003) 'The Question of Information Technology in International Relations', *Millennium: Journal of International Studies*, Vol. 32, No. 3, pp. 441–56.

Derrida, Jacques (1982) *Margins of Philosophy*. Chicago: University of Chicago Press.

Derrida, Jacques (1987) *Positions*. London: Athlone Press.

Devetak, Richard (1995) 'The Project of Modernity and International Relations Theory', *Millennium: Journal of International Studies*, Vol. 24, No. 1, pp. 27–51.

Devji, Faisal (2005) *Landscapes of the Jihad: Militancy, Morality, Modernity*. London: Hurst.

Dorman, William A. and Steven Livingston (1994) 'News and Historical Content', in W. Lance Bennett and David L. Paletz (eds.) *Taken by Storm: The Media, Public Opinion, and US Foreign Policy in the Gulf War*. Chicago: University of Chicago Press.

Dowden, Richard (1995) 'Covering Somalia – Recipe for Disaster', in Edward Giradet (ed.) *Somalia, Rwanda and Beyond: The Role of the International Media in Wars and Humanitarian Crises*. Dublin: Crosslines Global Report.

Drysdale, John (2001) *Whatever Happened to Somalia?* (New Edition). London: Haan Publishing.

Duffield, Mark (1998) 'Post-modern Conflict: Warlords, Post-adjustment states and Private Protection', *Journal of Civil Wars*, Vol. 1, No.1, Spring, pp. 65–102.

Edkins, Jenny and Véronique Pin-Fat (1999) 'The Subject of the Political', in Jenny Edkins, Nalini Persram and Véronique Pin-Fat (eds.) *Sovereignty and Subjectivity*. Boulder, CO: Lynne Rienner.

Elbe, Stefan (2003) 'Eurosomnia: Europe's "spiritual vitality" and the debate on the European idea', in Peter Mandaville and Andrew Williams (eds.) *Meaning and International Relations*. London: Routledge.

Elden, Stuart (2007) 'Blair, Neo-Conservatism and the War on Territorial Integrity', *International Politics*, No. 44 [accessed electronically].

Finnemore, Martha and Kathryn Sikkink (1998) 'International Norm Dynamics and Political Change', *International Organization*, Vol. 52, No. 4, Autumn, pp. 887–917.

Foucault, Michel (1991) *Discipline and Punish*. London: Penguin.

Franklin, Bob (2003) '"A Good Day to Bury Bad News?": Journalists, Sources and the Packaging of Politics', in Simon Cottle (ed.) *News, Public Relations and Power*. London: Sage.

Franklin, Jane (1998) 'Introduction', in Jane Franklin (ed.) *The Politics of Risk Society*. Cambridge: Polity.

Fukuyama, Francis (1989) 'The End of History?', *The National Interest*, Summer, http://www.wesjones.com/eoh.htm.

Furedi, Frank (1992) *Mythical Past, Elusive Future: History and Society in an Anxious Age*. London: Pluto Press.

Gearson, John (2002) 'The Nature of Modern Terrorism', in Lawrence Freedman (ed.) *Superterrorism: Policy Responses* (special issue of *The Political Quarterly*). Oxford: Blackwell.

Giddens, Anthony (1990) *The Consequences of Modernity*. Cambridge: Polity.

Giddens, Anthony (1994) *Beyond Left and Right: The Future of Radical Politics*. Cambridge: Polity.

Giddens, Anthony (2002) *Runaway World: How Globalisation is Reshaping our Lives* (Second Edition). London: Profile Books.

Gitlin, Todd (1994) 'From Universality to Difference: Notes on the Fragmentation of the Idea of the Left', in Craig Calhoun (ed.) *Social Theory and the Politics of Identity*. Oxford: Blackwell.

Gitlin, Todd (2003) 'Goodbye, New World Order: Keep the Global Ideal Alive', *Mother Jones*, 14 July, http://www.motherjones.com/commentary/columns/2003/29/we_478_01.html.

Gorz, André (1982) *Farewell to the Working Class*. London: Pluto Press.

Gourevitch, Alexander (2007) 'National Insecurities: The New Politics of the American National Interest', in Christopher J. Bickerton, Philip Cunliffe and Alexander

Gourevitch (eds.) *Politics without Sovereignty: A Critique of Contemporary International Relations*. Abingdon: University College London Press.

Gow, James (1997) *Triumph of the Lack of Will*. London: Hurst.

Gowing, Nik (1994) *Real-Time Television Coverage of Armed Conflicts and Diplomatic Crises: Does it Pressure or Distort Foreign Policy Decisions?* (Working Paper 94–1). Cambridge, MA: Shorenstein Barone Center, Harvard University.

Gray, Chris Hables (1997) *Postmodern War: The New Politics of Conflict*. London: Routledge.

Gray, Chris Hables (1999) 'Postmodernism with a Vengeance: The Vietnam War', in Michael Bibby (ed.) *The Vietnam War and Postmodernity*. Amherst, MA: University of Massachusetts Press.

Gray, Chris Hables (2002) 'War, Peace, and Complex Systems', *Borderlands*, Vol. 1, No. 1, http://www.borderlandsejournal.adelaide.edu.au/vol1no1_2002/gray_complexity.html.

Gupta, Jay A. (2004) 'Freedom of the Void: Hegel and Nietzsche on the Politics of Nihilism: Toward a Critical Understanding of 9/11', *Telos*, No. 129, Winter, pp. 17–39.

Guth, James L. (2000) 'Clinton, Impeachment and the Culture Wars', in Steven E. Schier (ed.) *The Postmodern Presidency: Bill Clinton's Legacy in US Politics*. Pittsburgh, PA: University of Pittsburgh Press.

Gutmann, Stephanie (2001) *The Kinder, Gentler Military*. San Francisco, CA: Encounter Books.

Hall, Stuart (1983) 'The Problem of Ideology – Marxism without Guarantees', in Betty Matthews (ed.) *Marx 100 Years On*. London: Lawrence and Wishart.

Hall, Stuart (1988a) *The Hard Road to Renewal*. London: Verso/*Marxism Today*.

Hall, Stuart (1988b) 'Brave New World', *Marxism Today*, October.

Hall, Stuart (1989) 'The Meaning of New Times', in Stuart Hall and Martin Jacques (eds.) *New Times*. London: Lawrence and Wishart.

Hall, Stuart (1996) 'Introduction: Who Needs "Identity"?', in Stuart Hall and Paul Du Gay (eds.) *Questions of Cultural Identity*. London: Sage.

Hallin, Daniel C. (1986) *The 'Uncensored War': The Media and Vietnam*. Oxford: Oxford University Press.

Hammond, Philip (2002) 'Moral Combat: Advocacy Journalists and the New Humanitarianism', in David Chandler (ed.) *Rethinking Human Rights*. Basingstoke: Palgrave.

Hammond, Philip (2007) *Framing Post-Cold War Conflicts: The Media and International Intervention*. Manchester: Manchester University Press.

Hansen, Lene (1998) 'Western Villains or Balkan Barbarism?', Ph.D. dissertation, University of Copenhagen.

Hardt, Michael and Antonio Negri (2000) *Empire*. Harvard, MA: Harvard University Press.

Harvey, David (1989) *The Condition of Postmodernity*. Oxford: Blackwell.

Hassan, Robert (2004) *Media, Politics and the Network Society*. Maidenhead: Open University Press.

Heartfield, James (1998) *Need and Desire in the Post-Material Economy*. Sheffield: Sheffield Hallam University Press.

Heartfield, James (2002) *The 'Death of the Subject' Explained*. Sheffield: Sheffield Hallam University Press.

Heartfield, James (2007) 'European Union: A Process without a Subject', in Christopher J. Bickerton, Philip Cunliffe and Alexander Gourevitch (eds.) *Politics without Sovereignty: A Critique of Contemporary International Relations*. Abingdon: University College London Press.

Hegarty, Paul (2004) *Jean Baudrillard: Live Theory*. London: Continuum.

Heng, Yee-Kuang (2006) *War as Risk Management: Strategy and Conflict in an Age of Globalised Risks*. Abingdon: Routledge.

Heuer, Uwe-Jens and Gregor Schirmer (1998) 'Human Rights Imperialism', *Monthly Review*, March, http://www.monthlyreview.org/398heuer.htm.

Hobsbawm, Eric (1981) 'The Forward March of Labour Halted?', in Martin Jacques and Frances Mulhern (eds.) *The Forward March of Labour Halted?* London: Verso.

Hughes, Robert (1994) *Culture of Complaint* (revised edition). London: Harvill.

Hume, Mick (1997) *Whose War is it Anyway?* London: Informinc.

Hume, Mick (2000) 'Nazifying the Serbs, from Bosnia to Kosovo', in Philip Hammond and Edward S. Herman (eds.) *Degraded Capability: The Media and the Kosovo Crisis*. London: Pluto Press.

Hunter, James Davison (1991) *Culture Wars: The Struggle to Define America*. New York, NY: Basic Books.

Huntington, Samuel P. (1993) 'The Clash of Civilizations?', *Foreign Affairs*, Vol. 72, No. 3, Summer, pp. 22–48.

Ignatieff, Michael (1998) *The Warrior's Honor: Ethnic War and the Modern Conscience*. London: Chatto and Windus.

Ignatieff, Michael (2000) *Virtual War: Kosovo and Beyond*. New York, NY: Metropolitan Books.

Ignatieff, Michael (2001) *Human Rights as Politics and Idolatry*. Princeton, NJ: Princeton University Press.

Ignatieff, Michael (2003) *Empire Lite: Nation-Building in Bosnia, Kosovo and Afghanistan*. London: Vintage.

International Commission on Intervention and State Sovereignty (2001) *The Responsibility to Protect*. Ottawa: International Development Research Center.

Jensen, Richard (1998) 'The Culture Wars, 1965–1995: A Historian's Map', (originally published in the *Journal of Social History*, 1995) revised version, 30 August, http://members.aol.com/dann01/cwar.html.

Johnston, Harry and Ted Dagne (1997) 'Congress and the Somalia Crisis', in Walter Clarke and Jeffrey Herbst (eds.) *Learning from Somalia: The Lessons of Armed Humanitarian Intervention*. Boulder, CO: Westview Press.

Johnstone, Diana (2000) 'The French Media and the Kosovo War', in Philip Hammond and Edward S. Herman (eds.) *Degraded Capability: The Media and the Kosovo Crisis*. London: Pluto Press.

Johnstone, Diana (2002) *Fools' Crusade: Yugoslavia, NATO and Western Delusions*. London: Pluto Press.

Kagan, Robert (2004) *Paradise and Power: America and Europe in the New World Order* (Revised Edition). London: Atlantic Books.

Kaldor, Mary (1999) *New and Old Wars: Organised Violence in a Global Era*. Cambridge: Polity.

Kaldor, Mary (2000) 'Europe at the Millennium', *Politics*, Vol. 20, No. 2, May, pp. 55–62.

Kampfner, John (2003) *Blair's Wars*. London: Free Press.

Kampmark, Binoy (2003) 'Wars that Never Take Place: Non-events, 9/11 and Wars on Terrorism', *Australian Humanities Review*, Issue 29, May–June, http://www.lib.latrobe.edu.au/AHR/archive/Issue-May-2003/kampmark.html.

Kaplan, Robert D. (1994) 'The Coming Anarchy', *The Atlantic Monthly*, Vol. 273, No. 2, http://www.theatlantic.com/politics/foreign/anarcf.htm.

Keeble, Richard (1997) *Secret State, Silent Press: New Militarism, the Gulf and the Modern Image of Warfare*. Luton: John Libbey.

Keeble, Richard (2000) 'New Militarism and the Manufacture of Warfare', in Philip Hammond and Edward S. Herman (eds.) *Degraded Capability: The Media and the Kosovo Crisis*. London: Pluto Press.

Kellner, Douglas (1999) 'From Vietnam to the Gulf: Postmodern Wars?', in Michael Bibby (ed.) *The Vietnam War and Postmodernity*. Amherst, MA: University of Massachusetts Press.

Kellner, Douglas (2004) 'Media Culture and the Triumph of the Spectacle', http://www.gseis.ucla.edu/faculty/kellner/papers/medculturespectacle.html.

Kellner, Douglas (2005) *Media Spectacle and the Crisis of Democracy*. Boulder, CO: Paradigm Publishers.

Kenny, Michael (1995) *The First New Left: British Intellectuals After Stalin*. London: Lawrence and Wishart.

Keohane, Robert O. and Joseph S. Nye (1977) *Power and Interdependence*. Boston, MA: Little, Brown.

Knaus, Gerald and Felix Martin (2003) 'Lessons from Bosnia and Herzegovina: Travails of the European Raj', *Journal of Democracy*, Vol. 14, No. 3, pp. 60–74, http://www.journalofdemocracy.org/Articles/KnaussandMartin.pdf.

Knightley, Phillip (2000) *The First Casualty: The War Correspondent as Hero and Myth-Maker from the Crimea to Kosovo* (Revised Edition). London: Prion Books.

Knightley, Phillip (2003) 'History or bunkum?', *British Journalism Review*, Vol. 14, No. 2, http://www.bjr.org.uk/data/2003/no2_knightley.htm.

Kumar, Krishan (1995) *From Post-Industrial to Post-Modern Society*. Oxford: Blackwell.

Laclau, Ernesto and Chantalle Mouffe (1985) *Hegemony and Socialist Strategy*. London: Verso.

Laïdi, Zaki (1998) *A World Without Meaning*. London: Routledge.

Lasch, Christopher (1995) *The Revolt of the Elites and the Betrayal of Democracy*. New York, NY: W. W. Norton.

Lehman, John F. and Harvey Sicherman, eds. (2000) *America the Vulnerable*. Philadelphia, PA: Foreign Policy Research Institute.

Lewis, Ioan and James Mayall (1996) 'Somalia', in James Mayall (ed.) *The New Interventionism, 1991–1994*. Cambridge: Cambridge University Press.

Livingston, Steven (1996) 'Suffering in Silence: Media Coverage of War and Famine in the Sudan', in Robert I. Rotberg and Thomas G. Weiss (eds.) *From Massacres to Genocide: The Media, Public Policy and Humanitarian Crises*. Washington, DC: Brookings Institution.

Livingston, Steven (1997) *Clarifying the CNN Effect*. Cambridge, MA: Joan Shorenstein Center on the Press, Politics and Public Policy, Harvard University, http://sparky.harvard.edu/presspol/publications/pdfs/70916_R-18.pdf.

Livingston, Steven and Todd Eachus (1995) 'Humanitarian Crises and US Foreign Policy: Somalia and the CNN Effect Reconsidered', *Political Communication*, Vol. 12, pp. 413–29.

Lupton, Deborah (1999) *Risk*. London: Routledge.

Lyman, Rick (1995) 'Occupational Hazards', in Edward Giradet (ed.) *Somalia, Rwanda and Beyond: The Role of the International Media in Wars and Humanitarian Crises*. Dublin: Crosslines Global Report.

Lyotard, Jean-François (1984) *The Postmodern Condition: A Report on Knowledge*. Manchester: Manchester University Press.

Lyotard, Jean-François (1989) 'Complexity and the Sublime', in Lisa Appignanesi (ed.) *Postmodernism: ICA Documents*. London: Free Association Books.

MacArthur, John R. (1993) *Second Front: Censorship and Propaganda in the Gulf War*. Berkeley, CA: University of California Press.

Mahajan, Rahul (2002) *The New Crusade: America's War on Terrorism*. New York, NY: Monthly Review Press.

Malik, Kenan (1996) *The Meaning of Race*. Basingstoke: Macmillan.

Malik, Kenan (2006) 'Setting the Stage', *Rising East Online*, No. 4, May, http://www.uel.ac.uk/risingeast/archive04/essays/malik.htm.

Mann, Michael (2003) *Incoherent Empire*. London: Verso.

Maren, Michael (1997) *The Road to Hell: The Ravaging Effects of Foreign Aid and International Charity*. New York, NY: Free Press.

Martin, Jerry L. and Anne D. Neal (2001) *Defending Civilization: How Our Universities Are Failing America And What Can Be Done About It*. Washington, DC: American Council of Trustees and Alumni.

Marx, Karl (1976) *Capital, Volume 1*. Harmondsworth: Penguin.

Mercer, Jonathan (1995) 'Anarchy and Identity', *International Organization*, Vol. 49, No. 2, Spring, pp. 229–52.

Mermin, Jonathan (1999) *Debating War and Peace*. Princeton, NJ: Princeton University Press.

Michalski, Milena, Alison Preston, Richard Paterson, Marie Gillespie and Tom Cheesman (2002) *After September 11: TV News and Transnational Audiences* (research report, undated, but c. 2002), http://www.afterseptember11.tv/download/11%20September%20Research.pdf.

Miller, Mark Crispin (2001) *The Bush Dyslexicon*. London: Bantam Books.

Mirza, Munira, Abi Senthilkumaran and Zein Ja'far (2007) *Living Apart Together: British Muslims and the Paradox of Multiculturalism*. London: Policy Exchange.

Møller, Bjørn (1996) 'Ethnic Conflict and Postmodern Warfare: What Is the Problem? What Could Be Done?', paper for the conference on *Anthropological Perspectives on the Roots of Conflict in the Eastern Mediterranean*, University of Malta, 4–5 October, http://www.ciaonet.org/wps/mub01/.

Morley, David and Kevin Robins (1995) *Spaces of Identity*. London: Routledge.

Moskos, Charles C. (2001) 'What Ails the All-Volunteer Force: An Institutional Perspective', *Parameters*, Summer, http://carlisle-www.army.mil/usawc/Parameters/01summer/moskos.htm.

Moskos, Charles C., John Allen Williams and David R. Segal (2000) 'Armed Forces after the Cold War', in Charles C. Moskos, John Allen Williams and David R. Segal (eds.) *The Postmodern Military*. Oxford: Oxford University Press.

Nicholls, Christine (2004) 'Postmodernity and September 11 2001 – Life Imitating Art? Art pre-empting Life? An Australian Perspective', *Altitude*, Vol 4, http://www.api-network.com/cgi-bin/altitude21c/fly?page=Issue4&n=1.

Norris, Christopher (1992) *Uncritical Theory: Postmodernism, Intellectuals and the Gulf War*. London: Lawrence and Wishart.

Patton, Paul (1995) 'Introduction', in Jean Baudrillard, *The Gulf War Did Not Take Place*. Bloomington, IN: Indiana University Press.

Persram, Nalini (1999) 'Coda: Sovereignty, Subjectivity, Strategy', in Jenny Edkins, Nalini Persram and Véronique Pin-Fat (eds.) *Sovereignty and Subjectivity*. Boulder, CO: Lynne Rienner.

Philo, Greg, Lindsey Hilsum, Liza Beattie and Rick Holliman (1999) 'The Media and the Rwanda Crisis: Effects on Audiences and Public Policy', in Greg Philo (ed.) *Message Received: Glasgow Media Group Research 1993–1998*. Harlow: Longman.

Poster, Mark (1988) 'Introduction', in Jean Baudrillard, *Selected Writings*. Stanford, CA: Stanford University Press.

Project for the New American Century (2000) *Rebuilding America's Defenses*. Washington, DC: PNAC, http://www.newamericancentury.org/RebuildingAmericasDefenses.pdf.

Prunier, Gérard (1997) 'The Experience of European Armies in Operation Restore Hope', in Walter Clarke and Jeffrey Herbst (eds.) *Learning from Somalia: The Lessons of Armed Humanitarian Intervention*. Boulder, CO: Westview Press.

Pupavac, Vanessa (2001) 'Therapeutic Governance: Psycho-social Intervention and Trauma Risk Management', *Disasters*, Vol. 25, No.4, pp. 358–72.

Rabinow, Paul (1984) 'Introduction' in Paul Rabinow (ed.) *The Foucault Reader*. Harmondsworth: Penguin.

Rampton, Sheldon and John Stauber (2003) *Weapons of Mass Deception*. London: Robinson.

Ricchiardi, Sherry (1996) 'Over the Line?', *American Journalism Review*, September [accessed electronically].

Rieff, David (1995) *Slaughterhouse: Bosnia and the Failure of the West*. London: Vintage.

Rieff, David (1999) 'A New Age of Liberal Imperialism?', *World Policy Journal*, Vol. 16, No. 2, Summer, pp. 1–10.

Rieff, David (2002) *A Bed for the Night: Humanitarianism in Crisis*. London: Vintage.

Rieff, David (2005) *At the Point of a Gun: Democratic Dreams and Armed Intervention*. New York, NY: Simon and Schuster.

Robins, Kevin and Frank Webster (1999) *Times of the Technoculture*. London: Routledge.

Robinson, Piers (2002) *The CNN Effect: The Myth of News, Foreign Policy and Intervention*. London: Routledge.

Roper, Jon (1995) 'Overcoming the Vietnam Syndrome: The Gulf War and Revisionism', in Jeffrey Walsh (ed.) *The Gulf War Did Not Happen: Politics, Culture and Warfare Post-Vietnam*. Aldershot: Arena.

Rose, Margaret A. (1991) *The Post-Modern and the Post-Industrial*. Cambridge: Cambridge University Press.

Rosenberg, Justin (1994) *The Empire of Civil Society: A Critique of the Realist Theory of International Relations*. London: Verso.

Rosenberg, Justin (2000) *The Follies of Globalisation Theory*. London: Verso.

Roy, Olivier (1994) *The Failure of Political Islam*. Cambridge, MA: Harvard University Press.

Roy, Olivier (2004) *Globalised Islam: The Search for a New Ummah* (Revised Edition). London: Hurst.

Ruggie, John Gerard (1998) *Constructing the World Polity*. London: Routledge.

Runciman, David (2004) 'The Precautionary Principle', *London Review of Books*, Vol. 26, No. 7 [accessed electronically].

Runciman, David (2006) *The Politics of Good Intentions*. Princeton, NJ: Princeton University Press.

Rutherford, Jonathan (1990) 'The Third Space: Interview with Homi Bhabha', in Jonathan Rutherford (ed.) *Identity: Community, Culture, Difference*. London: Lawrence and Wishart.

Sageman, Marc (2004) *Understanding Terror Networks*. Philadelphia, PA: University of Pennsylvania Press.

Sahnoun, Mohamed (1994) *Somalia: The Missed Opportunities*. Washington, DC: United States Institute of Peace Press.

Schivelbusch, Wolfgang (2003) *The Culture of Defeat*. London: Granta.

Shaw, Martin (1993) 'Grasping the nettle', *New Statesman and Society*, 15 January, pp. 16–17.

Shaw, Martin (1996) *Civil Society and Media in Global Crises: Representing Distant Violence*. London: Pinter.

Shaw, Martin (2002) 'Risk-transfer Militarism, Small Massacres and the Historic Legitimacy of War', *International Relations*, Vol. 16, No. 2, pp. 343–60.

Shaw, Martin (2005) *The New Western Way of War: Risk-Transfer War and its Crisis in Iraq*. Cambridge: Polity.

Shawcross, William (2000) *Deliver Us From Evil: Warlords and Peacekeepers in a World of Endless Conflict*. London: Bloomsbury.

Simpson, John (1998) *Strange Places, Questionable People*. London: Macmillan.

Snider, Don M. and Gayle L. Watkins (2000) 'The Future of Army Professionalism: A Need for Renewal and Redefinition', *Parameters*, Autumn, http://carlisle-www.army.mil/usawc/Parameters/00autumn/snider.htm.

Sokal, Alan D. (1996) 'Transgressing the Boundaries: Toward a Transformative Hermeneutics of Quantum Gravity', *Social Text*, No. 46–47, http://.physics.nyu.edu/faculty/sokal/transgress_v2/transgress_v2_singlefile.htm.

Spence, Keith (2005) 'World Risk Society and War Against Terror', *Political Studies*, No. 53 [accessed electronically].

Steigerwald, David (1995) *The Sixties and the End of Modern America*. New York, NY: St. Martin's Press.

Stelzer, Irwin, ed. (2004) *Neoconservativism*. London: Atlantic Books.

Stern, Jessica and Jonathan B. Wiener (2006) 'Precaution Against Terrorism', *Journal of Risk Research*, Vol. 9, No. 4, June [accessed electronically].

Taylor, Philip (2003) *Munitions of the Mind: A History of Propaganda from the Ancient World to the Present Day* (Third Edition). Manchester: Manchester University Press.

Toulmin, Stephen (1990) *Cosmopolis: The Hidden Agenda of Modernity*. Chicago: University of Chicago Press.

Tuathail, Gearóid Ó (1999) 'A Strategic Sign: The Geopolitical Significance of Bosnia in U.S. Foreign Policy', *Environment and Planning D: Society and Space*, No. 17, http://toal.net/Publish/papers/stratsign.html.

van Creveld, Martin (2000) 'The Great Illusion: Women in the Military', *Millennium: Journal of International Studies*, Vol. 29, No. 2, pp. 429–42.

van Ham, Peter (2001) *European Integration and the Postmodern Condition*. London: Routledge.

Vaux, Tony (2001) *The Selfish Altruist: Relief Work in Famine and War*. London: Earthscan Publications.

Walker, R.B.J. (1993) *Inside/Outside: International Relations as Political Theory*. Cambridge: Cambridge University Press.

Waltz, Kenneth (1979) *Theory of International Politics*. Reading, MA: Addison-Wesley.

Weber, Cynthia (1999) 'Masquerading and the US "Intervasion" of Haiti', in Jenny Edkins, Nalini Persram and Véronique Pin-Fat (eds.) *Sovereignty and Subjectivity*. Boulder, CO: Lynne Rienner.

Webster, Frank (1995) *Theories of The Information Society*. London: Routledge.

Wendt, Alexander (1992) 'Anarchy is what States Make of it: The Social Construction of Power Politics', *International Organization*, Vol. 46, No. 2, Spring, pp. 391–425.

Wendt, Alexander (1999) *Social Theory of International Politics*. Cambridge: Cambridge University Press.

Williams, Andrew (2003) 'Meaning and International Relations: Some Thoughts', in Peter Mandaville and Andrew Williams (eds.) *Meaning and International Relations*. London: Routledge.

Williams, John Allen (2000) 'The Postmodern Military Reconsidered', in Charles C. Moskos, John Allen Williams and David R. Segal (eds.) *The Postmodern Military*. Oxford: Oxford University Press.

Williams, Raymond (1980) *Problems in Materialism and Culture*. London: Verso.

Woods, James (1997) 'US Government Decisionmaking Processes During Humanitarian Operations in Somalia', in Walter Clarke and Jeffrey Herbst (eds.) *Learning from Somalia: The Lessons of Armed Humanitarian Intervention*. Boulder, CO: Westview Press.

Woodward, Susan L. (1995) *Balkan Tragedy: Chaos and Dissolution After the Cold War*. Washington, DC: The Brookings Institution.

Zehfuss, Maja ((2002) *Constructivism in International Relations: The Politics of Reality*. Cambridge: Cambridge University Press.

Zehfuss, Maja ((2007) 'Subjectivity and Vulnerability: On the War with Iraq', *International Politics*, No. 44 [accessed electronically].

Žižek, Slavoj (2000) *The Ticklish Subject: The Absent Centre of Political Ontology*. London: Verso.

Žižek, Slavoj (2002) *Welcome to the Desert of the Real!* London: Verso.

Žižek, Slavoj (2003) 'Paranoid Reflections', *London Review of Books*, Vol. 25, No. 7, [accessed electronically].

Index